Eyewitness Accounts of the American Revolution

Account
of Arnold's Campaign
against Quebec

John Joseph Henry

The New York Times & Arno Press

Arnold's Campaign Against Quebec

MAP

<small>OF THE</small>

ROUTE OF ARNOLD'S CAMPAIGN.

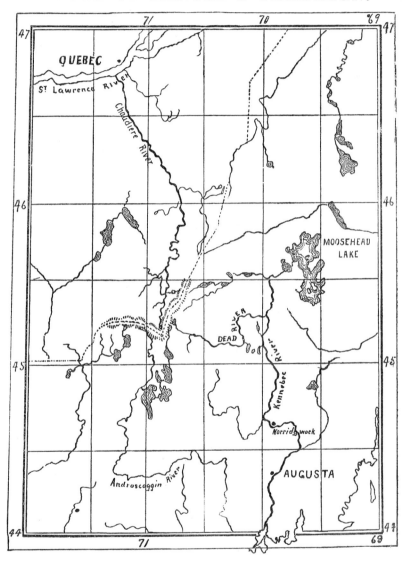

ACCOUNT

OF

Arnold's Campaign Against Quebec

AND OF THE

HARDSHIPS AND SUFFERINGS OF THAT BAND OF HEROES

WHO

TRAVERSED THE WILDERNESS OF MAINE

FROM

CAMBRIDGE TO THE ST. LAWRENCE,

IN THE

AUTUMN OF 1775.

———

By JOHN JOSEPH HENRY,

One of the Survivors.

————•◆•————

ALBANY:

JOEL MUNSELL.

1877.

MEMOIR

OF

JOHN JOSEPH HENRY,

BY HIS GRANDSON.

John Joseph Henry, the author of the Campaign against Quebec, was born at Lancaster, Pennsylvania, on the 4th of November A.D. 1758. His ancestors came to Pennsylvania with the first great wave of Scotch-Irish immigration. His father, William Henry, in a brief memoir of himself, written in the German tongue a few weeks before his death, says :

"I was born May 19th, 1729. My grandparents on my father's side came from Scotland, and on my mother's side were descendants of French refugees. My parents on both sides came from Ireland to Pennsylvania and were married in this country. My father was a Presbyterian and my mother a member of the Church of England, but as there was then no Anglican church in Pennsylvania the whole family felt drawn to join the Presbyterians."[1]

Robert Henry, the Scottish grandfather, with his wife Mary and their three sons John, Robert and James, arrived in the Delaware in 1722. He settled in the pleasant valley of Doe Run in the wide county of Chester and there, in 1735, he and his wife ended their pilgrimages on the same day and were buried together at the historic Octorara Meeting House.

Of the three sons James died early leaving a single child who did not survive infancy, and Robert, following the current of Scotch-Irish emigration went into the valley of Virginia where he left many sons and daughters, and they many descendants.

John Henry married the daughter of Hugh De Vinney, one of the Huguenots of the Pequea valley. He remained upon and added to the lands

---

[1] This statement is not strictly accurate. There was more than one Anglican church in the vicinity of Philadelphia previously to 1722.

1

of his father, but dying in middle life his family, consisting of five sons and several daughters, was in the language of the memoir "entirely scattered."

William Henry, the eldest of the sons, then in his fifteenth year, was sent to Lancaster to learn the trade of gunsmith with Matthew Roeser.

Lancaster county had been set off from the vast county of Chester in 1729 and itself included "all and singular the lands within the province of Pennsylvania lying to the northward of Octorara creek and to the westward of a line of marked trees running from the north branch of Octorara creek northeasterly to the river Schuylkill." Lancaster, the county seat, was laid out by James Hamilton, afterwards governor of Pennsylvania, in 1728, and was in 1745 an active and prosperous town with about two thousand inhabitants.

Emigrants in large numbers and in some cases in organized bodies, from Ireland, Scotland, France, Germany and Switzerland, had poured into the fertile wilderness of southern Pennsylvania. Flying for the most part from oppressive land laws or from religious persecution they brought with them their clergy, their school masters and their books and that intensity of faith and purpose which had sent them forth to found new homes across the sea. Lancaster, situated in the midst of a great valley of unsurpassed fertility soon became not only the seat of an active commerce and manufacture connected with the Indian trade but the home of many men well cultivated in the learning of the day, especially in its theological departments.

William Henry possessed in full measure the perfervid imagination of his race, and at early age turned his thoughts upon those great religious questions which are so seldom solved by ratiocination. He tells the story of his spiritual experiences at length in his memoir, but it is enough to say that he did not find the peace he sought, till middle life, when in 1763 he and his wife joined themselves to the Moravians, then known only as the Church of the United Brethren.

His work in worldly matters prospered, however, for like many of his race he was prudent in action, though speculative in thought. He became early the head of a large establishment for the manufacture of arms and equipments for the Indian trade. In 1754 he was appointed armorer for the troops collecting in Virginia for Braddock's expedition, and in 1757 he was, with apparent reluctance, called again to go to Virginia as "gun contractor for the whole army."

From this time forward he was much engaged in public affairs, especially in those which related to the Indian tribes. Possessing the confidence both of the whites and the Indians, he was able to render essential service in the settlement of many of the questions which arose between the races. The Delaware hero, Koquethagachton or White Eyes, and his successor Gelelemend or Leader called Killbuck by the whites, were among his friends.

Between him and the latter the tie of friendship was so strong that in 1784, after the Delaware custom, they agreed to exchange names. Gelelemend, a few years later, was baptized by the Moravians as William Henry and his descendants in Fairfield, Canada, still bear the name and claim kinship with the posterity of their ancestor's friend.

When the disputes between the colonies and the crown grew serious, William Henry, though a magistrate under the proprietary government, gave his support with characteristic ardor to the cause of the patriots. His activity and vigor were conspicuous during the war of the revolution. His factory was busy in the making of arms and he himself as deputy commissary general, exercised freely the almost unlimited authority given him by Washington, in the matter of raising supplies for the army. After the termination of the war he was called to fill a number of posts of honor and responsibility. It will seem strange to us, when the holding of a plurality of offices is deemed an abuse, that at the time of his death in 1786, he was a judge of the court of common pleas, a member of the general congress, and the treasurer of Lancaster county; and what may seem stranger still his wife, Anne Henry, succeeded him in the last office and continued to fill it with entire acceptation for many years and nearly up to the time of her own decease.

John Joseph Henry grew up in troublous times. In early childhood he and his elder brother William Henry, the younger, were witnesses of the Paxtang massacre. His own recollection was only of the hurrying and shouts of men, the firing of guns and the retreat at a gallop of those who had slain the helpless prisoners. His brother, two years his senior, was able, however, in later years to give a vivid account of the slaughter (*Heckewelder's Narrative*, p. 78). Strenuous efforts were made to bring the murderers to trial by William Henry and others, but the state of feeling on what was then the frontier, was such that no success followed their efforts. Even the detachment of Highlanders quartered in the town at the time would do nothing to stay the carnage or arrest the perpetrators of it.

Judge Henry was accustomed to say, late in life, that he had watched the careers of all of those lawless men who had murdered the Conestogas, and that the retribution which man denied had been awarded by Providence, for that nearly all of them died violent deaths. Tradition tells that the last of them broke his neck by falling from a loaded wagon near his own house.

As young Henry grew towards manhood the mutterings of the revolutionary storm were in the air. He drank in the passions of the time with eager spirit and with parental precept and example to justify him, gave up his whole heart to the strife. He had been sent in 1772, with his uncle John Henry, who was a gunsmith and Indian trader, to the remote frontier post of Detroit. Returning the next year on foot with a single guide, who died in the wilderness, he found his way after much suffering to the house of his relative General John Gibson, who dwelt at Logstown on the Ohio. He was kindly received by General Gibson and when restored to health was sent forward by him to his home in Lancaster.

General Gibson was himself one of the leading men of the frontier. He it was to whom the Mengwe chief, Logan, addressed the speech which Jefferson, in his *Notes on Virginia*, has made immortal. He was a brother of Colonel George Gibson, who was mortally wounded at St. Clair's defeat. Col. Gibson was the father of the late Hon. John Bannister Gibson, chief justice of Pennsylvania.

The Gibsons were all men of force of character combined with a gay humor. The story is told of Colonel Gibson that a couple of days after the defeat, whilst the army was still in great peril, as he lay in his rough shelter in the forest, his nephew, Lieutenant Slough of Lancaster, who had been slightly wounded in the arm, but had lent his blanket to his uncle, came to demand its return, saying that he had leave to go home to see his father and mother. The dying man turned to him with a smile and said "take it Jake, and go home and honor your father and mother that your days may be long in the land."

William Henry had designed that his sons William and John Joseph should follow his own avocation. The former acceded to his father's wishes and was the second in a line of prosperous makers of arms extending to the present day. But when the command was laid on the younger son to enter the factory he so far disobeyed it as to incur the serious displeasure of his father. Not long after the question between them was settled by the outbreak of the war. In 1774 the quarrel between the colonies and England was probably past cure. Both sides were making ready for the conflict.

In southern Pennsylvania the dour frontiersmen might differ as to the murder of Indian prisoners but they were of one mind as to fighting the British. They or their ancestors had fled across the ocean from the tyrannical land and church laws of England and they would resist to the death a new oppression in America.

In the spring of 1775 two companies of riflemen were enlisted at the first tap of the drum for the army before Boston — one from the county of Cumberland under Captain William Hendricks, the other from Lancaster county under Captain Matthew Smith. Young Henry, by this time a tall and hardy youth, well skilled in the use of the rifle and the ways of the forest, joined the latter without the knowledge of his father. His good mother, however, whose patriotism may have been a shade less prudent than that of her husband, was made the confidante of his intention and gave her consent to an act which was but the natural corollary of her own teaching. She made with her own hands in secret his rifleman's uniform, if such it could be called, consisting as he himself tells of leggings, moccasins and a deep ash colored hunting shirt.

When the day of departure came and the company was drawn up for inspection before starting, his father passed along the line but did not recognize his own son in the tall rifleman on its right.

The story of the campaign so well told by himself needs not to be rehearsed here. It is enough to say that he came home in the fall of 1776, apparently in health but with the seeds of disease deeply planted in his constitution. In a few weeks after this, he tells us, " a slight cold caught while skating on the Susquehannah or hunting the wild turkey among the Kittatinny mountains, put an end to all his visionary schemes of ambition." The scurvy, from which he suffered in the prison at Quebec, attacked with terrible force the knee which had been injured at the assault. The joint became the seat of violent inflammation, disease of the bone followed and when two years afterwards he left his couch it was only to walk with a crutch through life. Some good, however, came out of so much evil. The house of William Henry had long been the resort of the educated men of the Lancaster community and of such strangers as visited the place. During the revolution the leading men of the day found quarters there. Franklin, Rittenhouse, Paine and others were among his guests. (*Marshall's Diary* passim.) The Juliana library founded in 1750, so called from Lady Juliana Penn, wife of Thomas Penn and daughter of the Earl of Pomfret, was kept there. Constant access to books with abundant leisure to read them and the society of the foremost men of the time made up for a somewhat desultory early training and probably determined his ultimate choice of the law as his profession.

The memoir of his life by his daughter, the mother of the present writer, tells us all that is known of him till he came to the bar. His preceptor, Colonel Stephen Chambers, whose youngest sister he afterwards married, was an Irishman by birth. He had come to Pennsylvania with his father, mother and sisters in the great Scotch-Irish immigration of 1772 and 1773. The father being a man of property had educated his son at Trinity college, Dublin, intending him for the bar. He had the misfortune, however, at an early age to kill his antagonist in a duel, whereupon the whole family came to America. He also entered the army and did good service for some years but resigned his commission and came to the bar of Lancaster county in 1780 where he attained a large practice. He was a delegate to the Pennsylvania convention which ratified the federal constitution. He fell in a duel with Dr. Reger in 1789.

Mr. Henry, after several years of assiduous study, was admitted to practice in 1785. He too was soon largely employed. But the conditions of success in the law at that time, were very different from those which command it now. Beyond the statutes of the states there were practically no books on the law written or printed in America, no text-books, no digests, no reports. The first volume of *Dallas's Reports* was published in 1790, the second in 1798, and the third in 1799. With these exceptions no regular series of reports had been published in America up to the year 1800. The entire vast array of American reports, both state and federal, has come into existence since that day. The lawyers of that time were thrown for aid wholly on English resources, and English law books exclusively composed their modest libraries. It is perhaps a fortunate thing for the jurisprudence of the country that such was the case. Where all sound learning in the law was drawn from one source, it was but natural that the several jurisprudences established on that basis should have a substantial uniformity though the peculiar political institutions of the country might seem to disfavor such a result. Many men of great ability and profound learning were trained in this early school. They sought their knowledge at the very fountain heads of the law and grew strong in the mastery of its principles by tracing them to their foundation. Among these George and James Ross, Duncan, Charles Hall, Yeates, Watts and Charles Smith were among the associates and friends of Judge Henry.

In 1793 Mr. Henry was appointed by Governor Mifflin, the president of the second judicial district of Pennsylvania. His commission, bearing date the 18th day of December, 1793, appoints him "President of the Several Courts of Common Pleas in the Circuit consisting of the Counties of Chester, Lancaster, York and Dauphin," a vast territory whose features were fertile valleys and rugged hills with the hard wood forests every where predominant.

Of his work as a judge but little remains. It may be said of him, as has been said of his kinsman and youthful friend, the late Chief Justice Gibson, who at one time presided over another Pennsylvanian circuit, that so far as his work in that circuit was concerned " he has left no monument of his labors. Like the fruits of much of the best ability of the state, displayed in the same sphere, they perished on the spot without a record to perpetuate their worth." (*Essay on the Life and Writings of John B. Gibson, LL.D.*, by William A. Porter.) The words of Judge Porter have a sad aptitude to many cases.

The only case tried by Judge Henry, which is known to have been fully reported, is that of the Commonwealth vs. Hauer, et als., 2 *Chandlers Criminal Trials*, 353. The case in Chandler is but a feeble abridgment of a remarkable pamphlet printed at Harrisburg in 1798, giving a full account of the trials of the seven persons charged with complicity in the murder. It has been said that " few events ever caused more excitement and alarm amongst the German population than the murder of Francis Shitz in 1797. The trials of the parties implicated in this singular transaction are interesting as exhibiting the low state of public morals at that day in the interior of the state, especially amongst the foreign population, and also as involving some legal points of great importance in criminal law." (Prefatory note to the Report in Chandler.)

The counsel on both sides were of great ability and the many questions of law and of fact were argued with much learning and fullness. The rulings of Judge Henry throughout the case were briefly and clearly made, and his charge to the jury correctly stated the principles of the law applicable to it.

Two of the prisoners were found guilty of murder in the first degree and expiated their crime upon the gallows.

The pamphlet report, by an anonymous author, is a model of completeness. It gives a statement of the case, the pleadings, the evidence in full, the motions made at the several stages of the very complex proceedings, the rulings of the court on the points raised, the arguments of the counsel and the charge of the judge. It is a conscientious history by a fully competent hand of a celebrated case, from the perusal of which a lawyer may derive greater profit than by reading volumes of such reports as slip-shod indolence too often imposes on the profession.

About the year 1804, the constitution of Judge Henry, so severely tried in youth, began to give way under repeated attacks of the gout, which in a letter written to his brother William in 1807, he speaks of as an inheritance from his mother. That it is transmissible by descent many others have grievous reason to testify.

In succeeding years the severity of his attacks increased so greatly that he was unable longer to fill the arduous duties of his office. He therefore, in the latter part of the year 1810, tendered his resignation to the governor of the state. Four months later, on the 15th April, 1811, he rested finally from his labors. His remains lie in the burial ground of the Moravian church at Lancaster.

Judge Henry was a man of great stature and strength, and of grave and leonine aspect—yet he was of jovial temper and quick and warm sensibilities. His religious faith was cast in the antique mold which would not admit of a doubt and somewhat scorned the doubter. By the testimony of all who knew him he was a brave, just and honorable gentleman.

The *Campaign against Quebec* was dictated to his daughter, Anne Mary, the mother of the writer, with the aid of casual notes and memoranda from his bed of sickness in his latest years. The manuscript received no revision at his hands, for he was called away very shortly after its last pages were written. His widow gave it to the press in 1812, and it was printed without even the correction of verbal and typographical errors.

He left two sons, Dr. Stephen Chambers Henry, late of Detroit, and Dr. Julien Henry of St. Louis, also deceased, and several daughters, one only of whom, Anne Mary, the wife of the late Honorable Thomas Smith, of Delaware county, has left issue.

A portrait of Judge Henry in the stately dress of a gentleman of the old time, from the hand of his youngest brother, Benjamin West Henry, a pupil of Gilbert Stuart, represents him as a man of massive features, broad shoulders and grave yet kindly expression, and is in full harmony with what is remembered of him.

AUBREY H. SMITH.

Philadelphia, May 25th, 1877.

LIFE OF THE AUTHOR.

WRITTEN BY HIS DAUGHTER.

———— •• ————

There is an observation trite, true, and universally admitted, that the lives of those who have not embraced a wide sphere of action, are uninteresting and perfectly devoid of any incitements to attention. Biographies of warriors and statesmen are perused with avidity; but it is not merely their own history, but that of the times in which they lived, at least partially so. But descending to the quieter walks of life, when we trace the history of a good and unfortunate man, through all the varied evolutions that peculiarly mark his fate, and prevent him from being enrolled in the list of those beings who have found the path divested of thorns, it is, to some, still interesting; and although the incidents are not of a nature to excite wonder or astonishment, they may still possess the power to call forth the sympathy of minds of feeling — minds that have been taught to feel another's woe.

John Joseph Henry, the author of the following pages, was born November 4th, 1758, at Lancaster, Pennsylvania. His father, William Henry, was a man whose memory is still revered by those who possessed any knowledge of him, his strict honesty and known probity rendering it sacred to such as claimed him as their friend. He was possessed of a mechanical genius in a strong degree. He it was who invented the well known screw-auger.

Warmly addicted to this his favorite passion, he wished to instil into the minds of his children, a taste for mechanics. With some of them he succeeded. As soon as his son John Joseph had attained the age of fourteen, he bound him an apprentice to an uncle, who was a gunsmith, then a resident at Lancaster, but after sometime removed to Detroit, taking his nephew with him. At that place, his stay was but short, on account of scarcity of business. He returned on foot with a single guide, who died in the wilderness which lay between Detroit and his home. It was here that hardships and misfortune first were felt, his future companions during a length of years devoted to God and his country. Young Henry returned to his parents and home, dissatisfied with the employment a judicious father had pointed out for him, as the means by which he wished him to gain a future subsistence. His ardent mind panted after military glory. The troubles of his country, which was then making vigorous, and ultimately successful struggles for a total emancipation from slavery, wrought strongly upon one, the acme of whose hopes and wishes was, to be one of those who contended most for freedom. In the fall of 1775, he clandestinely joined a regiment of men raised in Lancaster county, for the purpose of joining Arnold, who at that time was stationed at Boston. His father was commissary to the troops, which office obliged him to attend them to Reading. It was at this time, under circumstances which rendered him most liable to detection from his parent, he left his home to wander, at the age of sixteen, in a strange land. Thus a thirst for glory inflamed his youthful breast, and superseded every other passion and affection of his heart. After enduring all the fatigues of a veteran soldier, they entered Canada on his birthday — an eventful one to him. He endured hardships here, which, in his own simple style, he fully enumerates. It was in prison, where he lay for nine months, that he contracted a disease (the scurvy), which at that time did not make its appearance, but six weeks afterwards, on his return home, at a time when least expected, it made its appearance under its most malignant form. It was at a time when it became a duty incumbent on him to continue in the army. A captaincy had been procured for him in the Virginia line, and a lieutenancy in that of Pennsylvania. He had designed to accept of the command under the hero Morgan, which was that of captain, but the disposer of all events arrested his career, and instead of his fond expectations being accomplished, all his hopes were blasted, his high prospects faded, and became a dreary void, by the order of that Omnipotence, who furnished him with that fortitude which enabled him, through all his misery, to kiss the rod that chastised him. It was after two years' continuance on the couch of sickness, his leg, which was the unfortunate cause of all his illness, began to heal, and renovated health to give hopes that peace yet remained for him.

As his lameness precluded all possibility of his again entering the army; as he had, by a disregard of parental authority, at least so far as concerned his trade, forfeited his claim to his father's exertions to place him in such a situation as would make him capable of rendering himself useful to society, a vigorous effort on his part was necessary; resolution was not wanting; it was made. He bound himself as an apprentice to John Hubley, Esq., prothonotary of the county of Lancaster, as a clerk in the office. Here for four years he pursued his business with the closest application, and discharged the duties of his office with unabated care and strictness; and when the labors of the day were over, his nights were consumed in study, endeavoring to compensate himself, in some measure, for the neglect that his education had suffered by his becoming a soldier. His frame, still somewhat debilitated by his illness, was not capable of sustaining the fatigues of office; his health suffered much from labor so severe and application so intense. The time of his indentures being expired, he commenced the study of law, under Stephen Chambers, Esq. Here he became acquainted with his future companion in life, the youngest sister of Mr. Chambers. He practised law from the year 1785, until December, 1793. As his law knowledge was known to be extensive, his abilities and talents met their due reward, with an appointment, by his excellency Thomas Mifflin, governor, to the office of president of the second judicial district of Pennsylvania.

A number of years had now elapsed, his family was large; by an unfortunate removal to a country, at that period sickly, he was attacked by the gout, which from inexperience, and owing to his having no knowledge as to the consequences that would necessarily ensue, did not take proper precautions, so as to render it a regular disease. Under that deceptious name, numerous disorders invaded his frame, and at times with so much severity, that he was necessitated to continue at home, which prevented him from executing his official duties as a judge. It was during seven long years of bodily suffering, that his mind and memory reverted to those scenes more forcibly than ever, which formed so eventful a period in a life of misfortune and vicissitude. The interesting narrative of the sufferings of that band of heroes, of which he was the youngest, is a simple tale of truth, which he undeviatingly throughout his book adheres to.

He is supported in all his assertions, by the testimony of a number of his companions in that arduous campaign, men of character and respectability. His relation of incidents, his descriptive accounts of the country they passed through, the situation of Quebec, and the disposition of the army, all mark him to have been a youth of accurate observation, of a comprehensive and intelligent mind. Possessing, as he must necessarily have done, activity of spirit and contempt of fatigue, he gained the approbation and esteem of his seniors. The buoyant spirits of youth rose high over misfortune; unde the pressure of the severest distress, vivacity was still retained, and burst forth at intervals to cheer his hopeless companions.

Disease had now made rapid progress on a constitution weakened by repeated attacks, and accumulation of disorders, which no skill could counteract or remedy. The nonperformance of his duties caused petitions from the several counties to be presented to the legislature, for his removal ; nothing was alleged against him but absence. That honorable house, having examined and considered the charges, acquitted him with honor. His commission he retained for the space of two years afterwards ; but illness and debility increasing, and a knowledge of his infirmities being incurable, compelled him to resign that office, which he had held with integrity, for seventeen years. Four months succeeding, his worn out frame was destined to feel the stroke of death, and his freed soul to seek refuge in the bosom of his Father and his God. He died at Lancaster, April 15th, 1811, aged 53.

ARNOLD'S CAMPAIGN AGAINST QUEBEC.

PRELIMINARY.

When the bold enterprise of invading Canada by the way of the Kennebec river and the uninhabited wilderness of Maine had been determined upon by Washington, in the autumn of 1775, he wrote to congress as follows, on the 21st September, from Cambridge, Mass., where the American army was encamped :

I am now to inform the honorable congress that, encouraged by the repeated declarations of the Canadians and Indians, and urged by their requests, I have detached Col. Arnold, with one thousand men, to penetrate into Canada by way of Kennebec river, and, if possible, to make himself master of Quebec. By this manœuvre I proposed either to divert Carleton from St. John's, which would leave a free passage to General Schuyler, or, if this did not take effect, Quebec, in its present defenceless state, must fall into his hands an easy prey. I made all possible inquiry as to the distance, the safety of the route, and the danger of the season being too far advanced, but found nothing in either to deter me from proceeding, more especially as it met with very general approbation from all whom I consulted upon it. But that nothing might be omitted to enable me to judge of its propriety and probable consequences, I communicated it, by express, to General Schuyler, who approved of it in such terms that I resolved to put it in immediate execution. They have now left this place seven days, and, if favored with a good wind, I hope soon to hear of their being safe in Kennebec river.

A copy of his plan of the proposed route was sent to congress, in the following words :

Route to QUEBEC, *from* KENNEBEC RIVER.

From the mouth of Kennebec river to Quebec, on a straight line, is two hundred and ten miles. The river is navigable for sloops about thirty-eight miles, and for flat-bottomed boats about twenty-two miles ; then you meet Taconick falls, and from Taconick falls to Norridgewock, as the river runs, thirty-one miles ; from thence to the first carrying place, about thirty miles ; carrying place four miles, then a pond to cross, and another carrying place, about two miles to another pond ; then a carrying place about three or four miles to another pond ; then a carrying place to the western branch of Kennebec river, called the Dead river ; then up that river, as it runs, thirty miles, some small falls and short carrying places around them intervening ; then you come to the height of the land, and about six miles carrying place, into a branch which leads into Ammeguntick pond, the head of Chaudière river, which falls into the St. Lawrence river about four miles above Quebec.

From the *American Archives* of PETER FORCE, Washington's instructions to Arnold are given, intrusting him with the command of the forces detached from the main army for the expedition, and the course he was to pursue in the execution of his important mission.

To Colonel BENEDICT ARNOLD, *Commander of the Detachment of the Continental Army destined against* QUEBEC :

SIR: You are intrusted with a command of the utmost consequence to the interest and liberties of America ; upon your conduct and courage, and that of the officers and soldiers detached on this expedition, not only the success of the present enterprise, and your own honor, but the safety and welfare of the whole continent, may depend. I charge you, therefore, and the officers and soldiers under your command, as you value your own safety and honor, and the favor·and esteem of your country, that you consider yourselves as marching, not through an enemy's country, but that of our friends and brethren — for such the inhabitants of Canada and·the Indian Nations have approved themselves in this unhappy contest between Great Britain and America ; that you check, by every motive of duty and fear of punishment, every attempt to plunder or insult any of the inhabitants of Canada. Should any American soldier be so base and infamous as to injure any Canadian or Indian, in his person or property, I do most earnestly enjoin you to bring him to such severe and exemplary punishment as the enormity of the crime may require ; should it extend to death itself, it will not be disproportioned to its guilt at such a time and in such a cause. But I hope and trust that the brave men who have voluntarily engaged in this expedition will be governed by different views ; that order, discipline, and regularity of behavior, will be as conspicuous as their courage and valor. I also give it in charge to you to avoid all disrespect or contempt of the religion of the country ; and if common prudence, policy, and a true Christian spirit, will lead us to look with compassion upon their errors, without insulting them, while we are contending for our own liberty, we should be very cautious of violating the rules of conscience in others, ever considering that God alone is the judge of the heart of man, and to him only in this case they are answerable.

Upon the whole, Sir, I beg you to inculcate upon the officers and soldiers the necessity of preserving the strictest order during their march through Canada ; to represent to them the shame, disgrace, and ruin, to themselves and country, if they should, by their conduct, turn the heart of our brethren in Canada against us ; and, on the other hand, the honors and rewards which await them, if, by their prudence and good behavior, they conciliate the affections of the Canadians and Indians to the great interests of America, and convert those favorable dispositions they have shown into a lasting union and affection.

Thus wishing you, and the officers and soldiers under your command, honor, safety, and success, I remain, Sir, your most obedient humble servant,

GEORGE WASHINGTON.

To Colonel BENEDICT ARNOLD :

1. You are immediately on their march from Cambridge to take the command of the detachment from the Continental Army against Quebec, and use all possible expedition, as the winter season is now advancing, and the success of this enterprise (under God) depends wholly upon the spirit with which it is pushed, and the favorable disposition of the Canadians and Indians.

2. When you come to Newburyport, you are to make all possible inquiry what men of war or cruisers there may be on the coast, to which this detachment may be exposed on their voyage to Kennebec river; and if you shall find that there is danger of being intercepted, you are not to proceed by water, but by land, taking care on the one hand not to be diverted by light and vague reports, and on the other not to expose the troops rashly to a danger which by many judicious persons has been deemed very considerable.

3. You are by every means in your power to endeavor to discover the real sentiments of the Canadians towards our cause, and particularly as to this expedition ; ever bearing in mind that if they are averse to it, and will not coöperate, or at least willingly acquiesce, it must fail of success. In this case you are by no means to prosecute the attempt. The expense of the expedition and the disappointment are not to be put in competition with the dangerous consequences which may ensue from irritating them against us, and detaching them from that neutrality which they have adopted.

4. In order to cherish those favorable sentiments to the American cause that they have manifested, you are as soon as you arrive in their country to disperse a number of the addresses you will have with you, particularly in those parts where your route shall lie, and observe the strictest discipline and good order, by no means suffering any inhabitant to be abused, or in any manner injured, either in his person or property ; punishing with exemplary severity every person who shall transgress, and making ample compensation to the party injured.

5. You are to endeavor, on the other hand, to conciliate the affections of those people, and such Indians as you may meet with, by every means in your power; convincing them that we come at the request of many of their principal people, not as robbers, or to make war upon them, but as the friends and supporters of their liberties as well as ours ; and, to give efficacy to these sentiments, you must carefully inculcate upon the officers and soldiers under your command, that not only the good of their country, and their honor, but their safety, depends upon the treatment of these people.

6. Check every idea and crush in its earliest stage every attempt to plunder, even those who are known to be enemies to our cause ; it will create dreadful apprehensions in our friends, and when it is once begun, none

can tell where it will stop. I therefore again most expressly order that it be discouraged and punished, in every instance, without distinction.

7. Whatever king's stores you shall be so fortunate as to possess yourselves of are to be secured for the continental use, agreeable to the rules and regulations of war published by the honorable congress. The officers and men may be assured that any extraordinary services performed by them will be suitably rewarded.

8. Spare neither pains nor expense to gain all possible intelligence on your march, to prevent surprises and accidents of every kind ; and endeavor, if possible, to correspond with General Schuyler, so that you may act in concert with him. This I think may be done by means of the St. François Indians.

9. In case of a union with General Schuyler, or if he should be in Canada upon your arrival there, you are by no means to consider yourself as upon a separate and independent command, but are to put yourself under him, and follow his directions. Upon this occasion, and all others, I recommend most earnestly to avoid all contention about rank. In such a cause, every post is honorable in which a man can serve his country.

10. If Lord Chatham's son should be in Canada, and in any way fall in your power, you are enjoined to treat him with all possible deference and respect. You cannot err in paying too much honor to the son of so illustrious a character and so true a friend to America. Any other prisoners who may fall into your hands you will treat with as much humanity and kindness as may be consistent with your own safety and the public interest. Be very particular in restraining not only your own troops but the Indians from all acts of cruelty and insult which will disgrace the American arms, and irritate our fellow-subjects against us.

11. You will be particularly careful to pay the full value for all provisions or other accommodations which the Canadians may provide for you on your march ; by no means press them or any of their cattle into your service, but amply compensate those who voluntarily assist you. For this purpose you are provided with a sum of money in specie, which you will use with as much frugality and economy as your necessities and good policy will admit, keeping as exact account as possible of your disbursements.

12. You are by every opportunity to inform me of your progress, your prospect, and intelligence, and upon any important occurrence to despatch an express.

13. As the season is now far advanced, you are to make all possible despatch ; but if unforeseen difficulties should arise, or if the weather should become so severe as to render it hazardous to proceed, in your own judgment and that of your principal officers, whom you are to consult, in that case you are to return, giving me as early notice as possible, that I may give you such assistance as may be necessary.

14. As the contempt of the religion of a country, by ridiculing any of its ceremonies or affronting its ministers or votaries, has ever been deeply resented, you are to be particularly careful to restrain every officer and soldier from such imprudence and folly, and to punish every instance of it. On the other hand, as far as lies in your power, you are to protect and support the free exercise of the religion of the country, and the undisturbed

enjoyment of the rights of conscience in religious matters, with your utmost influence and authority.

GEORGE WASHINGTON.

The address to the people of Canada was printed for distribution as opportunity offered, and was in the following words :

By his Excellency GEORGE WASHINGTON, *Esquire, Commander in Chief of the Army of the United Colonies of* NORTH AMERICA.

To the Inhabitants of CANADA :

FRIENDS AND BRETHREN : The unnatural contest between the English colonies and Great Britain has now risen to such a height, that arms alone must decide it. The colonies, confiding in the justice of their cause and the purity of their intentions, have reluctantly appealed to that Being in whose hands are all human events. He has hitherto smiled upon their virtuous efforts. The hand of tyranny has been arrested in its ravages, and the British arms, which have shone with so much splendor in every part of the globe, are now tarnished with disgrace and disappointment. Generals of approved experience, who boasted of subduing this great continent, find themselves circumscribed within the limits of a single city and its suburbs, suffering all the shame and distress of a siege, while the freeborn sons of America, animated by the genuine principles of liberty and love of their country, with increasing union, firmness, and discipline, repel every attack, and despise every danger. Above all, we rejoice that our enemies have been deceived with regard to you ; they have persuaded themselves, they have even dared to say, that the Canadians were not capable of distinguishing between the blessings of liberty and the wretchedness of slavery ; that gratifying the vanity of a little circle of nobility would blind the eyes of the people of Canada ; by such artifices they hoped to bend you to their views, but they have been deceived ; instead of finding in you that poverty of soul and baseness of spirit, they see, with a chagrin equal to our joy, that you are enlightened, generous, and virtuous; that you will not renounce your own rights, or serve as instruments to deprive your fellow-subjects of theirs.

Come, then, my brethren, unite with us in an indissoluble union ; let us run together to the same goal. We have taken up arms in defence of our liberty, our property, our wives, and our children ; we are determined to preserve them or die. We look forward with pleasure to that day, not far remote, we hope, when the inhabitants of America shall have one sentiment, and the full enjoyment of the blessings of a free Government. Incited by these motives, and encouraged by the advice of many friends of liberty among you, the grand American congress have sent an army into your province, under the command of General Schuyler, not to plunder, but to protect you ; to animate and bring forth into action those sentiments of freedom you have disclosed, and which the tools of despotism would extinguish through the whole creation. To coöperate with this design, and to frustrate those cruel and perfidious schemes which would deluge our frontiers with the blood of women and children, I have detached Colonel Arnold into your country, with a part of the army under my command. I have enjoined upon him, and I am certain that he will consider himself, and act as in the country of his patrons and best friends.   Necessaries and accommodations of every kind which you may furnish he will thankfully receive, and render the full value.   I invite you, therefore, as friends and brethren, to provide him with such supplies as your country affords ; and I pledge myself not only for your safety and security, but for ample compensation.   Let no man desert his habitation.   Let no one flee as before an enemy.   The cause of America and of liberty is the cause of every virtuous American citizen, whatever may be his religion or his descent.   The United Colonies know no distinction but such as slavery, corruption, and arbitrary domination, may create.   Come, then, ye generous citizens, range yourselves under the standard of general liberty, against which all the force and artifice of tyranny will never be able to prevail.

GEORGE WASHINGTON.

The following order is found among the general orders of the commander in chief, of Sept. 8, 1775 :

The detachment going under the command of Colonel Arnold, to be forthwith taken off the roll of duty, and to march this evening to Cambridge common, where tents and every thing necessary are provided for their reception.   The rifle company at Roxbury, and those from Prospect hill, to march early to-morrow morning, to join the above detachment.   Such officers and men as are taken from General Green's brigade, for the above detachment, are to attend the muster of their respective regiments to-morrow morning, at seven o'clock, upon Prospect hill ; when the muster is finished, they are forthwith to rejoin the detachment at Cambridge.

So many journals of this expedition have been preserved, and published with annotations and introductions more or less extensive, some of the more important of them are alluded to instead of going over the same ground with an elaborate introduction to the narrative which Judge Henry has left to us.

The most complete and circumstantial of these narratives that have attained to publication, are those of Henry, Thayer and Senter.   The former was published in a separate volume in 1812, and has since been republished. Senter's may be found in vol. 1 of the Penn. Hist. Society Bulletin.   The Journal of Melvin has been published in two or three editions.   Meigs's in the Mass. Hist. Soc. Collections.   Ware's in the New Eng. Hist. and Genealogical Register, annotated by Mr. Justin Winsor. The Maine Hist. Soc. Collections, vol. 1, 2d ed., gives several of Arnold's letters and orders during the expedition, and a narrative principally derived from the published journals.   The Journal of Capt. Thayer has been elaborately annotated by the Rev. Edwin M. Stone, and published by him with an exhaustive bibliographical and historical introduction, which has been published entire in the Rhode Island Hist. Soc. Collections.

In view of the well preserved narratives in the collections of the historical societies of this remarkable episode in the history of the revolution, the publication of a new edition of Judge Henry's simple but truthful account of the expedition, was thought to be an enterprise of doubtful utility, unless accompanied by new and important adjuncts, further illustrating its authenticity, and the movements of the actors in the scene.   Whatever it may lack therefore in bringing out new and startling facts, the contribution of a new memoir of Judge Henry, a few brief notes, and an index, so often omitted in such works, together with some documentary papers introductory to the narrative, are relied upon as an apology for the present edition, the previous crude ones being entirely out of print, and unattainable.

The narrative of Henry is the only one giving an account of the pioneer expedition of his party to discover the source of the Chaudière river, a service that was executed with much energy and expedition, and attended with great peril and hardship.   Looking at the exploit from this distant period, there seems to have been a good deal of misdirected energy and hardihood in the conduct of the enterprise, occasioning disaster and loss by unskillful management, amounting almost to recklessness, by which provisions and munitions of all kinds were wrecked, and time and human force inefficiently expended.   The pioneer detachment under Steele, and the advance party under Arnold made good progress, but there was apparent lagging in the rear in bringing up the supplies, and the final defection of Enos was fatal to the entire success of the expedition, which was the capture of Quebec.   The attainment of that object would have secured Canada to the revolutionists, and saved the valuable lives of Montgomery and others, and might have given another destiny to Arnold.

The original edition of the narrative was published at Lancaster, Pa., in 1812, with the following notice, and recommendation by one of the compatriots of the author.

To the Public.

This work is given to the world, as left by Judge Henry. Had he lived to superintend the printing of it himself, many alterations would, no doubt, have been made, many passages which may at present appear obscure, would have been fully explained, and many differences of style corrected. As the work purports to be written by Judge Henry, it was thought improper to make any alterations or additions, trusting that the world, when acquainted with the circumstances under which it was published, will be disposed to pardon trivial errors as to the truth of the principal facts. The following letter from General Michael Simpson, is ample testimony :

Dear Sir : I have read your work " of the expedition through the wilderness in 1775." So far as I was concerned in the transactions related in the work, they are truly stated. That expedition, perhaps the most arduous during the revolutionary war, is truly represented. The public may, in the general, be assured that the account is genuine.

Your humble servant,

Michael Simpson.[1]

---

[1] For a notice of Michael Simpson see a subsequent page.

CAMPAIGN AGAINST QUEBEC.

By John Joseph Henry.

My dear Children:

There is a point in the history of the American revolution, hitherto little attended to ; as yet imperfectly related, and now at this late day almost forgotten ; which would deserve and require the talents and genius of a Xenophon, to do it real justice. As your father in early life had a concern in that adventure, permit him to relate to you in the words of truth, a compendious detail of the sufferings of a small band of heroes ; unused, to be sure, to military tactics and due subordination, but whose souls were fired by an enthusiastic love of country, and a spirit such as has often inspired our ancestors, when determined to be free. In giving you this relation, knowing him as you do, you will scarcely call in question his veracity ; particularly when he assures you upon the honor of a gentleman and an honest man, that every word here related, to the best of his recollection and belief, is literally true. He could not be so unjust to your morals, your veracity, or integrity, as to state any thing to you which he knew, or even suspected to be untrue. He has himself been too much the victim of base liars, not to endeavor to eradicate so vile a principle from your minds. His own education, though made by his truant-isms (in avoidance of the bounteous and liberal designs of his good father), an incorrect one, yet the piety and real religious fervor of his parents, never would tolerate a lie. This mental vice, to them, was the greatest of all abominations, as it is with your father : it is also his most fervent hope and prayer, that every one of you, will not only contemn the lie, but hold in sovereign detestation the liar.

Persons at your age, and at this advanced stage of the improvement and melioration of our soil, in a climate so far south as ours, can scarcely form a correct conception, but from actual observation, of the sterility, the dreariness and the destitution of every comfort of life, which a wilderness in a high northern latitude exhibits. A confidence however in your good sense, encourages, and in fact animates him, to put that upon paper, which has a thousand times, in detached parcels, been the subject of amusing prattle around the fireside.   This is done the rather at this time, as some very atrocious scoundrels who never looked an enemy in the eye, now assume the garlands and honors which ought to adorn the brows of more worthy men.

In the autumn of 1775, our adorable Washington thought it prudent to make a descent upon Canada.   A detachment from the American grand army, then in the vicinity of Boston, Massachusetts, was organized, to fulfil this intention, by the route of the Kennebec and Chaudière rivers.   It was intended as a coöperation with the army of General Montgomery, who had entered the same province, by the way of Champlain and Montreal. Colonel Benedict Arnold was appointed the commander in chief of the whole division.   The detachment consisted of eleven hundred men.   Enos[1] was second in command. Of this I knew nothing, but from report.   Riflemen composed a part of the armament.   These companies, from sixty-five to seventy-five strong, were from the southward : that is, Captain Daniel Morgan's company

[1] The expedition consisted of two battalions ; the first commanded by Lieut. Col. Christopher Greene ; the second under Lt. Col. Roger Enos. It was subdivided into three divisions, the rear division being under the command of Enos, who, 25th October, abandoned the enterprise with his division, ignominiously taking the provisions, and returned to Cambridge.—*M*.

from Virginia ; that of Captain William Hendricks from Cumberland county in Pennsylvania, and Captain Matthew Smith's company from the county of Lancaster, in the latter province.[1]   The residue, and bulk of this corps consisted of troops from Massachusetts, Rhode Island and Connecticut.   It has flown from my memory, whether we had any from New Hampshire ; but there is an impression on my mind that we had, as General Dearborn, who was of the latter province, commanded a company in the expedition.   All these men were of as rude and hardy a race as ourselves, and as unused to the discipline of a camp, and as fearless as we were.   It fell to me to know many of them afterwards intimately ; speaking generally, without any allusion to particulars, they were an excellent body of men, formed by nature as the stamina of an army, fitted for a tough and tight defence of the liberties of their country.   The principal distinction between us, was in our dialects, our arms, and our dress.   Each man of the three companies bore a rifle-barreled gun, a tomahawk, or small axe, and a long knife, usually called a scalping-knife, which served for all purposes, in the woods.   His under-dress, by no means in a military style, was covered by a deep ash-colored hunting-shirt, leggings and moccasins, if the latter could be procured.   It was the silly fashion of those times, for riflemen to ape the manners of savages.[2]

---

[1] No sooner was a call for volunteers issued in 1775, than we find a company formed in Paxton and Derry in Pa., to march to Quebec ; having as officers and privates Matthew Smith, James Crouch, Richard Dixon, Robert McClure, Archibald Steele, Michael Simpson, John Joseph Henry, John Harris, eldest son of John Harris founder of Harrisburgh, and other honored names, now seldom recalled, but the remembrance of whose valiant deeds, hardy endurance, and patriotic sacrifices will never be forgotten by a grateful people.   Dixon and Harris never returned from Quebec.   One of them certainly was killed there ; the fate of the latter is quite uncertain.— *Centennial Address at Harrisburgh,* July 4, 1876, by A. B. HAMILTON.—*M.*

[2] The Canadians who first saw these men emerge from the woods, said they were *vetu en toile,* clothed in linen.   The word *toile* was changed to *tole,* iron plate.   By a mistake of a single word the fears of the people were greatly increased, for the news spread that the mysterious army that descended from the wilderness was clad in sheet iron.—*M.*

Our commander, Arnold, was of a remarkable character. He was brave, even to temerity ; was beloved by the soldiery, perhaps for that quality only. He possessed great powers of persuasion, was complaisant ; but, withal, sordidly avaricious. Arnold was a short, handsome man, of a florid complexion, stoutly made, and forty years old at least.[1]

On the other hand Morgan was a large, strong bodied personage, whose appearance gave the idea history has left us of Belisarius. His manners were of the severer cast ; but where he became attached he was kind and truly affectionate. This is said, from experience of the most sensitive and pleasing nature ; activity, spirit and courage in a soldier, procured his good will and esteem.

Hendricks was tall, of a mild and beautiful countenance. His soul was animated by a genuine spark of heroism. Smith was a good looking man, had the air of a soldier, was illiterate and outrageously talkative. The officers of the eastern troops were many of them men of sterling worth. Colonel Christopher Greene seemed too far advanced in life for such hard service, yet he was inspired by an ardor becoming a youth. He afterwards did the public good service at Redbank on the Delaware, in the autumn of 1777. Majors Meigs, Febiger and Bigelow, were excellent characters. As we acted in the advance, the latter gentlemen were not well known to us, until sometime afterwards. Your father was too young to enjoy any other honor than that of exposing himself, in the character of a cadet, to every danger. This little army in high spirits, marched from Prospect hill near Cambridge in Massachusetts, on the 11th of September, 1775, and on the following day[2]

---

[1] Arnold was but thirty-four years of age at this time. Notices of Arnold are found in the biographical dictionaries and elsewhere, and a pedigree of his family is given in HOUGH's *Am. Biog. Notes*, p. 8.—*M.*

[2] Portions of the army took different routes to Newburyport. The companies under Major Return J. Meigs marched from Roxbury, through Cambridge, Mystick, Malden, Lynn, Salem, Danvers, Beverly, Wenham, and Rowley. – *Mass. Hist. Soc. Coll.*, 2d series, II, 227, 228.

arrived at Newburyport (which is formed by the waters of the Merrimac river). This place, at that time, was a small but commercial town, near the border of Massachusetts. Here we remained encamped five days, providing ourselves with such articles of real necessity, as our small means afforded. On the afternoon of the sixth day, we embarked aboard of ten transports;[1] sailed in the evening, and at dawn of day descried the mouth of the Kennebec river. The wind was strong but fair. The distance of this run was 150 miles. We ascended the river to Colonel Colborn's ship yard;[2] here we left our vessels, and obtained bateaux, with which we proceeded to Fort Western. At this place, on the day of our arrival, an arrangement was made by the commander in chief, which in all probability sealed the destiny of your parent. It was concluded to dispatch an officer and seven men in advance, for the purposes of ascertaining and marking the paths, which were used by the Indians at the numerous carrying-places in the wilderness, towards the heads of the river; and also, to ascertain the course of the river Chaudière, which runs from the height of land, towards Quebec.

To give some degree of certainty of success to so hazardous an enterprise, Arnold found it necessary to

---

[1] On the 19th the detachment, consisting of ten companies of musketmen, and three companies of riflemen, amounting to 1100 men, embarked on board of ten transports, and sailed for the Kennebec river.—*Ibid,* 228.—*M.*

[2] The bateaux were built at Agry's point, about two miles below Gardiner, the residence of Major Colborn. It is mentioned in Meigs's Journal of the expedition, that but fourteen days had elapsed since orders had been given for building two hundred bateaux, collecting provisions for and levying eleven hundred men, and marching them to this place. Here the army embarked, on the 22d September, having taken two days to transfer their baggage and stores. It is mentioned in HANSON's *History of Gardner and Pittston,* that Col. Colborn, who built the bateaux, was never paid for them, and that his heirs unsuccessfully petitioned congress for remuneration. In Thayer's Journal the construction of the bateaux is most severely condemned as a fraud upon the government. See p. 6, THAYER's *Journal, R. I. Collections,* vol. 6.—*M.*

select an officer of activity and courage ; the choice fell upon Archibald Steele[1] of Smith's company, a man of an active, courageous, sprightly and hardy disposition, who was complimented with the privilege of naming his companions.   These consisted of Jesse Wheeler, George Merchant, and James Clifton, of Morgan's ; and Robert Cunningham, Thomas Boyd, John Tidd, and John

---

[1] Archibald Steele, a brother of Gen. John Steele, was a man of great intrepidity and resolute daring.   Upon the breaking out of the Revolution he and a man named Smith raised a company in Lancaster county and marched to Boston, where they were organized into a regiment and placed under the command of Benedict Arnold.   This was the regiment that made the celebrated march through the wilderness of Maine to Quebec, in the winter of 1775, which has ever been remembered as one memorable in the annals of American history.   During this march Archibald Steele had the command of a party of men who were selected to go before the army and mark out the roads and crossing places ; and on the arrival of the army at the St. Lawrence he was appointed superintendent of the crossing of the river.   At the head of his company Steele marched with the army to the attack upon Quebec, but upon the fall of Gen. Montgomery the Americans retreated, and Arnold's division were all taken prisoners.   He was badly wounded in the left hand, two of his fingers having been carried away by a musket shot.   The following may be cited as showing the heroic daring of Capt. Archibald Steele : On one occasion as the Americans were crossing a river in bark canoes, these were filled to their utmost capacity with men, and Capt. Steele seeing no room in the canoe leaped into the river, rested his hands on the stern of the boat whilst one of the men therein sat upon them, and thus was he dragged through the floating ice to the opposite shore.   When they reached the shore, life was almost extinct ; the soldiers wrapped him in their blankets, and rolled him over the ground to infuse new life in him.   On his return home from the Quebec expedition he met the American army in New Jersey, and was informed by Gen. Hand that two of his brothers, John Steele and Wm. Steele, were then serving with the army.   Capt. Archibald Steele asked Gen. Hand if he thought his brother John would be competent to assume the command of a company (being but eighteen years of age.)   Hand replied that he would warrant his qualification, and the commission was produced.   Archibald Steele was afterwards appointed deputy quartermaster general, a position he retained for some considerable time.   He was appointed by Washington colonel of a western expedition, but sickness prevented the acceptance of this command.   He held for some time in Philadelphia his position of military storekeeper.   He died in Philadelphia, Oct. 19, 1832, aged 91 years.   He had three sons in the naval service during the war of 1812 (George, William and Matthias), who were captured, taken to England, and there for a time detained as prisoners of war. — Harris's *Biog. Hist. Lancaster Co., Pa.*, 561.

M'Konkey, of Smith's company.   Though a very youth,
yet in a small degree accustomed to hardships, derived
from long marches in the American woods, Steele's
course of selection next fell upon your father, who was
his messmate and friend.   Two birch-bark canoes were
provided; and two guides, celebrated for the management of such water craft, and who knew the river as
high up as the great carrying-place were also found.
These were Jeremiah Getchel, a very respectable man,
and John Horne, an Irishman who had grown gray in
this cold climate.

This small party, unconscious of danger, and animated
by a hope of applause from their country, set forward
from Fort Western in their light barks, at the rate of
from fifteen to twenty, and in good water, twenty-five
miles per day.   These canoes are so light, that a person
of common strength may carry one of the smallest kind,
such as ours were, many hundred yards without halting.[1]
Yet they will bear a great burden, and swim nearly
gunwale deep ; an admirable description of them is given
by Hearne, in his Journey to the Coppermine river.
Steele's canoe bore five men with their arms and
baggage, which last was indeed light in quantity and
quality, one barrel of pork, one bag of meal, and 200
weight of biscuit.   The other canoe carried seven men,
their arms and baggage, and a due proportion of provisions.

---

[1] The gentlemen composing this party were unwilling to impose upon
me, any thing above my apparent strength, yet in the heyday of youth, I
would clap a canoe on my back, and run a hundred yards across a carrying-
place.   This is done by a particular mode of management.   There is a
broad stave, something like a flour barrel-stave, but straight and thicker,
with two perforations in it, an inch or more apart, towards the middle of
the stave.   A thong of stout leather is inserted through those holes, and
tightly bound to the central cross-bar of the canoe.   The carrier swings
the canoe by a sudden jerk upon his shoulders, and which he can handle
with ease, throwing the hollow side of the canoe on his back, the stave, if
it may be so called, resting principally on the hind part of the head, and
the prominences of the shoulders.   Thus he may, if a strong man, pass
over a considerable space of ground of a difficult nature, in a short time
with much speed.— *Henry.*

On the evening of the 23d of September, our party
arrived at Fort Halifax,[1] situated on the point formed by
a junction of the Sebasticook and Kennebec rivers.
Here our commander, Steele, was accosted by a Captain
Harrison, or Huddlestone, inviting him and the company
to his house.   The invitation was gladly accepted, as the
accommodation at the fort, which consisted of old block
houses and a stockade in a ruinous state, did not admit
of much comfort ; besides it was inhabited, as our friend
the captain said, by a *rank tory*.   Here for the first time
the application of the American term *tory*, was defined
to me by the captain.   Its European definition was well
known before.   Another interesting conversation upon
the part of the captain, struck my mind as a great
curiosity in natural history, and well deserving com-
memoration ; he observed that he had immigrated to the
place he then resided at, about thirty years before, most
probably with his parents, for he did not then appear to
be much beyond forty.   That at *that* period the common
deer which now inhabits our more southern climate, was
the only animal of the deer kind which they knew, unless it was the elk ; and them but partially.   In a short
space of time the moose deer appeared in small numbers,
but increased annually afterwards, and as the one species
became more numerous, the other diminished : so that
the kind of deer first spoken of, at the time of this information, according to the captain, was totally driven from
that quarter.   The moose deer reigned the master of
the forest.   This anecdote, if true, might in such minds

---

[1] Fort Halifax was built by Gov. Shirley of Massachusetts in 1754, by
engagement with the Plymouth company, who were to build Fort Western
at Cushnoc now Augusta.   It was located at Ticonic, the confluence of the
Sebasticook with the Kennebec, and was built of hewn timber, with a block
house at opposite angles of the fort, and picketed.   Plans of both forts are
given in NORTH's *History of Augusta*.   At Ticonic was the first carrying
place, where all the provisions and baggage had to be transported by land a
distance of eighty rods, and the bateaux dragged over by human force aided
by a yoke of oxen.— *M.*

as those of Buffon, or De Pauw, give occasion to systems in natural history, totally inconsistent with the laws of nature; still there may be something in it; animals, like human beings, whether forced by necessity or from choice, do migrate. Many instances might be given of this circumstance of the animal economy, in various parts of the world. The above relation is the only instance which has come to my knowledge, where one species has expelled another of the same genus. If the fact be true, it is either effected by a species of warfare, or some peculiarity in the appearance of the one kind, and of horror or perhaps of disgust in the other; we know the rock goat (*steinbock* of the Germans and *boquetin* of the French) formerly inhabited the low hills of southern France and of the Pyrenees; they have been driven thence by some peculiar cause, for they are now confined to the tops of the highest mountains in Europe. It is true, it has been frequently advanced by men of respectability and information in Pennsylvania, that the grey fox which is indigenous in the United States, and all North America, has been driven from the Atlantic sea coast into the interior, by the introduction of the red fox from Europe. But we have no sufficient data to warrant this assertion. The truth probably is, that as the grey fox is a dull and slow animal, compared with the sprightliness, rapidity, and cunning of the red fox, that the first has been thinned by the huntsmen, and gradually receded from the seacoast to the forest, where, from his habits, he is more secure. The cunning and prowess of the latter, has enabled him to maintain his station among the farms, in despite of the swiftness and powerful scent of the dogs. But that which puts this assertion out of view, is that the red fox is indigenous throughout North America. He and the grey fox are found in the highest latitudes, but there, their skins are changed into more beautiful furs than those of ours, by the effects of climate. Another notion has been started within these twenty years past, of the fox squirrel expelling the large grey squirrel : but it is fallacious.

Be these things as they may, we spent an agreeable and most sociable evening with this respectable man, and his amiable family. On the following day, our party rose early, and accompanied by our host, waited upon the *tory,* who then showed himself to be an honest man, of independent principles, and who claimed the right of thinking for himself. He exchanged a barrel of smoke-dried salmon for a barrel of pork, upon honest terms.

We set out from this place, well pleased with our host, the old tory, and our bargain. In a very few days, without other accident than the spraining of Lieut. Steele's ancle, by his slipping, when carrying a canoe over the path, at one of the intermediate portages, we arrived safely at Norridgewock falls. Coming to the landing place, the water being smooth and very deep, a rock, as we passed it, drew my attention very particularly, it was standing in a conical form, five feet in perpendicular height, and ten or twelve feet in diameter at the base. I observed that next the water, the face of the rock, which was a bluish flint, was, as it were, scalloped out, down to the very water's edge. Asking Getchel how this had occurred, his reply was that the Indians, in former times, had from thence obtained their spear and arrow points. It seems unreasonable that without a knowledge of iron, they should have been capable of executing such a labor. However, upon observation and reflection, since Getchel's time, an inducement from experience and reasoning occurs, which influences me to believe that he might have been correct in his observation. The rock, no doubt, still remains, and there is leisure for inquiry and discussion.

We were hurried. The village within one hundred yards of the pitch of the fall, was evidently a deserted

Indian town.[1] We saw no one there. It was without
the vestige of inhabitants. Dressing our victuals here
at mid-day, an occurrence happened, which disgusted me
in an extreme degree. On this day, an estimate of our
food was made, and an allotment in quantity to each man,
though no actual separation of shares took place, as *that*,
it was agreed, should happen at the twelve-mile carrying
place.   By the estimate now made, it seemed that there
was something of a surplus. As we had had hard work,
that and some preceding days, and harder fare, our good
commander was inclined to indulge us.   The surplus
was allotted for this day's fare. It happened that
M'Konkey was, by routine, the cook. He boiled the
meat (vegetable food of any kind was not attainable),
and when sauntering towards the fall, he called us to
dinner.   We came eagerly. He was seated on the earth,
near the wooden bowl. The company reclined around
in a like posture, intending to partake ; when M'Konkey
raising his vile and dirty hands, struck the meat, exclaim-
ing, " By G—d this was our last comfortable meal."
The indelicacy of the act, its impiety, and the grossness
of the expression, deprived the company of appetite.   On
several subsequent occasions M'Konkey showed himself
as mean in spirit, as he was devoid of decency.   We soon
rid ourselves of him.   Many years afterwards, at Lancaster, in Pennsylvania, he applied and received a loan
by way of charity from me, which he meanly solicited
with the most abject sycophancy.   So true it is, in
general, that those who disregard the social decencies of

---

[1] The advanced party arrived at Norridgewock on the 2d of October.
This was the third carrying place, and had been the residence of the noted
Jesuit missionary, Rale, among the Conibas, usually called the Norridgewock
Indians, who for many years were a great scourge to the advancing English.
A vigorous attack was made upon the place in 1724, when Rale was killed
on the 24th of August, and the Indian village destroyed.   Vestiges of it,
and of a Catholic chapel, as well as the priest's grave still remained.   Here
were repaired their hastily constructed bateaux, which in the end caused
great loss of provisions and munitions, and here they left the abode of man,
and entered upon the uninhabited wilderness.—*M.*

life, are equally incapable of those virtues which make man respectable in society.

On the afternoon of this day, we crossed to the west side of the river below the fall: searched for, and with difficulty found the carrying place. Having marked it with precision, we rested awhile. On the west side of the river, not very distant from us, there was a considerable extent of natural meadow.[1] One of our party, ex-

---

[1] In traversing this meadow, which was a beautiful plain, one of the party found the horns of a moose-deer, which from appearances had been shed in the foregoing summer, or perhaps in the beginning of autumn; being then about five feet ten inches high. Getchell, facetiously, yet gravely, insisted by way of measurement, that I should stand under the main fork. The crown of my head rubbed against the crown-work of the horns. This, to all of us, was matter of great surprise. However, in a short time afterwards the circumstance of size was thought little of, when we came into contact with the living animal, upon whose head such horns grew. There is a paucity of words for a description upon paper, of the enormous dimensions of the male moose, which we saw, and of their horns. The male-deer bears horns; the female bears none. Those horns, which we examined minutely, were of a large size, but not so large as some we saw on the living deer. About midway of the horn, from the crown of the head, there is a broad, flat part of the horn, called the blade, which, in the specimen under examination, was full two of my spans, or nearly twenty inches from whence branched the proud antlers or prong. There is no beast of the forest more handsomely decorated, unless it be the reindeer of the north of Europe and Asia. In the evenings, in the first ascension of the Kennebec and Dead rivers, sitting around our solitary smoke fires, we have often seen those stately deer passing the river in droves, sometimes of fifteen or twenty in number, the one walking after the other in the accustomed path, but due care and discipline kept our arms quiet. The country around Natanis's house, a circle of ten or fifteen miles, was at that time an admirable hunting ground. One day, suddenly passing a sharp point of the river about five miles below Natanis's cabin, we as suddenly fell back. We wanted fresh food. Regardless of what might follow, Steele permitted us to fire. We had seen five or six of those monstrous deer, standing in the water knee-deep, feeding on their favorite food, the red willow. Boyd, Wheeler and myself passed the river, out of sight of the moose, in the most cautionary manner. The stream here was not more than sixty yards wide. We approached them through the thick underwood, which clothed the bank. Boyd preceded. The rustling of the leaves alarmed the deer. They threw up their heads. What a sight! The antlers of several of them, seemed to exceed in size, those we had already seen. Boyd, apprehensive they were about to run from us, fired without giving Wheeler and myself an opportunity to take a stand, but the greatest misfortune was, that the worthy Boyd had neglected to clean his gun that day, it made long fire, and but a trifling

ploring the country for deer, met with two white men
who had come from a distance, mowing the wild grass
of the meadow.   An agreeable barter ensued ; we gave
salted pork, and they returned two fresh beaver tails,
which, when boiled, renewed ideas imbibed with the
May-butter of our own country.   Taste, however, is
arbitrary, and often the child of necessity.   Two years
before this, acorns had supplied me with a precarious
sustenance, on a journey from Sandusky to Pittsburg ;
it momentarily sustained life and bodily labor, but the
consequence was ill health.   Your respectable kinsman,
General Gibson, received me into his house at Logstown
on the Ohio, and restored me sound to my parents.
These minute matters are noted here from an expectation
that, knowing the privations men may suffer in respect
to food, you will each of you remember to receive the
dispensations of Providence, of every kind, if not with
thankfulness, at least with submission.

We passed the portage of Norridgewock falls.   Thence
for several days, the navigation for such canoes as ours
was tolerable, and in the most part convenient.   We
ascended the river rapidly, blazing every carrying-place.
Having now receded many miles from the last white
inhabitants at Norridgewock, it became us therefore to
proceed cautiously.   A circumspection was adopted,
which, though prudent in the predicament we were in,
appeared to be rather harsh to the feelings ; the firing of
a gun was prohibited ; though the weather was chilling,

---

report.   The bullet scarcely reached the deer.   Wheeler and myself were
creeping to our places when Boyd's gun disturbed the animals.   The guns
in our hands were ineffectually discharged.   This jejune occurrence is related
merely for the introduction of a single observation.   When the bull moose,
at the rustling of the leaves, and afterwards when Boyd fired, threw up
their heads, the tips of their horns seemed to me to stand eighteen feet in
the air.   The ridge of the shoulder seemed seventeen hands high.   The
largest of these animals was a *lusus naturæ.*   The moose in ordinary, is of
an ash-colored grey.   The one I speak of was flecked, in large spots of red,
on a pure white ground.   His skin, if we could have obtained it, would
have been a valuable curiosity. — *Henry.*

we dared scarcely make a smoke at night. Angling for trout and chub in the morning and evening, made up our stock of fresh food. We frequently saw ducks, etc., and many moose deer, yet we discharged not a gun; in truth we had been made to believe that this country had numerous Indians in it.

The party proceeded without molestation but from natural rock, and a strict current (by the 27th of September)[1] to the twelve-mile carrying-place.[2] Here a new scene opened. Our guides professed that neither of them had ever been north of this place across the carrying-place, but Getchel alleged he had hunted to the east of the river.

Now we assumed the title of being our own guides, giving to Getchel due respect and attention for his information relative to the route north. He informed me that the course of the river, which is injudiciously called the Dead river, tended sixty or one hundred miles northerly, took a short turn southwardly, and was then within twelve miles of us. That that part was full of rapids, and impassable to boats, or even canoes. We searched for the carrying-place, and found a path tolerably distinct, which we made more so by blazing the trees and snagging the bushes with our tomahawks; proceeding until evening, the party encamped at the margin of a

---

[1] It will be remembered that this was the advanced party. Other divisions were nearly two weeks later in reaching this point. The divisions do not seem to have followed each other in the same route, some going by water, others seeking better paths than had been taken by their predecessors.—*M.*

[2] This celebrated portage is through the third range of townships of the Bingham purchase, in latitude 45° 15′, and is about fourteen miles long from the Kennebec to Dead river. It is divided into four carrying places by three ponds. The first carry is three and three-fourths miles to the first pond, which is one-fourth of a mile wide; the second carry a mile to the second pond, about as wide as the first; the third about the same length as the second, to the third pond about four miles wide. From this the fourth carry of four miles reaches to the Dead river. — NORTH's *History of Augusta,* 127-8. The map facing the title page, gives a tolerably correct plan of the route pursued, on as small a scale as it is possible to represent it.—*M.*

small lake, perhaps about half a mile wide, where there was plenty of trout, which old Clifton, who was good at angling, caught in abundance.   Here, in a conference on the subject, it was resolved that two persons of the party should remain (with about one-half of the provisions), until the return of our main body, calculating the return would be in eight or ten days.   It had been observed that Clifton, being the oldest of the company, yet brave and a good shot, from the fatigues we had endured, had begun to flag.   With the assent of our chief, the younger part of us proposed to him to remain where we then were, with the better part of the provisions. After considerable altercation he assented, on condition of his having a companion.   The youngest of the party nominated M'Konkey, who could not restrain his joy at the proposal.   It was advised for them to retire to the south end of the pond, perhaps a mile, and there, as in a perfect recess, remain concealed ; knowing M'Konkey, the consequences were foreseen.   After the accomplishment of this affair, Lieutenant Steele parted the provision appropriated for the marchers, not by pounds or ounces, my dear children but by : " Whose shall be this." Some of you have been taught how this is done ; if you should have forgotten, it will be well now to tell you of it. The principal of the party, if he is a gentleman and man of honor, divides the whole portion equally into as many parts as there are men, including himself; this is done under the eyes of all concerned, and with their approbation the officer then directs some one of the company to turn his back upon him, and laying his hand on a particular portion, asks, " Whose shall be this ?" The answer is hap-hazard, A, S, etc., or any other of the party. It has frequently occurred that we were compelled to divide the necessaries of life in this way, and it could not be fairly said, that any fraud or circumvention took place.

September 28th, we left Clifton and his companion in a most dreary wild, but with enough to support them ;

and if they would act honorably, to assist us. A laughable occurrence ensued. Sergeant Boyd and myself had,
that day, the charge of unloading and loading the canoes,
which, as customarily, being very light and easily blown
off shore by a puff of wind, were drawn half their lengths
on the beach ; we ran a race who should perform his
duty soonest — he arrived first. Taking up his canoe
suddenly, but hoping to have a better stand than the
shore presented, he set his foot on a large bed of moss
seemingly firm, and sunk ten feet into as cold water,
while fluid, as was ever touched. We soon passed the
pond, found the path, marked it, and came, at the end of
several miles, to a second pond, if my recollection serves,
larger than the former : traversing this, we encamped
more cautiously than ever. On the next day, pursuing
the path, and marking it, a third pond of small diameter
was presented to our view. Passing this, by the evening
we encamped on the north bank of the Dead river.

This river, which is nothing more than an extension
of the Kennebec,[1] is called by this remarkable name,
because a current, a few miles below the place we were
now at, and for many miles above it, is imperceptible.
It is deep and perhaps two hundred and fifty yards wide.
The ground we footed within the last three days, is a
very rugged isthmus, which forms the great bend of the
Kennebec. Coming from the high ground towards the
Dead river, we passed a bog which appeared, before we
entered it, as a beautiful plat of firm ground, level as a
bowling green, and covered by an elegant green moss.
That day, to save my shoes for severer service, moccasins had been put in their place. Every step we made,
sunk us knee-deep in a bed of wet turf. My feet were
pained and lacerated by the snags of the dead pines, a foot
and more below the surface of the moss ; these and many
other occurrences, which happened afterwards, con-

---

[1] The Dead river is a western branch of the Kennebec, as will be seen
by reference to the map.—*M.*

vinced me more than reading could, of the manner of
the formation of turf. Sometimes, to lighten the canoes
when ascending strict water, several of us would disem-
bark, and proceed along shore, and on many occasions,
traverse a point of land to save distance. Doing this, we
often met with what we thought a flat ground covered
by moss. Entering the parterre, as it might be called,
and running along that which we found to be a log
covered with moss, the moisture on the log, would cause
a foot to slip — down we would come, waist deep in a
bed of wet moss; such incidents always created a laugh.
A spark, if these beds of moss had been dry, as they
were wet, would have made a dreadful conflagration: the
upper country seemed throughout as if covered with it.
To the south and west of the bog first mentioned, there
was a natural meadow of great extent. On the west it
reached, seemingly, to the foot of the mountains several
miles off. A beautiful creek serpentined through it and
formed a convenient harbor and landing place, opposite
to our camp, and directly to which the Indian path led us.

The timber trees of this, are in great measure different
from those of our country. Here are neither oaks,
hickories, poplars, maples nor locusts; but there is a
great variety of other kinds of excellent timber, such as
the white and yellow pines, hemlock, cedar, cypress, and
all the species of the firs.[1] These trees, in the low
grounds, grow to a very large size; on the hills, as we
approach northwardly, they seem to dwindle, particularly
as we come to the height of land; but again rise to a
superb height, as we descend into the intervale, on the
streams running into Canada. Among the trees of this
country, there are two which deserve particular notice,
because of their remarkable qualities. These are the

---

[1] The balsam fir (*pinus fraseri*), overlooked by Michaux, but differing
from the silver fir, was found to be very abundant (Pres. ALLEN in vol. 1,
Maine Hist. Coll., 160). It was this fir which Henry mentions, the liquid
of which he was taught to gather.— *M.*

balsam fir, Canada balsam. Balm of Gilead fir, or *balsamum Canadense, pinus balsomea,* which produces the purest turpentine, and the yellowbirch The first, as its vulgar name imports, yields a balsamic liquid, which has been, and perhaps now is, much esteemed by the medical profession. The bark is smooth, except that there are a vast number of white and lucid protuberances upon it, of the size of a finger or a thumb nail, bulging from the surface of the bark. This tree grows to the size of from fifteen to twenty inches in diameter. From the essays made, it seems to me that a vial containing a gill might be filled in the space of an hour. Getchel, our guide, taught me its use. In the morning when we rose, placing the edge of a broad knife at the under side of the blister, and my lips at the opposite part, on the back of the knife which was declined, the liquor flowed into my mouth freely. It was heating and cordial to the stomach, attended by an agreeable pungency. This practice, which we adopted, in all likelihood contributed to the preservation of health. For though much wet weather ensued, and we lay often on low and damp ground, and had very many successions of cold atmosphere, it does not now occur to me, that any one of us was assailed by sickness, during this arduous excursion. The yellow birch is useful in many particular instances to the natives. They form the body of the tree into setting-poles, paddles, spoons and ladles. The bark, its better property, serves as a covering for the frame of the canoe, much in the same manner as the Esquimaux and Greenlanders apply the seal skin. To you it may appear to be a strange assertion, but to me it seems true, that the birch-bark canoe is the most ingenions piece of mechanism man, in a rude state, is capable of performing. This bold idea requires a disclosure of the means and the manner of the work, which shall be done before I leave the subject.[1]

---

[1] The birch-bark canoe, as intimated before, in the body of the work, is not only a curious, but a most ingenious machine. So far as my descrip-

From the bark of the yellow-birch the Indian also forms bowls, and baskets of a most beautiful construction, and it even serves as a wrapper for any nice matter which it is wished to keep securely, much in the manner we use brown wrapping-paper. The appearance of the yellow birch tree at a distance, is conspicuous. Approaching near it, in the autumn, it seems involved in rolls, something resembling large circular rounds of parchment, or yellow-paper. There is in my mind no question, but that among a numerous and industrious people, such as the

---

tive powers extend, you shall have its construction, described in writing but without the aid of the pencil it seems to be almost impossible to convey to you a just and accurate comprehension of the distinct parts of this beautiful piece of water-craft. Having had several opportunities to observe the manner of the formation of the birch-bark canoe, in its various stages, a description of its sections may not be disagreeable to you. In the construction of the canoe, the bow and stern pieces are separate frames, alike in dimensions, and made of cedar, cypress, or any other light wood ; yet very light, and so well or tightly bound by tenons, as to require a considerable effort to break them. These bow and stern pieces, suppose a canoe of ten, or even fifty feet, are connected by laths, with that which I have called gunwales (gunnels), correspondent in size with the intended length of the canoe. These gunwales are made from the toughest and best of the timber that the country produces. The gunwales are strongly secured to the head and stern by tenons and the cedar root in a most neat and strong manner. The ribs of the canoe, according to its size, are from two to five inches in diameter, of the straightest cedar or fir, without knots, closely fitted together, side by side, and well sewed by means of an awl to the gunwales. This frame is covered with the yellow-birch-rind, an eighth, a sixth, or a fourth of an inch thick. This bark, when applied to canoes, is from two to four feet in length ; commensurate with the extension of the bow and stern from each other. Each part of this bark, where the seams meet, is nicely sewed together by the split cedar root ; these seams are then pitched over in a ridge, by a hard pitch, in the width of perhaps an inch or more, so as to make the vessel, truly that which seamen call water-tight. But to this clumsy attempt to describe to you a boat, which you have never seen, and perhaps never will see, it seems requisite to add another observation. The bark which encircles the bottom of the canoe, is strongly attached to the gunwales by cedar root, much in the same manner as I have seen you threading wire, for the making of artificial flowers. This bark, thus prepared and applied, speaking comparatively (great with small), is a much stronger material, than your thread, either of flax or silk. The gunwale was as neatly laced by the cedar, and almost as ornamental, and equally strong in texture, as the canes we sometimes see from India, covered with splits of rattan, or some other pliant plant, of southern growth. The

Chinese, this indigenous product would become an article of general use in various ways. The bark, when taken from the tree, may be obtained lengthwise of the tree, from one to four feet in breadth, and of a length equal to the circumference. It is sometimes white with a yellowish cast, but more usually of a pale, and sometimes of a deep gold color. It is partible, when ever so thick, into the most filmy sheets. The Indians, for canoes, use it of the thickness of from a fourth, down to the eighth of an inch, according to the size of the vessel. Curiosity and convenience made us reduce it often to a

---

paddles are uniformly made of ash, where it can be obtained, but most usually of birch, or even of softer wood, in this part of Canada. Many of the paddles which I saw, were double-bladed, that is a blade at each end of the handle or pole, and in the hands of a strong person would be, from its formation, apparently as light as a feather. The pushing-pole was of the same kind of materials, but light, and if iron could be had, was shod at the but-end. The rapid and rocky rivers which those poor people, the Indians, must ascend and descend in their hunting excursions, and which they do with inconceivable dexterity, requires a quickness of motion of the body, particularly the arms, which is truly astonishing. The paddle, at this moment used on the right, and then instantly cast on the left hand of the canoe, requires a celerity of action which none but such as are used to those exercises dare undertake. In those instances the double-bladed paddle, saves half the time which would be employed by the single bladed, in these arduous but necessary labors. Activity and agility, from the circumstance of the precariousness of an Indian life, and their manner of subsisting, become in their education a primary parental motive ; without those qualities, an Indian can never acquire fame, and is often starved.

It often reëxhilerates my mind, when reflecting on the waywardness and unhappiness of my life, to remember the occurrences (July 1773), in a part of a days journey from the windlass of the old carrying place, on the south side of the river, west of Niagara, by a path which led us to a celebrated fountain, a little below the brow of the hill, called Mount Pleasant, and thence to the falls. My youthful imagination was greatly excited. The company consisted of a French gentleman, my uncle John Henry, and myself. The Frenchman was a trader who had but just arrived from the Illinois country, and had dealt beyond the Mississippi. When we came to Stedman's, his canoe, attended by three or four *couriers de bois*, lay on the beach turned upside down, with an immense number of packs of beaver, press-packed, strewed around, perhaps the whole might have been 3000 lb. weight. The canoe was of birch, fifty feet in'length, most beautifully made, its breadth was probably from six to seven feet in the middle, I examined with a curiosity, such as a boy of my age might possess.— *Henry*.

film, by no means thicker or more substantial than the silky paper we obtain from India.   It serves equally well for the pencil as paper.   Ink, however, flows upon it. In the course of time a medium may be discovered to preclude this inconvenience — this bark will preserve better than paper.

September 30th.   The company, not apprehending the reverses which fortune had in store for them, left the encampment full of courage and hope, though a strong drift of snow, which whitened all the surrounding hills, had fallen during the night.   Having smooth water, we paddled away merrily, probably for thirty miles. Getchel, besides his *sheer* wisdom, possessed a large fund of knowledge concerning the country, which he had derived from the aborigines, and much humorous anecdote with which, in spite of our privations, he made us laugh.   It was omitted to be mentioned that, before we left our last encampment, it became a resolution of the whole party that the pork in the possession of each one should be eaten raw, and to eat but in the morning and evening.   As we could not obtain food in this miserable portion of the globe, even for money, if we had it, and having nothing else than our arms and our courage to depend on; unacquainted with the true distance of our expedition, for we had neither map nor chart, yet resolved to accomplish our orders at the hazard of our lives — we prudently began to hoard our provision ; half a biscuit and half an inch square of raw pork, became this evening's meal.   The day's journey brought us to the foot of a rapid, which convinced us that the term Dead river was much misapplied.   The night was spent, not upon feathers, but the branches of the fir or the spruce.   It would astonish you, my dear children, if there was leisure to explain to you, the many comforts and advantages those trees afford to the way-worn traveler.   Suffice it now to say, we rested well.

October 1st.   The morning brought on new labors. Our secondary guide and myself, thinking that we could manage the water, slipped into our canoe.   Getchel and another worked Steele's, while our companions, crossing the hill, marked the carrying-place.   From our camp two-thirds at least of these rapids were concealed from our view.   In much danger, and by great exertion, we surmounted them in less than an hour.   Taking in our company, we had good water till the evening, when we were impeded by a precipitate fall of four feet.   We encamped.

October 2d.   Carrying here, we had good water all the next day.   Mere fatigue and great lassitude of body, most likely, in a good measure, owing to the want of food, caused us to sleep well.   From cautionary motives our guns, though not uncared for, were considered as useless, in the way of obtaining food.   Several of our company angled successfully for trout, and a delicious chub, which we call a fall fish.   This place became remarkable to me, as, sometime afterwards, my friends Gen. Simpson,[1] Robert Dixon, and myself were here at the point of death.   This you will find in the sequel. Carrying a few perches around this precipice, we got into good water, and then performed a severe day's labor.

October 3d.   The evening brought us to our encampment, on the south side of the river.   Angling was

---

[1] Michael Simpson was a native of Paxtang, Penn., born about 1740. He entered the company of Capt. Matthew Smith, of Paxtang, as second lieutenant, his commission bearing date June 25, 1775.   At the time of the assault upon Quebec he was, by order of Arnold, in command as lieutenant at the isle of Orleans.   After the termination of the attack on Quebec he returned with the remnant of the army.   On the 1st of Dec., 1776, he was appointed captain in Col. Thompson's regiment.   He served in the battles of Trenton, Princeton, Brandywine, and White Plains.   Also served in Sullivan's campaign against the Northern Indians in 1779, but upon the consolidation of the regiments he was retired in Jan. 1781.   After the close of the war he married, removed to his farm two miles below Harrisburgh on the west side of the Susquehanna.   He died June 1, 1813, at the age of 73, and lies in the grave yard at Paxtang church.   The general was possessed of amiable qualities, was a warm friend, kind, liberal and obliging (*Letter from Dr. Ogle*).   His death is mentioned in Drake's Biog. Dictionary as having occurred 15 June, 1813, aged 80. — *M.*

resorted to for food. Sergeant Boyd, observing low ground on the other side of the river, and an uncommon coldness in the water, passed over, and in an hour returned with a dozen trout of extraordinary appearance, long, broad and thick. The skin was of a very dark hue, beautifully sprinkled with deep crimson spots. Boyd had caught these in a large and deep spring-head.[1] Contrasting them with those we caught in the river, they were evidently of a different species. The river trout were of a pale ground, with pink spots, and not so flat or broad.

October 4th. The next day, proceeding onward, we here and there met with rough water. In the evening we were told that on the next day we probably should arrive at the camp of Natanis, an Indian, whom our commander was instructed to capture or kill. Natanis was well known to the white inhabitants of the lower country : they knew from him the geographical position of his residence. The uninstructed Indian, if he possesses good sense, necessarily from his wanderings as a hunter, becomes a geographer. This good man (as we subsequently knew him to be), had been wrongfully accused to Arnold, as a spy, stationed on this river to give notice to the British government of any party passing this way into Canada : hence that cruel order. We landed some miles below where we supposed his house was. Our canoes were brought upon the shore, and committed to the care of two of the party. We arrived at the house of Natanis, after a march, probably of three miles, over a flat country covered with pines, etc. Approaching on all sides with the utmost circumspection, we ran quickly to the cabin, our rifles prepared, and in full belief that we had caught Natanis. Some were

---

[1] This peculiarity of the trout is said to be common in deep water; exposure to light affecting the color and structure of the fish. This is ventured upon the remark of a trout fisherman without having given the subject investigation.— *M.*

persuaded, at the distance of two hundred yards from the place, that they saw the smoke of his fire. But the bird was flown. He was wiser and more adroit than his assailants, as you will afterwards learn. The house was prettily placed on a bank twenty feet high, about twenty yards from the river, and a grass plat extended around, at more than shooting distance for a rifle, free from timber and brushwood. The house, for an Indian cabin, was clean and tight, with two doors, one fronting the river, the other on the opposite side. We found many articles of Indian fabrication, evidently such as would not be totally abandoned by the owner : besides, it was remarked, that the coals on the hearth, from their appearance, had been burning at least within a week past. These notions did not allay our apprehensions of meeting with Indian enemies. The canoes, in the meantime, having been brought up, we embarked and proceeded with alacrity.

This afternoon, in a course of some miles, we came to a stream flowing from the west, or rather the northwest. As we were going along in uncertainty, partly inclined to take the westerly stream, one of the party fortunately saw a strong stake, which had been driven down at the edge of the water, with a piece of neatly folded birch-bark, inserted into a split at the top. The bark, as it was placed, pointed up the westerly stream, which at its mouth seemed to contain more water than that of our true course. Our surprise and attention were much heightened, when opening the bark, we perceived a very perfect delineation of the streams above us, with several marks which must have denoted the hunting camps, or real abodes of the map maker. There were some lines, in a direction from the head of one branch to that of another, which we took to be the course of the paths which the Indians intended to take that season. This map we attributed to Natanis ; if not his, to his brother Sabatis, who, as we afterwards knew, lived about seven miles up this westerly stream. For when our party,

after returning to the twelve mile carrying-place, had
again reascended the river, we were told, by the crew of
one of Morgan's boats, that they had mistaken the
westerly stream as the due route, and had found deserted
cabins at the distance already mentioned, and the property
of the late inhabitants placed in a kind of close cages,
made of birch-bark, in the forks of the trees ; these they
most iniquitously plundered. Venison, corn, kettles,
etc., were the product. Inspecting the map thus acquired,
we pursued our journey fearlessly. Now the river
became narrower and shallower. The strength of each
of us was exerted at poling or paddling the canoes. Some
strict water interfered, but in a few days we came to the
first pond, at the head of the Dead river.

October 7th. This first pond, in the course of the
traverse we made, might be about a mile, or a little more,
in diameter. Here, on a small island, scarcely containing one-fourth of an acre, we discovered and ate a
delicious species of cranberry, entirely new to us. It
grew upon a bush from ten to twelve feet high, the stock
of the thickness of the thumb, and the fruit was as large
as a may-duke cherry.[1] In the course of one or two
miles, we reached a second pond. Between this pond
and the third, we carried ; the communication, though
not long, was too shallow for our canoes. The carrying-
place was excessively rugged, and in high water formed
a part of the bed of the stream. The country around
us had now become very mountainous and rough.
Several of these mountains seemed to stand on insulated
bases, and one in particular, formed a most beautiful
cone, of an immense height. We rested for the evening.

October 8th. Being near the height of land which
divides the waters of New-England from those of
Canada, which run into the St. Lawrence, the weather

---

[1] This was doubtless the acid fruit of *viburnum oxycoccus,* which I found
on the river De Loup, a branch of the Chaudière, in Sept., 1824 (**Pres.**
Allen, in *Me. Hist. Soc. Coll.,* 1, 507).— *M.*

in consequence of the approaching winter, had become piercingly cold. My wardrobe was scanty and light. It consisted of a roundabout jacket, of woolen, a pair of half worn buckskin breeches, two pair of woolen stockings (bought at Newburyport), a hat with a feather, a hunting-shirt, leggings, a pair of moccasins, and a pair of tolerably good shoes, which had been closely hoarded.

We set out early, yet jovially. We entered a lake surrounded by high and craggy mountains, and perpendicular rocks of very considerable altitude, which about eleven o'clock, A.M., cast us into a dusky shade. Pulling the paddle, as for life, to keep myself warm, some trifling observation which fell from me, relative to the place we were in, such as its resemblance to the vale of death, which drew the attention of the company : Getchel, in his dry way, turning toward me, said, " Johnny, you look like a blue leather whet stone." The simplicity and oddity of the expression, and the gravity of his manner, caused great merriment at my expense ; it was enjoyed on my part, certain that it was not an expression of disesteem, but affection, for the man liked me. These minim tales and jejune occurrences are related to convey to your minds an idea, how men of true spirit will *beard* death in every shape, even, at times, with laughter, to effectuate a point of duty which is considered as essential to the welfare of their country. Thus we went on, incessantly laboring, without sustenance, until we came, about three o'clock, to the extreme end of a fifth and the last lake. This day's voyage might amount to fifteen or twenty miles.[1]

[1] In the fall of 1858 a young man passing up the Dead-river valley and across the chain of ponds, the head of the river, landing at the Arnold trails, found by the side of the trail between the Dead-river waters and the Chaudière, the remains of an old musket, apparently having been left standing against a tree, where it had rotted down. The stock was entirely gone, and the barrel and mountings had fallen down together at the foot of the tree. It is conjectured that the musket had been left there by one of Arnold's soldiers, and the barrel is now in the possession of Mr. Columbus Steward, of North Anson, Maine, who says that the Arnold trail

On this lake we obtained a full view of those hills which were then, and are now, called the height of land. It made an impression upon us that was really more chilling than the air which surrounded us. We hurried ashore, drew out our canoes, and covered them with leaves and brush-wood. This done, with our arms in our hands, and our provision in our pockets, we made a race across the mountain, by an Indian path, easily ascertainable, until we arrived on the bank of the Chaudière river. The distance is about five miles, counting the rising and descent of the hill as two. This was the acme of our desires. To discover and know the course of this river, was the extent of our orders : beyond it, we had nothing to do. Our chief, wishing to do every thing a good officer could, to forward the service, asked, if any one could climb a tree, around the foot of which we then stood ? It was a pine of considerable height, without branches for forty feet ; Robert Cunningham, a strong athletic man, about twenty-five years old, presented himself. In almost the twinkling of an eye, he

---

on the divide as it is called, between the head waters of Dead river and the Chaudière is still easily followed, and is often passed over by lumbermen and hunters. The following appeared in the *Maine Farmer* in 1877 : —*M.*

"*A Centennial Relic.* Mr. Sheppard Harville of Lincolnville, has in his possession a French rifle gun barrel, that he found over thirty years ago, on Dead river at the foot of Arnold's falls, so called from the fact of its being on the route that Arnold marched with his army, through the wilderness to Point Levi, Quebec. It is one of the numerous falls by which he was obliged to carry his bateaux ; Skowhig falls, Skowhegan ; Bombazee falls, Norridgewock ; Carratunk falls, Solon ; and Hurricane falls, near White's ferry, Dead river.

Arnold's falls are a few miles below Flagstaff village, where Arnold raised his flag. He then sent Sergeant Bigelow and a few chosen men up on a high mountain, near by, to see if they could discover settlements in Canada ; hence the name, Mt. Bigelow.

" Mr. Harville then of Solon, Charles Folsom and others of Skowhegan, Hartly Green and Asa Green of Dead river, were driving logs for Captain John Wheeler of Skowhegan. Hartly and Asa Green being the boatmen on the drive near where this gun barrel was found by Mr. Harville. When discovered by him on the trail near the falls, it was resting against a rock. The stock had entirely rotted off ; and it is supposed to have been left there by one of Arnold's men one hundred years ago last September."

climbed the tree. He fully discerned the meandering course of the river, as upon a map, and even descried the lake Chaudière, at the distance of fourteen or fifteen miles. The country around and between us and the lake was flat. Looking westward, he observed a smoke; intimating this to us, from the tree where he sat, we plainly perceived it. Cunningham came down; the sun was setting seemingly in a clear sky.

Now our return commenced. It so occurred, that I was in the rear, next to Getchel, who brought it up. We ran in single file, and while it was light, it was observed by me, as we tried to stride into the footsteps of the leader, that he covered the track with his feet; this was no mean duty. It required the courage, the vigor, and the wisdom, which designates genuine manhood. Our object was to be concealed from a knowledge of any one who might communicate our presence there, to the Canadian government. The race was urged, and became more rapid by the indications of a most severe storm of rain; we had scarcely more than gotten half way up the hill, when the shower came down in most tremendous torrents. The night became dark as pitch; we groped the way across the ridge, and in descending, relied on the accuracy of our leader, we continued with speed. The precipice was very steep; a root, a twig, perhaps, caught the buckle of my shoe: tripped, I came down head foremost, unconscious how far, but perhaps twenty or thirty feet. How my gun remained unbroken, it is impossible to say. When I recovered, it was in my hands. My companions had outstripped me. Stunned by the fall, feeling for the path with my feet, my arrival at the canoe-place was delayed, till ten at night, an hour and more later than my friends. An erection called a tent, but more correctly a wigwam, was made in the hurry with forks, and cross-poles, covered by the branches of fir. It rained incessantly all that night. If the clothes we wore had been dry, they would have become wet — so we laid down in

all those we had on.   Sleep came to my eyes, notwithstanding the drippings of the pelting storm, through the
humble roof.

October 9th.   We arose before day.   The canoes
were urged suddenly into the water, it still rained hard,
and at daylight we thought of breakfasting.   Gracious
God! what was our fare? What could we produce for
such a feast?   Rummaging my breeches pockets, I found
a solitary biscuit and an inch of pork.   Half of the
biscuit was devoted to the breakfast, and so also by each
person, and that was consumed in the canoes as we
paddled over the lake.   The rain had raised the lake,
and consequently the outlets about four feet.   We slided
glibly along, over passages where a few days previously
we had carried our canoes.   At the outlet of the fourth
lake, counting as we came up, a small duck appeared
within shooting distance.   It was a diver, well known
in our country — a thing which we here contemn.
Knowing the value of animal food, in our predicament,
several of us fired at the diver : Jesse Wheeler, however
(who all acknowledged as an excellent shot), struck it
with his ball.   A shout of joy arose — the little diver
was safely deposited in our canoe.   We went on quickly,
without accident, till the evening, probably traversing a
space of more than forty miles.   At night-fall we halted,
weary and without tasting food since morning.   Boyd
and Cunningham, who were right-hand men on most
occasions, soon kindled a fire against a fallen tree.   An
occurrence this evening took place, which my dear
children you will hardly credit, but which (permit me to
assure you) is sacredly true ; the company sat themselves gloomily around this fire.   The cooks, according
to routine (whether our chief or others), picked the duck,
and when picked and gutted, it was brought to the fireside.   Here it became a question how to make the most
of our stock of provisions.   Finally it was concluded to
boil the duck in our camp-kettle, together with each
man's bit of pork, distinctively marked by running a

4

small skewer of wood through it, with his particular and private designation. That the broth thus formed should be the supper, and the duck on the ensuing morning should be the breakfast, and which should be distributed by " whose shall be this." Strange as this tale may appear to you, in these times, the agreement was religiously performed. Being young, my appetite was ravenous, as that of a wolf, but honor bound the stomach tightly.

We rose early and each person selected his bit of pork, which made but a single mouthful ; there was no controversy. The diver was parted most fairly, into ten shares, each one eyeing the integrity of the division. Lieutenant Steele causing the turning of the back, the lottery gave me a victory over my respectable friend Cunningham. His share, was the head and the feet, mine one of the thighs. Hungry and miserable as we were, even this was sport to our thoughtless minds. In fact, we were sustained by a flattering hope that we should soon meet our friends, the army.

October 10th. Setting out early, by the evening we made nearly fifty miles. The bit of pork and the rest of the biscuit became my supper. My colleagues were similarly situated. The morning sun saw us without any food. We did not despond. The consolatory idea, that on that, or the next day, we should certainly join the army, infused energy into our minds and bodies. Yet being without food, though we loved each other, every endearment which binds man to man was, as it were, forgotten in a profound silence. After a long day's journey still we were supperless.

11th. The succeeding morning, starting early, we ran at a monstrous rate. The waters by additional rains above, had risen greatly. By ten or eleven o'clock A.M., we observed a great smoke before us, which from its extent, we could ascribe to nothing else, than the encampment of the army, our friends and fellow soldiers. After some time the light canoe, several hundred yards before us (with Steele and Getchel in it), passed between

the forks of a tree, which lay rooted in the middle of
the stream, where most likely it had lain for many years.
All its branches had been worn away by the annual fric-
tions of the ice or waters, except those which formed
the fork, and those stood directly against the current,
nearly a foot out of water, and ten or more feet apart.
Seeing our friends pass through safely, and being unconscious that we were worse or less adventurous watermen
than they were, we risked it. We ran with great velocity. My good Irishman steered. By an unlucky
stroke of some one of our paddles (for each of us had
one), but from his situation and power over the vessel it
was fairly attributable to the steersman, the canoe was
thrown a little out of its true course, just as it was entering the prongs of the fork. Trifling as this may appear
to you, to us it was the signal of death. One of the
prongs took the right hand side of the canoe, within six
inches of the bow, immediately below the gunwale.
Quick as lightning that side of the canoe was laid open
from stem to stern, and water was gushing in upon us,
which would inevitably have sunk us in a second of time,
but for that interference of Providence, which is atheist-
ically called presence of mind, otherwise a host of men
could not have saved us from a watery grave. Instinct-
ively leaning to the left, we sunk the gunwale of that
side down to the water's edge, by which we raised the
broken side an inch and more out of it. Calling loudly
to our companions ahead, they soon saw our distress and
put in, at the great smoke. Carefully and steadily sitting, and gently paddling, many hundred yards, we landed
safely. Here was no army, no friends, no food, only a
friendly fire, kindled by ourselves as we ascended the
river ; it had been our camp. The fire we had made
had scarcely more than smoked, but now it had crept
into the turfy soil, and among the roots of trees, and was
spread over half an acre. Our situation was truly hor
rible. When we had examined the broken canoe, and
had rummaged both for the means of mending it, every

heart seemed dismayed. Our birch-bark and pitch had been exhausted in former repairs, we were without food, perhaps one hundred miles from the army, or perhaps that army had returned to New England. That sensation of the mind called *the horrors,* seemed to prevail. Getchel alone was really sedate and reflective. He ordered the other guide to search for birch-bark, whilst he would look among the pines for turpentine. We followed the one or the other of these worthies, according to our inclinations, and soon returned with those desirable materials. The cedar root was in plenty under our feet. Now a difficulty occurred, which had been unforeseen, and which was seemingly destructive of all hope. This was the want of fat or oil of every kind, with which to make the turpentine into pitch. A lucky thought occurred to the youngest of the company, that the pork bag lay empty and neglected, in one of the canoes. The thought and the act of bringing it were instantaneous. The bag was ripped, and as if it had been so much gold dust, we scraped from it about a pint of dirty fat. Getchel now prepared an abundance of pitch. The cedar root gave us twine. The canoe was brought up to the fire. We found every rib, except a few at the extreme points, actually torn from the gunwale. All hands set to work — two hours afterwards the canoe was borne to the water.

We embarked, and proceeding cautiously, as we thought, along the shore (for we dared not yet, with our craggy vessel, venture into deep water), a snag, standing up stream, struck through the bottom of the canoe. This accident happened about five hundred yards from the fire. We put back with heavy hearts and great difficulty — our friends followed. It took an hour to patch the gap. The cup of sorrow was not yet full. As the men were bearing the wounded canoe to the water, Sergeant Boyd who paddled in the small canoe, which was drawn up as usual, taking hold of the bow raised it waist high (as was right) intending to slide it gently into the water — the bank was steep and slippery. Oh ! my dear children, you cannot conceive the dread and horror the succeeding part of this scene produced in our minds : Mr. Boyd's own feet slipped — the canoe fell from his hands — its own weight falling upon the cavity formed by the declivity of the bank and the water — broke it in the center, into two pieces, and which were held together by nothing but the gunwales. Now absolute despair for the first time seized me. A thought came across my mind, that the Almighty had destined us to die of hunger, in this inhospitable wilderness. The recollection of my parents, my brothers and sister, and the clandestine and cruel manner of my deserting them, drew from me some hidden, yet burning tears, and much mental contrition. This was unknown, unseen and un-heard of by any, but he who is present everywhere, knows everything, and sees our inmost thoughts. Getchel (comparing small things with great, who much resembled Homer's description of Ulysses, in his person, and whose staid and sober wisdom and foresight, also bore a like-ness to the talents of that hero), resigned, yet thoughtful and active, instantly went to work. The canoe was brought to the fire and placed in a proper posture for the operation. The lacerated parts were neatly brought together, and sewed with cedar root. A large ridge of pitch, as is customary in the construction of this kind of water craft, was laid over the seam to make it water-tight. Over the seam a patch of strong bark a foot in width, and of a length sufficient to encircle the bottom even to the gunwales, was sewed down at the edges and pitched. Again over the whole of the work, it was thought prudent to place our pork bag which was well saturated with liquid fat. It was a full yard wide, and was laid down in the same manner. This work which was laborious nearly consumed the rest of the day.

We set out notwithstanding the lateness of the hour, and would it is likely have gone all night, well knowing the water below to be good, but for an enlivening occurrence which soon after happened. Hunger drove us along at a cautious but rapid rate. The sterility of the country about had afforded us no game, neither moose, bear nor wolf: nothing in short, but the diver and a red pine squirrel which was too small and quick to be killed by a bullet. These squirrels did not much exceed in size our striped ground squirrel. About dusk the lieutenant's canoe, four hundred yards before us, had within view turned a sharp point of land, when we heard the crack of a rifle, and presently another and a huzza. Apprehending an attack from an enemy, we pulled hard to be enabled to sustain our friends. In a moment or two, observing them pulling for the north shore which was steep, we looked up it for the enemy. Good Heavens! what a sight! We saw a moose-deer, falling on the top of the bank. A cry of exultation seemed to burst the narrow valley of the river. Steele had struck the deer in the flank, as it was leaving the water, but it sprung up the bank with agility. Wheeler, with better fortune for us all, pierced its heart as it arrived at the top. Seeing this you can scarcely imagine the celerity of our movements. We were ashore in a moment. A fire was kindled, the secondary guide cut off the nose, and upper lip of the animal, instantly, and had it on the fire. What a feast! But we were prudent. We sat up all night, selecting the fat and the tit-bits — frying, boiling, roasting, and broiling, but carefully eating little at a time. Towards morning, we slept a few hours, absolutely careless of consequences. We knew that we had arrived in a land where game was plentiful, and where there were no foes superior to our number, to oppose us.

October 12. We rose after sunrise, and began, according to practice, to examine and prepare our guns. Prepared, mine was placed against a tree; my duty, in course, was of the culinary kind. George Merchant, my coadjutor, had gone to the river for water. He ran back, seized his own gun, and intimated that a bull moose was swimming across the river towards the camp.

We jumped to our arms — it so happened that my station was rearward. The enormous animal was coming towards us, and not more than fifty paces off, his head and horns only above water. The sight was animating. Wheeler and some others fired at his head, but without effect. The extreme desire they had to possess so noble a prey, probably caused a tremor of the hand, or that part of his body was impenetrable to our small balls, which is most likely. The moose turned and swam to the opposite bank. Having got to the verge of the river, his emerging was awaited. My ball struck precisely where it ought to kill. The huge animal rose the bank by several boggling leaps, but seemed unknowing which way to run — we thought he would fall. Wheeler, and some others, getting into the canoes, pursued him by his blood half a mile. When Wheeler returned, he overloaded me with praises for the accuracy of the shot, and was confident that the deer was killed. We had no time to spare. We feasted till noon, and in the intermediate moments, culled the entrails for the fat ; we even broke the bones, and extracted the marrow, under the full persuasion that food of an oily nature is one of the strongest mainstays of human life. Of this principle, if we had a doubt, we were shortly afterwards most irrefragably convinced. We departed from our camp joyously, untortured by the fear of starving ; our canoe sunk deep by the weight of our venison. Running some miles and suddenly doubling a point, we saw a large grey wolf sitting on his haunches ; he was fired at, but the distance was too great ; he escaped. Looking down the river we saw a moose swimming from the main to an island ; it was soon brought down. It proved to be young, of about 300 weight. Its ears and flanks were much torn by the wolf. This prize constituted veal in our larder. The choice parts were deposited in the canoes, the residue was at the disposal of the wolf.

October 13th, the following morning, embarking early, after noon we arrived at our first encamping ground on the Dead river, in good health and spirits ; though pallid and weak, for the want of substantial food in due quantity.

By this time the fat and marrow of the animals we had killed were exhausted, and our stock of salt had been long since expended. One who has never been deprived of bread and salt, nor known the absence of oleaginous substances in his food, cannot make a true estimate of the invaluable benefits of such ingredients, in the sustentation of the bodily frame ; nor of the extremity of our corporeal debility.

We ascended the bank, which is steep, and about fourteen feet high, carrying our baggage, arms and venison, leisurely, by piecemeal. The canoes, as being too heavy for our strength, were secured below, in the water, by withes. It was immediately concluded to preserve our provisions by jerking. This operation is done by slicing the meat into thin strips. Then driving four forks into the earth, in a square position, at the required distance perpendicularly, and laying poles from fork to fork, and poles athwart from pole to pole. A rack is thus made, about four feet high, on which the sliced meat is laid, and smoke-fires are made underneath. This duty was soon performed. We now began to look about us, and discuss the subject of our return to the army, which we had, before this time, persuaded ourselves we should meet at this place. The non-appearance of the army and our distress, induced a conclusion that we were deserted, and abandoned to a disastrous fate, the inevitable result of which would be, a sinking into eternity for want of food, for though we might have killed more deer, the vigor of our bodies was so reduced, that we were convinced that that kind of food could not restore us to our wonted energy, and enable us to perform so rugged and long a march, as that to the frontiers of Maine. The notion of navigating the river, was scouted as a fallacy, because we did not possess a sufficient degree of bodily force to bear the canoes across the twelve-mile carrying-place. As, in the case of the retreat of the army, we had determined to follow, it became requisite to finish the jerking, which would take six days, to make it the more portable for our feebleness, and preservable if we should have wet weather on the march. It was further concluded "That Lieut. Steele, Getchel and Wheeler, should immediately proceed on foot across the twelve-mile carrying-place, to meet the army : if they did meet it, that they should return to us with supplies by the end of three days, but in all events to return." Having no doubt of the honor of those gentlemen, the rest of the party remained cheerfully jerking the meat. Now we experienced the full extent of a new species of starving. Having neither bread, nor salt, nor fat of any kind, every day we remained here, we became more and more weak and emaciated. We had plenty of meat, both fresh and dried, of which we ate four, five and six times a day, in every shape we had the means of dressing it. Though we gorged the stomach, the appetite was unsatiated. Something like a diarrhœa ensued, which contributed to the imbecility of our bodies. Bear's oil would have made our venison savory, but such an animal as a bear we had as yet not seen in all our wanderings. On the evening of the fourth day, we looked out for our absent companions with much heartfelt anxiety. They came not. In the morning of the next day, we consulted upon the question whether we should follow the army. A majority voted for staying a few days longer to complete the jerking. To show you the great bodily weakness we were brought to, it may be proper to relate the following anecdote as more evincive of the fact, than any other method which might be adopted, to bring it fully to your minds. Sergeant Boyd (the strongest and stoutest man of the party and perhaps of the army), and myself, taking our arms, descended into a canoe, and passed the river to the mouth of the creek before mentioned, intending to go to the next pond on the carrying-place, there to meet, as we hoped, the advance of the army. We staggered along through the plain, falling every now and then, if our toes but touched a twig or tuft of grass. Thus going forward, we arrived at the edge of the moss-bog, which is mentioned as we ascended the river, and which is one and a half or two miles from the pond. Here my worthy friend Boyd, unable to proceed, sunk down upon a log. My seat, in tears of excruciating grief, was taken beside him, endeavoring to infuse comfort and courage into his manly mind — it was in vain. The debility of his body had disarmed his courageous soul. Every art in my power was exercised to induce him to pass the bog ; he would not listen to me on that subjeet. Melancholy of the desperate kind oppressed me. Convinced that the army had retreated, a prognostication resulted in my mind, that we should all die of mere debility in these wilds. We sat an hour. At length we agreed to return to our camp, though it was yet early in the afternoon. Our companions were pleased to see us, thinking our coming so soon indicated good news ; but a gloom of desperation followed. As a last effort to save our lives, we all agreed to pass the river the next morning and follow the army, which we were now assured had returned to Fort Western. Each one put into his knapsack as much of our mawkish food, as he could conveniently carry.

October 17. We started early, passed the river, but from mere inability to carry our canoes, left them behind us, at the bank of the creek. Marching forward as fast as our feeble limbs would carry us, when we came to the log where Boyd had seated himself, we were filled with extatic joy to observe, on the far side of the bog, a party of pioneers forming a causeway for the passage of the army. Our strength redoubled — we passed the bog with considerable speed. Our wan and haggard faces and meagre bodies, and the monstrous beards of my companions, who had neglected to carry a razor with them, seemed to strike a deep sorrow into the hearts of the pioneers. They gave us a little of their food, but

what exhilerated us more, was the information that
Major Febiger, with the advanced-guard, lay at the next
pond.   We urged forward as fast as we could.   Arriving at his fire a little before my company, an incapacity
to stand compelled me to sit.   Febiger, in a hurried
manner, asked who we were? and from whence we
came?   A few words explained the mystery and cause
of our distress.   A glistening tear stood in this brave
soldier's eye.   As it were with a sudden and involuntary
motion and much tenderness, he handed me his wooden
canteen (which contained the last spirits in the army),
from me it passed to Cunningham, who had just come
up, the most ghastly and way-worn figure in nature,
from him it went round to the rest, who arrived gradually, but slowly.   The heart of Febiger [1] seemed over-
joyed at the relief he had and could afford us.   The
liquor had restored our fainting spirits, but this was not
enough for his generosity to exhibit.   He requested us
to take seats around the fire, and wait the boiling of his
kettle, which was well replenished with pork and dump-
lings.   This was all devoted to our use, accompanied by
an open heartedness and the kindest expressions of interest
for our sufferings, and regard for our perseverance in
our duty as military men.   This meal to all of us seemed
a renewal of life.   It was accustomed food.   Febiger,
ere this time, was unknown to us, but in the process of
events, he acquired our esteem and entire confidence,
as a friend and a real soldier.   Our more immediate and
intimate friends were still beyond the pond, but coming

---

[1] Christian Febiger, colonel in the Revolutionary army, born Denmark,
1747; died, Phila. Sept. 20, 1796.   He had seen service before en-
listing April 28, 1775, and at Bunker's Hill led a portion of Gerrish's
regiment, of which he was adjutant, to the scene of battle in season to do
good service.   He served with marked ability throughout the war; accompanied Arnold to Quebec, and was made prisoner in the attack on that
citadel; was conspicuous at the capture of Stony Point, where he led a
column of attack, and at Yorktown, where he commanded the 2d Va.
regiment.   From 1789 until his death, he was treasurer of Pensylvania.—
Drake's Biographical Dictionary, 319.

forward.   By-and-by Morgan came, large, a commanding aspect, and stentorian voice.   He wore leggings, and
a cloth in the Indian style.   His thighs, which were
exposed to view, appeared to have been lacerated by the
thorns and bushes.   He knew our story from Steele and
Wheeler, and greeted us kindly.   We now found ourselves at home, in the bosom of a society of brave men,
with whom we were not only willing, but anxious to
meet the brunts of war.   This was the twenty-sixth day
we had been absent from the army.   In the evening we
resumed our stations in our respective messes.   It was
now fully explained to us, why Steele had not brought
us relief.   He had met the advance of the army on the
Kennebec side of the carrying-place.   Always alert and
indefatigable, when any duty was to be done, the
labors of the men in carrying boats, barrels of flour,
etc., were intolerable, and required the strength and
athletic exertions of the officers, and particularly, such
as Lieut. Steele, to enliven them in their duty.   In bearing a heavy burden over rugged ground, he fell and
sprained or dislocated his shoulder.   Notwithstanding
this accident, he had sent us supplies, but the bearers,
either from cowardice or other cause, never came near
us.   Getchel and Wheeler had other duties to attend
to — they were under immediate command.   We also
discovered from Steele, that Clifton and M'Konkey,
soon after we left them, had deserted their post, carrying all they could on their backs, to meet the army.
The dastardly vices of the latter, prevailing over the
known courage, good sense, and sedate age, of the
former : nothing occurs to me contributory to the fame
of these men afterwards.   The first was an invalid, the
latter a caitiff coward.   In your scanning the characters
of men, which you will be compelled to do in
your own defence, in the course of your lives, it
will be a good general rule for you to adopt : that
whether you be in the company of military men, scholars,
men of the law, legislators, etc., etc., in short, persons

of any profession or class, if you find a person very loquacious, dragging the conversation to himself, and in a dictatorial way taking the lead ; but more especially if he talks of his own prowess, deep reading, causes he has gained, eloquence, etc., etc., but still more so if the party boasts of wealth or ancestry : in the first instance, without hesitation, set such a person down in your memory as a braggadocio, a mere puffer, until you can inquire further for a proof to the contrary.   There are, to my knowledge, exceptions to this general rule, but few in number, particularly in the military class.   M'Konkey was of the puffing sect, and there never was a more consummate scoundrel and coward.

October 18th. Now we turned our faces towards the north.   Having rejoined our messmates, enjoying substantial food and warm tents, we soon recruited a good degree of strength, and our former gayety of temper and hilarity returned to us.   We accompanied the army, and became a kind of guides in minute matters, for the paths and carrying places we had sufficiently developed, for Captain Ayres and his pioneers, by strong blazing and snagging of bushes, so that he might proceed in perfect security, in the performance of the duties of his office.   The three companies of riflemen under Morgan took up our old encamping ground·on the Dead river, during the afternoon of the following day.[1]

---

[1] The place on the Kennebec where the *carry* commenced is now definitely known to lumbermen and inhabitants of that region ; indeed the route to the ponds, and between them and the Dead river is distinctly marked by a growth of evergreens passing through a growth of hard wood growth, they having taken the place of the original wood cut by the army to facilitate the crossing.   It is said that some of the bateaux which were abandoned at the ponds, and sunk there, are occasionally found on the bottom.— *Letter from Hon. James W. North.*

During the survey of the north-eastern boundary in 1844, one of the engineers traversing the swampy highland observed a hollow sound where he struck down his Jacob staff, he discovered on scraping away the moss an entire bateau, composed of sawed wood which was not indigenous to the locality, that rendered it more than probable that it was one of Arnold's bateaux.— *Letter of Mr. John F. Anderson.— M.*

October 19th and 20th. Here we lay encamped for
several days, waiting the arrival of the rear of the New
England troops: they came up hourly. During our
stay here, it pleased me internally, to observe that Morgan adopted certain rules of discipline, absolutely necessary to the state we were in, but discordant with the
wild and extravagant notions of our private men.[1]
Powder and ball, particularly the first, to us riflemen,
was of the first consequence. At Cambridge the horns
belonging to the men were filled with an excellent rifle
powder, which, when expended, could not be replaced
in Canada by any powder of an equal quality. The men

---

[1] Morgan was a strict disciplinarian. Permit an anecdote. He had
obtained the command of the rifle corps from Arnold, without any
advertence to the better claim of Hendricks, who, though the youngest
man was of the three captains, in point of rank, by the dates of commis-
sions, the superior officer. Hendricks, for the sake of peace in the army,
and of good order, prudently and good naturedly acquiesced in his assumption of the command, for Morgan had seen more service in our former wars.
At this place Morgan had given it out in orders, that no one should fire.
One Chamberlaine, a worthless fellow, who did not think it worth while
to draw his bullet, had gone some hundreds of yards into the woods, and
discharged his gun. Lieut. Steele happened to be in that quarter at the
time; Steele had but arrived at the fire, where we sat, when Morgan,
who had seen him coming, approached our camp, and seated himself within
our circle. Presently Chamberlaine came, gun in hand, and was passing
our fire, towards that of his mess. Morgan called to the soldier, accused
him as the defaulter; this the man (an arrant liar) denied. Morgan
appealed to Steele. Steele admitted he heard the report, but knew not the
party who discharged the gun. Morgan suddenly springing to a pile of
billets, took one, and swore he would knock the accused down unless he
confessed the fact. Instantly, Smith seized another billet, and swore he
would strike Morgan if he struck the man. Morgan knowing the tenure
of his rank, receded. This was the only spirited act I knew of Smith.
Such were the rough-hewn characters which, in a few subsequent years, by
energy of mind and activity of body, bore us safely through the dreadful
storms of the revolution. Morgan was of an impetuous temper, yet withal,
prudent in war, as he was fearless of personal danger. His passions
were quick and easily excited, but they were soon cooled. This observation is applicable to many men of great talents, and to none more than
Morgan. His severity, at times, has made me shudder, though it was
necessary, yet it would have been a pleasing trait in his character if it had
been less rigid.— *Henry.*

had got into a habit of throwing it away at every trifling
object.   Upon our return from the Chaudière, this circumstance raised disgust in us ; for we had been studi-
ously careful of our ammunition, never firing but at
some object which would give us the means of subsistence.   Though we drew our loads every morning, from
a fear of the dampness of the atmosphere, yet the ball
and powder were never lost.   Our bullet screws brought
the first out with ease, and it was recast, the latter was
carefully returned to the horn, where, if moist, it soon
became dry.   The principal of Morgan's rules were,
that there should be no straggling from the camp ; and
no firing without authoritative permission.   Reasonable
as these injunctions were, they were opposed.   Being
young and my friend Steele absent, a whisper of approbation did not fall from me, which, in my subordinate
station, might have been indelicate.   It was left to the
energy of Morgan's mind, and he conquered.   During
our resting here, Arnold, accompanied by Steele and
some excellent boatmen, proceeded to the head of the
river.   The rifle corps preceded the main body of the
army, both by land and water.   The boats, which were
heavily laden with baggage and provisions, took in no
more men than were necessary to navigate them, that is,
three to a boat.   The remainder of the army marched
by land, the river being generally the guide.

Here, my dear children, permit me to give you the
genuine character of my friend, General Simpson, whom
you all know personally.   He was among my earliest
and best friends.   He was then as apparently eccentric,
as he is at this time : there is no obvious difference in
his manners between the two periods.   As an officer,
he was always active and keen in the performance of
his duty.   Hard was the service ; but his heart was soft
to his friend.   Simpson invited his messmate aboard his
boat, being still somewhat feeble from our late privations :
the invitation was gladly accepted.

October 21st.   We embarked.   Having Lieut.

Simpson for a steersman, and John Tidd and James Dougherty as boatmen, we went gaily on for that and the next day: able to lead any boat in the river.

October 22d. On the evening of this second day, we encamped on a bank eight or nine feet high, at a place where we had rested when ascending the river the first time. In the evening a most heavy torrent of rain fell upon us, which continued all night. Having now a good tent over our heads, the inconvenience was not much felt. We slept soundly. Towards morning, we were awaked by the water which flowed in upon us from the river. We fled to high ground.

October 23. When morning came the river presented a most frightful aspect: it had risen at least eight feet, and flowed with terrifying rapidity. None but the most strong and active boatmen entered the boats. the army marched on the south side of the river, making large circuits to avoid the overflowings of the intervale or bottom lands. This was one of the most fatiguing marches we had as yet performed, though the distance was not great in a direct line. But having no path and being necessitated to climb the steepest hills, and that without food, for we took none with us, thinking the boats would be near us all day. In the evening we arrived at the fall of four feet, which was mentioned when ascending the river. Alas! all the boats of the army were on the opposite side of the river. The pitch of the fall made a dreadful noise, and the current ran with immense velocity. We sat down on the bank sorely pinched by hunger, looking wistfully towards our friends beyond the torrent, who were in possession of all the provisions, tents and camp equipage, convinced however, that the most adventurous boatmen would not dare the passage, for the sake of accommodating any of us. We were mistaken. There were two men, and only two, who had skill and courage to dare it. Need Lieut. Simpson, on an occasion like this, be named? he, accompanied by John Tidd, entered his empty boat.

What skill in boatmanship! what aptitude with the paddle was here exhibited. The principal body of the water ran over the middle of the fall, and created a foaming and impetuous torrent, in some measure resembling, at this particular time, of a very high freshet, that of the Oswego falls, which has been known to me ere this. The river was about one hundred and fifty, or two hundred yards in breadth, counting on the increase of water by the rains. The force of the central current naturally formed considerable eddies at each side of the river, close under the pitch. Simpson now disclosed his amazing skill. Though there was an eddy, even that was frightful, he came by its mean nearly under the pitch, and trying to obtain an exact start, failed. The stream forced his boat down the river, but he recovered and brought it up. Now we, who were trembling for the fate of our friends, and anxious for our own accommodation, began to fear he might be drawn under the pitch. Quick, almost in a moment, Simpson was with us. He called in his loud voice to Robert Dixon, James Old (a messmate) and myself to enter the boat. We entered immediately. He pushed off; attempting the start by favor of the hither eddy, which was the main thing -- we failed. Returning to the shore, we were assailed by a numerous band of soldiers, hungry, and anxious to be with their companions. Simpson told them he could not carry more with safety, and would return for them. Henry M'Annaly, a tall Irishman, who could not from experience comprehend the danger, jumped into the boat; he was followed by three or four other inconsiderate men. The countenance of Simpson changed, his soul and mine were intimate. "O God," said he, "men we shall all die." They would not recede. Again we approached the pitch; it was horrible. The bateau swam deep, almost ungovernable by the paddle. Attempting again to essay the departure —we failed. The third trial was made: it succeeded. As lightning we darted athwart the river. Simpson with his

paddle, governed the stern.   The worthy Tidd in the
bow.   Dixon and myself, our guns stuck in the railing
of the bateau, but without paddles, sat in the stern next
to Simpson.   Mr. Old was in the bow near Tidd.
Henry M'Annaly was adjoining Mr. Old.   The other
men sat between the stern and bow.   Simpson called to
the men in the bow to lay hold of the birch bushes ;
the boat struck the shore forcibly : they caught hold
M'Annaly in particular (this was in the tail of the eddy),
but like children, their holds slipped, at the only spot
where we could have been saved ; for the boat had been
judiciously and safely brought up.   Letting go their
holds, the bow came round to the stream, and the stern
struck the shore.   Simpson, Dixon, and myself, now
caught the bushes, but being by this time thrown into the
current, the strength of the water made the withes as so
many straws in our hânds.   The stern again swung
round: the bow came again ashore.   Mr. Old, Tidd,
and M'Annaly, and the rest, sprung to the land to save
their lives.   Doing this, at our cost, their heels forced
the boat across the current.   Though we attempted to
steady it, the boat swagged.   In a moment after, at
thirty feet off shore, it being broad side to the current,
turned ; borne under, in spite of all our force, by the
fury of the stream.   The boat upsetting, an expression,
as going into the water, fell from me, " Simpson we
are going to heaven."   My fall was head-foremost.
Simpson came after me — his heels, at the depth of fifteen
feet or more, were upon my head and neck ; and those
grinding on the gravel.   We rose nearly together, your
father first — my friend followed.   The art of swimming,
in which, I thought myself an adept, was tried, but it
was a topsy-turvy business.   The force of the water
threw me often heels-over-head.

In the course of this voyage, after a few hundred
yards, Simpson was at my side, but the force of the
stream prevented the exertion of swimming ; yet the
impetuosity of the current kept us up.   It drove us

toward the other side of the river, against a long ridge of perpendicular rocks of great extent. Luckily, in the course of some hundred yards, the current changed, and brought us perforce to the north side of the river. Floating along with my head just above water — prayers in sincere penitence having been uttered, a boat's crew of the eastern men handed me a pole. It was griped as by the hand of death — but griped the pole remained to me. The strength of water was such, that the boat would inevitably have upset, if the boatman had kept his hold. A glance of the eye informed me that my companion in misfortune had shared the same fate. Resigned into the bosom of my Savior, my eyes became closed; the death appeared to me a hard one; sensibility in a great degree forsook me. Driving with the current some hundreds of yards more, the most palpable feeling recollected, was the striking of my breast against a root or hard substance. My head came above water. Breathing ensued; at the same moment Simpson raised his head out of the water, his gold laced hat on it, crying "Oh!" neither of us could have crept out; we should have there died but for the assistance of Edward Cavanaugh, an Irishman, an excellent soldier, who was designated in the company by the appellation of Honest Ned. Passing from the lower part of the river, he happened to come to the eddy, at the instant of time my breast struck. He cried out "Lord, Johnny! is this you?" and instantly dragged me out of the water. Simpson immediately appearing, he did him the same good office. Lying on the earth perhaps twenty minutes, the water pouring from me, a messenger from the camp came to rouse us. Roused we went to it. But all eyes looked out for Dixon, all hearts were wailing for his loss. It was known he could not swim, but none of us could recollect whether he had dropped into the water or had adhered to the boat. In some time we had the inexpressible pleasure of Dixon in our company. He had stuck to the side of the boat, which lodged on a vast pile of drift wood some miles below, and in this way he was saved. Arriving at the camp our friends had a large fire prepared, particularly for our accommodation ; heat upon such an occurrence is most agreeable. My two friends in distress, whose clothing was principally woolen — felt none of my private disaster. My leather breeches attached closely and coldly to the skin. Modesty prohibited a disclosure. The sense of pain or inconvenience which was observed by my seniors, caused an inquiry. Immediately the breeches were off and stuck upon a pole to dry. Simpson was so much exhilerated by our escape, that seated on a stump, he sung *Plato* in great glee. It became a favorite with us. During all this time, perhaps till one or two o'clock, my breeches were in my hand almost in continued friction. The laugh of the company was against me, but it was borne stoically.

October 24, the following morning, presented me with many difficulties ; to be sure my horn, with a pound of powder, and my pouch, with seventy bullets, were unharmed by the water, though around my neck in the course of our swimming. Yet I had lost my knapsack, my hat, and my most precious rifle. Awaking, the world appeared to be a wild waste. Disarmed, my insignificance pressed strongly on my mind — dishonor seemed to follow of course. Without the armor of *defence*, men and nations are mere automatons, liable to be swayed by the beck of power and subject to the hand of oppression. Young as your father was, his soul was oppressed. To return with the invalids was dreadful, and without arms, he could not proceed. Comfort came to me in the shape of Lieutenant, now General Nichols, then of Hendricks. He had two hats — he presented me one ; but what was more to my purpose, he, or General Simpson, informed me that some of the invalids wished to dispose of their rifles. With the assistance of Nichols and Simpson, a bargain was struck with a person called William Reynolds, or Rannals, of our company ; who was miserably sick, and returned in the boats. Money was out of the question, an order upon my father, dated at this place, for the price of twelve dollars was accepted, and afterwards, in due time, paid honorably. This gun was short, about forty-five balls to the pound, the stock shattered greatly, and worth about forty shillings. Necessity has no law. Never did a gun, ill as its appearance was, shoot with greater certainty, and where the ball touched, from its size, it was sure to kill. This observation, trifling as it may seem, ought to induce government to adopt guns of this size, as to length of barrel, and size of ball. There are many reasons to enforce this opinion. We departed from this place without any material occurrence, and went rapidly forward.

October 27th. Somewhat laughable ensued on this morning near the first pond, at the head of the river. The Virginians (though it is not probable that any of the officers excepting one) had taken up the idea, that they were our superiors in every military qualification, and ought to lead. Hendricks, though the oldest commissioned officer of the rifle companies, was still the youngest man. For the sake of peace and good order, he had not assented to, but merely acquiesced in Morgan's assumption of the command of our corps, as the elder *person.* Those men, who were clever and brave, were just such in that behalf, as we were ourselves : but a Mr. Heath, who was blind of an eye, a lieutenant of Morgan's, seemed to think, that all others were inferior to those of the ancient dominion. We had a hard morning's *pushing,* when coming up to the first pond, at the head of the Dead-river, we saw Heath before us. Observing to Simpson, "*push him,*" we went up with much force ; poor Heath laboring as a slave to keep his place. Tidd and Dougherty felt my spirit as much as Simpson did. At the moment of our passing, for we went up on the outside of him, towards the middle of the current, his pole stuck, upon which he gave us a few hearty curses. Entering the lake, the boat under my guidance and information, steered directly for the passage to the second lake. Humphreys (Morgan's first lieutenant) a brave and most amiable man, whom we highly esteemed, was in a boat far to the left, searching for a passage. Simpson, at my instance, hailed him to come on. He answered there was no passage *there*, alluding to the place we steered for. Encouraging my friend to go on, the deception Humphreys lay under was soon discovered. The creek was soon discovered. The creek was deep and serpentine, and the country around, for a considerable distance, a flat. A log brought down by the last freshet, lay across the stream, so as to give to a stranger the idea that the mouth of the creek was merely a nook of the lake. Setting the log afloat, as was easily done, the boat proceeded.

October 28. Continuing rapidly, for now we had no carrying, nor marking of trees, there being plenty of water, the evening was spent at the foot of that mountain called the Height-of-land.[1] This was a day of severe labor. The navigation of the Chaudière, being, so far as our information went, represented to the captains, Hendricks and Smith, as very dangerous, they, to save their men, concluded to carry over the hill, but one boat for each of their companies. This resolution was easily accomplished. Morgan, on the other hand, determined to carry over all his boats. It would have made your heart ache, to view the intolerable labors his fine fellows underwent. Some of them, it was said, had the flesh worn from their shoulders, even to the bone. The men said it; but by this time an antipathy against Morgan, as too strict a disciplinarian had arisen.

October 29th. The following day, the army, disjointed as was our corps, at least Hendricks's and Smith's, encamped on the plain, on the bank of the Chaudière.

---

[1] The Hon. Miles Standish lives on what is termed the Flag Staff Plantation, at the foot of Mount Bigelow, on Arnold's route, the mountain on which Maj. Timothy Bigelow planted a flag staff, which gave name to the mountain and place.— *Letter from Hon. James W. North.*— M.

Morgan afterwards took his station near us. Here it first became generally known, that Enos had returned from the twelve mile carrying-place, with 500 men, a large stock of provisions, and the medicine chest.[1]   It

---

[1] The desertion of Enos was known by a portion of the army as early as the 23d.   He made an ingenious defence of his retreat, and at the trial the witnesses being his own officers, who were all in favor of returning, he was acquitted, but never survived the stigma of having done a disreputable act.— *M.*

Head-Quarters, Cambridge, November 30, 1775.
A General Court Martial to sit to-morrow morning, at eleven o'clock, at Mr. Pomeroy's, in Cambridge, to try Lieutenant-Colonel Enos, for "quitting his commanding-officer without leave." President, Brigadier-General Sullivan, with the twelve field-officers next for court-martial duty.

COLONEL ROGER ENOS TO THE PUBLIC.

I esteem it the duty of every man not only to merit a good name, but to appear in defence of it when unjustly attacked, and, if possible, to clear it from groundless aspersions.   Great numbers, for want of proper information, or by artful misrepresentations, imbibe unreasonable prejudices against their fellow men, and form conceptions greatly to their disadvantage, who, on a full and impartial knowledge of the facts, will essentially alter their opinions, and applaud those actions which, from misrepresentation, they were inclined to censure and condemn.   As my character, both as an officer and soldier, hath of late suffered much in the view of many, and as I value my reputation as high as my life (indeed, I consider it as the greatest curse that can befall a man to outlive his character), I must beg leave, through the channel of the press, to exhibit to the world the following representation of my case; which I trust will sufficiently clear up my character, and convince the impartial, that my conduct, instead of the censure, merits the approbation of the public.

At a Court of Inquiry held at Cambridge, on Wednesday, the 29th day of November, 1775, by order of his excellency the commander-in-chief of the forces of the United Colonies, to examine into the conduct of Lieutenant-Colonel Enos, for leaving the detachment under Colonel Arnold and returning home, without permission from his commanding officer, present :
Major-General Lee, president; Brig. General Greene, Brig. General Heath, Colonel Nixon, Colonel Stark, Major Durkee, Major Sherburne.
The court are of opinion, after receiving all the information within their power, that Colonel Enos's misconduct (if he has been guilty of misconduct) is not of so very heinous a nature as was first supposed, but that it is necessary, for the satisfaction of the world, and for his own honor, that a court-martial should be immediately held for his trial.

CHARLES LEE, *Maj. General, President.*
A true copy, from the minutes of said court, compared and examined by
W. TUDOR, *Judge Advocate.*

damped our spirits much, but our commander conceived it was better to proceed than return. We were about a hundred miles from the frontier of Canada, but treble that distance from that of New-England. Our provisions

---

Proceedings of a general court-martial of the line held at head-quarters at CAMBRIDGE, *by order of his Excellency* GEORGE WASHINGTON, *Esq., Commander-in-chief of the Forces of the* UNITED COLONIES, DECEMBER 1, *A.D.* 1775.

Brigadier-General Sullivan, president; Colonel Bridge, Colonel Sergeant, Colonel Greaton, Lieutenant-Colonel Cleveland, Lieutenant-Colonel Marsh, Lieutenant-Colonel Reed, Lieutenant-Colonel Brown, Lieutenant-Colonel Vose, Major Poor, Major Wood, Major Woods, Major Johnson; W. Tudor, judge advocate.

The court, being duly sworn, proceeded to the trial of Lieutenant-Colonel Enos, of the Twenty-Second Regiment, under an arrest for leaving the detachment under Colonel Arnold, and returning home, without permission from his commanding officer.

Lieutenant-Colonel Enos, being arraigned on the above charge, says, that true it is, he did return without permission from Colonel Arnold, his commanding officer; but the circumstances of the case were such as obliged him so to do.

Captain Williams. At the great carrying-place, I heard that the men ahead were in want of provision. About two-thirds across the great carrying-place, I met Major Bigelow coming back with ninety-five men, who said they wanted provision; I dealt out to them a barrel of pork and one of flour; I delivered Major Bigelow six barrels more of provision. We proceeded forward, and met several parties returning home, and we had orders to supply them with provision to reach the English settlements. When I came up with Colonel Enos, I was informed by Major Bigelow there had been a council of war, and that it was settled that, for want of provisions, the whole detachment under Colonel Enos should return. Colonel Enos proposed to go forward, and let his division return; but as there was a large number, besides those which belonged properly to our division, and as we had several invalids to bring back, and were very short of provision (for we had but three days' provision, and were above one hundred miles from the English settlements), I thought it was absolutely necessary for Colonel Enos to take the command of the party back, and protested against his going on to join Colonel Arnold; at the same time, not knowing that Colonel Enos had any orders from Colonel Arnold to join him. That division which went on to join Colonel Arnold had not more than five days' provision. We supplied Colonel Greene's division with most of their provision, and left ourselves but three days' provision.

Captain McCobb. About fifty miles up the Dead river we held a council of war, at which I assisted as a member; and it was agreed that the whole division under Col. Enos should return, there not being sufficient provision to carry both divisions through. Colonel Greene's division being some way ahead, it was found that we should save two days' time by letting that

were exhausted. We had no meat of any kind. The flour which remained, so far as I know, was divided fairly and equally, among the whole of the troops, the *riflemen* shared *five pints of flour* per man. During the

division go forward, and time was too precious and provision too scarce to enter into disputes. It was thought best for the service, that Colonel Greene's division should proceed, and we left them with about five days' provision, and returned with three ourselves. Lieutenant-Colonel Enos was for going forward without his division; but, for the same reasons which have been mentioned by Captain Williams, I protested against his going on.

Captain Scott confirms all that Captain McCobb deposes, and adds, that he himself protested against Colonel Enos's going forward ; that he thought, and is now confirmed in the opinion, that the presence of Colonel Enos was very necessary to preserve the harmony and order necessary to secure the safe retreat of the men who were ordered to return.

Lieutenant Hide. I assisted at the council of war up the Dead river. We found, by the best computation, that it would take fifteen days to reach any French inhabitants, and that it would be impossible for both divisions of Greene's and Enos's to go through, the provision being so short. It was adjudged that there was about four days' provision for those who went forward, and we returned with three. I protested against Colonel Enos's going on to join Colonel Arnold, his presence being necessary for our safe retreat, as we had a number of invalids, and a considerable number of men who did not belong to either of the companies in our division.

Lieutenant Buckmaster confirms what Lieutenant Hide deposes ; and adds, that it was the opinion of all the officers of Colonel Enos's division, that he should return with his division, as we had one hundred and fifty men who did not belong to our division, who had only a subaltern to command them, and whom it would have been impossible to manage without Colonel Enos's presence.

The court being cleared, after mature consideration, are unanimously of opinion, that Colonel Enos was under a necessity of returning with the division under his command, and therefore acquit him with honor.

JOHN SULLIVAN, *President.*

A true copy of the proceedings.

Attest : W. TUDOR, *Judge Advocate.*

———

New-York, April 28, 1776.

I hereby certify that I was president of a court-martial, in Cambridge, when Colonel Enos was tried for leaving Colonel Arnold with the rear division of the detachment under his command, bound for Quebec ; and, upon the trial, it clearly appeared to me, as well as to all the other members of the court, that Colonel Enos was perfectly justifiable in returning with the division, being clearly proved, by the testimony of witnesses of undoubted veracity (some of whom I have been personally acquainted with for a number of years, and know them to be persons of truth), that so much provision had been sent forward, to support the other divisions, as

night and the ensuing morning, the flour was baked into
five cakes per man, under the ashes, in the way of Indian
bread.

October 30th. We set forward. The men were
told by the officers " that orders would " not be required
in the march, each one must " put the best foot foremost."
The first day's march was closed by a charming sleep on
fir-branches. The gentlemen of our mess lay together,
covering themselves with the blankets of each one. My
memory does not serve, to say, that any stir was made
by any one, during the night. Happening to be the first

---

left them so small a quantity that their men were almost famished with
hunger on their return; and some would undoubtedly have starved, had
they not, by accident, come across and killed a large moose. Upon their
evidence, there remained no doubt in the mind of myself, or any of the
members, that the return of the division was prudent and reasonable; being
well convinced that they had not provision sufficient to carry them half
way to Quebec, and that their going forward would only have deprived
the other division of a part of theirs, which, as the event has since shown,
was not enough to keep them all from perishing; we therefore unanimously acquitted Colonel Enos with honor.

I further certify, that by a strict inquiry into the matter since, from persons who were in the divisions that went forward, I am convinced that had
Colonel Enos, with his division, proceeded, it would have been a means of
causing the whole detachment to have perished in the woods, for want of
sustenance.

I further add, that I have been well informed, by person acquainted
with Colonel Enos, that he has ever conducted as a good and faithful officer.

JOHN SULLIVAN.

TO THE IMPARTIAL PUBLIC.

The case of Lieutenant-Colonel Enos having engaged the attention of
many officers of the army, as well as others, and as we are informed he is
much censured by many persons, for returning back from the expedition to
Canada, under the command of Colonel Arnold, by which Colonal Enos's
character greatly suffers, we think it our duty to certify, that some of us,
from our own personal knowledge of the military abilities of Colonel Enos,
and others of us from information, are fully convinced that he is a gentleman fully acquainted with his duty as an officer, a man of fortitude and
prudence, and, in our opinion, well calculated to sustain, with honor, any
military character; and, from the fullest inquiry, we are satisfied that
(whatsoever different representations may be made) in returning to camp,
with the division under his command, he is justifiable, and conducted as an
understanding, prudent, faithful officer, and deserves applause rather than

who awaked, in the morning, the blanket was suddenly thrown from my head, but what was my surprise to find that we had lain under a cover of at least four inches of snow. We scarcely had risen and had our kettle on the fire, when our drummer (we had no bugles), John Shaeffer, came slipshod to our fire, complaining that all his cakes had been stolen from him. A more wretched figure was scarcely ever beheld. He was purblind. This circumstance, though he was my townsman, and acquainted with me from my earliest infancy, was yet unknown to me until this last march, ascending the

---

censure; and we can safely recommend him as a person worthy to be employed in any military department.

WILLIAM HEATH, Brig.-Gen.	JOEL CLARK, Lieut.-Col.
JAMES REED, Colonel.	EBENEZER SPROUT, Major.
J. BREWER, Colonel.	EBENEZER CLAP, Lieut.-Col.
SAMUEL H. PARSONS, Colonel.	SAMUEL PRENTICE, Major.
JOSEPH REED, Colonel.	CALVIN SMITH, Major.
JONATHAN NIXON, Colonel.	JOSIAH HAYDEN, Major.
CHARLES WEBB, Colonel.	JOHN BAILY, Colonel.
DANIEL HITCHCOCK, Colonel.	JOHN TYLER, Lieut.-Col.
JOHN STARK, Colonel.	THOMAS NIXON, Lieut.-Col.
LEVI WELLS, Major.	LOAMMI BALDWIN, Colonel.
SAMUEL WYLLYS, Colonel.	JAMES WESSON, Lieut.-Col.
WILLIAM SHEPARD, Lieut.-Col.	ISAAC SHERMAN, Major.
ANDREW COLBURN, Major.	

Now, let Dr. Smith, of Philadelphia, display the malignity of his heart in another funeral oration, in attempting to stab my reputation, and render me infamous in the view of the world. However, I will venture to assert, that if ill-nature, and a fondness to raise his reputation on the ruin of his fellow-men, are as discernible in his other political writings as in this oration, so far as it respects my character, he is one of the most dangerous writers, and, perhaps, the most consummate villain, that walks on the face of God's earth. Ignorance of my real character, and of the grounds and reasons of my conduct in returning from the expedition to Canada, was no warrant for such indecent freedom as he has used in his malicious, though feeble attempt to ruin my reputation. He ought to have waited till a true and impartial history of the facts had enabled him to talk on the subject with propriety, and not have uttered things at random; and, for the sake of furnishing matter for declamation, have undertook, with such violence, to blacken the character of an innocent man.   ROGER ENOS.

New London, May 31, 1776.

Dead river, commenced. My station in the line of march, which was in the single file (or Indian, as it was then called), was next to the captain; the drummer followed. Here it was his defect of sight was most effectually shown. Smith was lithsome and quick afoot, as we all were, except poor Shaeffer. In the course of this toilsome march, without a path, many deep ravines presented, over these lay many logs, fallen perhaps many years before. The captain took the log, preferring it to a descent of twenty or thirty feet into the gulf below, which at times was quite abrupt. Following me, Shaeffer would frequently, drum and all, tumble headlong into the abyss. His misfortunes in this way, for he was a laughing stock, excited contempt in the soldiers, but in me compassion.[1] Often, he required my aid. On this

---

[1] I cannot exactly recollect the time, but the records of government will show, that this miserable man was indicted of a burglary and convicted. His respectable brother, Mr. Jacob Shaeffer of Lancaster (Penn.), applied to me to certify in his favor [it was in 1780 or 1781] to the president and council, who had the power of pardon. The representation was, in substance similar to the present. This part of our transactions rests in my memory; but the impression is so strong, that I cannot forget it. It gave me great pleasure to imagine, that probably I might again contribute to the saving the life of a man, which I had actually saved once before. At that time, by our law, the punishment of burglary was death, and my compatriot Shaeffer, was under that sentence. My soul was grieved.

In a drunken bout at Philadelphia, he had blindly stumbled into a house, which he took to be his lodgings. Here detected in one of the chambers, he was charged as a felon. Gracious God! upon the superfices of thy earth, there was never a more unoffending soul. He could scarcely see a yard before him.

It has amused and pleased me often to hear that he extols me. He is now industrious.

The fate of James Warner, among others, was really lamentable. He was young, handsome in appearance, not more than twenty-five years of age; he was athletic and seemed to surpass in bodily strength. Yet withal he was a dolt. His wife was beautiful, though coarse in manners. The husband on the other hand, was a poor devil, constantly out of view, or in the background of the pictures.

We heard nothing of them after entering the marsh, and until a month had elapsed at Quebec. In December, the wife or widow of poor James Warner, came to our quarters on the Low-grounds, bearing her husband's

latter occasion, our kettle, boiling a bleary, which was no other than flour and water, and that without salt, my solicitations prevailing, the mess gave him a tin cup full of it. He received from me my third cake. This man, blind, starving and almost naked, bore his drum (which was unharmed by all its jostlings) safely to Quebec, when many other hale men died in the wilderness.

November 1st. This morning, breakfasting on our bleary, we took up the line of march through a flat and boggy ground. About ten o'clock A.M., we arrived by a narrow neck of land at a marsh which was appalling. It was three-fourths of a mile over, and covered by a

---

rifle, his powder-horn and pouch. She appeared fresh and rosy as ever. This arose from the religious and gratuitous spirit of the Canadians.

The story Mrs. Jemima Warner told, was extremely affecting, and may be worth remembering, as it is something like a sample of the whole of our distresses and intolerable disasters.

The husband was a great eater. His stores of provisions after the partition, at the head of the Chaudière, were in a little time consumed. The consummate wife ran back from the marsh, and found her beloved husband sitting at the foot of a tree, where he said he was determined to die.

The tender-hearted woman attended her ill-fated husband several days, urging his march forward; he again sat down. Finding all her solicitations could not induce him to rise, she left him, having placed all the bread in her possession between his legs with a canteen of water. She bore his arms and ammunition to Quebec, where she recounted the story. The nephews of Natanis, afterwards at Quebec, confirmed the relation of this good woman. For when going up, and returning down the river with our inestimable friend M'Cleland, she urged them, suffused in tears, to take her husband on board. They were necessarily deaf to her entreaties. Thus perished this unfortunate man at a period of his age when the bodily powers are generally in their full perfection. He and many others, who died in the wilderness, lost their lives by an inconsiderate gluttony. They ate as much at a meal as ought to have been in our circumstances the provision of four days, and a march of one hundred miles. Young men without knowledge or previous experience are very difficult to govern by sage advice, when the rage of hunger assails.

To conclude this lengthy note, allow me to introduce to you another instance of human misery, which came under my eye, in this dolorous and dreadful march. As was before observed in the body of the work " At the head of the Chaudière, it was given out by the officers, that order would not be required from the soldiery in the march, etc." Yet the companies, being in the most part either fellow-townsmen, or from the same county, adhered together, bound by that affectionate attachment which is engen-

coat of ice, half an inch thick. Here Simpson concluded to halt a short time for the stragglers or maimed of Hendricks's and Smith's companies to come up. There were two women attached to those companies, who arrived before we commenced the march. One was the wife of Sergeant Grier, a large, virtuous and respectable woman. The other was the wife of a private of our company, a man who lagged upon every occasion. These women being arrived, it was presumed that all our party were up. We were on the point of entering the marsh, when some one cried out " Warner is not here." Another said he had " sat down sick under a

---

dered by the locality of birth, or the habitudes of long and severe services, in a communion and endurance of hardships and desperate adventures. It appears to me to be a principle of the human mind, " that the more hardships we endure in company of each other, the greater becomes our esteem and affection for our fellow-sufferers." For myself, this is said from experimented woe and extreme calamity.

We had no path, the river was our guide. One day, either the second or third of this march, a mountain jutting in a most precipitate form into the river compelled us to pass the margin of the stream upon a long log, which had been brought thither by some former freshet. The bark and limbs of the tree had been worn away by the rubbings of the ice, and the trunk lay lengthwise along the narrow passage, smooth and slippery, and gorged the pass. This difficulty had collected here a heterogeneous mass of the troops, who claimed the right of passage according to the order of coming to it. The log was to be footed, or the water, of the depth of three or four feet, must be waded. There was no alternative. An eastern man, bare-footed, bare-headed, and thinly clad, lean and wretched from abstinence, with his musket in hand, passed the log immediately before me. His foot slipped, and he fell several feet into the water. We passed on regardless of his fate. Even his immediate friends and comrades, many of whom were on the log at the same moment, did not deign to lend him an assisting hand. Death stared us in the face. I gave him a sincere sigh at parting, for to lose my place in the file, might have been fatal. This pitiable being died in the wilderness. The hard fate of many others might be recapitulated, but the dreadful tale of incidents, if truly told, would merely serve to lacerate the heart of pity, and harrow up the feelings of the soul of benevolence. Tears many years since, have often wetted my cheeks, when recollecting the disasters of that unfortunate campaign, the memorable exit of my dearest friends, and of many worthy fellow-citizens, whose worth at this time, is embalmed solely in the breasts of their surviving associates. Seven died sheerly from famine ; and many others by disorders arising from hard service in the wilderness.— *Henry.*

tree, a few miles back." His wife begging us to **wait a**
short time, with tears of affection in her eyes, ran back
to her husband.   We tarried an hour.   They came not.
Entering the pond (Simpson foremost), and breaking
the ice here and there with the buts of our guns and feet,
as occasion required, we were soon waist deep **in the**
mud and water.   As is generally the case with youths,
it came to my mind, that a better path might be **found**
than that of the more elderly guide.   Attempting **this,**
in a trice the water cooling my armpits, made me gladly
return into the file.   Now Mrs. Grier had got before
me.   My mind was humbled, yet astonished, **at the**
exertions of this good woman   Her clothes more than
waist high, she waded before me to the firm ground.
No one, so long as she was known to us, dared intimate
a disrespectful idea of her.   Her husband, who was an
excellent soldier, was on duty in Hendricks's boat, which
had proceeded to the discharge of the lake with Lieutenant
M'Cleland.   Arriving at firm ground, and waiting again
for our companions, we then set off, and in a march of
several miles, over a scrubby and flat plain, arrived at a
river flowing from the east into the Chaudère lake.
This we passed in a bateau, which the prudence of
Colonel Arnold had stationed here, for our accommodation ; otherwise we must have swam the stream, which
was wide and deep.   In a short time we came to another
river flowing from the same quarter, still deeper and
wider than the former.   Here we found a bateau, under
the superintendency of Capt. Dearborn, in which we
passed the river.   We skirted the river to its mouth,
then passed along the margin of the lake to the outlet of
Chaudière, where we encamped with a heterogeneous
mass of the army.   It was soon perceived that the
French term *Chaudière,* was most aptly applied to the
river below us.   Indeed every part of it, which came
under our view, until we arrived at the first house in
Canada, might well be termed a *caldron* or boiler, which
is the import of its French name.   It is remarkable of

this river, and which, to me, distinguishes it from all others I had seen, that for sixty or seventy miles it is a continued rapid, without any apparent gap or passage, even for a canoe. Every boat we put into the river was stove in one part or other of it. Capt. Morgan lost all his boats, and the life of a much valued soldier. With difficulty he saved his own life and the treasure committed to his care. Arnold, accompanied by Steele, and John M. Taylor, and a few others, in a boat, were in the advance of the army. He may have descended in a boat, it is most likely he did.[1]

November 2d, in the morning we set off from the Chaudière lake, and hungered, as to my own particular, almost to death. What with the supplies to Shaeffer, and my own appetite, food of any kind, with me, had become a nonentity. My own sufferings, in the two succeeding marches, from particular causes, were more than ordinarily severe. My moccasins had, many days since, been worn to shreds and cast aside ; my shoes, though they had been well sewed and hitherto stuck together, now began to give way, and that in the very worst part (the upright seam in the heel). For one to save his life, must keep his station in the rank. The moment that was lost, as nature and reason dictate, the following soldier assumed his place. Thus, once thrown out of the file, the unfortunate wretch must await the passage of many men, until a chasm, towards the rear, happened to open for his admission. This explanation will answer some questions which you might naturally put. Why did you not sew it ? Why did you not tie the shoe to your foot ? If there had been awl, and thread, and strings at command, which there was not, for the causes above stated, one dared not have done either, as the probable consequences would ensue " Death by hunger in a dreary wilderness." For man when thrown

---

[1] June 26th, 1809.   John M. Taylor tells me, that they descended by land.— *Henry.*

out of society is the most helpless of God's creatures. Hence you may form a conception of the intolerable labor of the march. Every step taken the heel of the foot slipped out of the shoe : to recover the position of the foot in the shoe, and at the same time to stride, was hard labor, and exhausted my strength to an unbearable degree. You must remember that this march was not performed on the level surface of the parade, but over precipitous hills, deep gullies, and even without the path of the vagrant savage to guide us. Thus we proceeded till towards mid-day, the pale and meagre looks of my companions, tottering on their feeble limbs, corresponding with my own. My friend Simpson, who saw my enfeebled condition and the cause, prevailed with the men to rest themselves a few minutes. Bark, the only succedaneum for twine, or leather, in this miserable country, was immediately procured and the shoe bound tightly to the foot. Then marching hastily, in the course of an hour or more, we came within view of a tremendous cataract in the river, from twelve to twenty feet high. The horror this sight gave us, fearing for the safety of our friends in the boats, was aggravated, when turning the point of a steep crag, we met those very friends ; having lost all but their lives, sitting around a fire on the shore. Oh God ! what were our sensations ! Poor M'Cleland, first lieutenant of Hendricks's, and for whose accommodation the boat was most particularly carried across the mountain, was lying at the fire ; he beckoned to us. His voice was not audible ; placing my ear close to his lips, the word he uttered scarcely articulate, was, " Farewell." Simpson, who loved him, gave him half of the pittance of food which he still possessed ; all I could was — a tear. The short, but melancholy story of this gentleman, so far as it has come to my knowledge, may be detailed in a few words. He had resided on the Juniata at the time he was commissioned. My knowledge of him commenced in the camp near Boston. He was endowed with all those qualities which win the affections of men. Open, brave, sincere and a lover of truth. On the Dead river, the variable weather brought on a cold which affected his lungs. The tenderness of his friends conducted him safely, though much reduced, to the foot of the mountain, at the head of the Dead river. Hence he was borne in a litter across the mountain by men. If you had seen the young, yet venerable Capt. Hendricks bearing his share of this loved and patriotic burden across the plain to our camp, it would have raised esteem, if not affection, towards him. From our camp, M'Cleland was transported, in the boat, to the place where we found him. The crew, conducting the boat, though worthy men and well acquainted with such kind of navigation, knew nothing of this river. They descended, unaware of the pitch before them, until they had got nearly into the suck of the falls. Here, luckily, a rock presented, on which it was so contrived as to cause the boat to lodge. Now the crew, with great labor and danger, bore their unfortunate lieutenant to the shore, where we found him. We passed on, fearful for our own lives. Coming to a long sandy beach of the Chaudière, for we sometimes had such, some men of our company were observed to dart from the file, and with their nails, tear out of the sand, roots which they esteemed eatable, and ate them raw, even without washing. Languid and woe-begone as your father was, it could not but create a smile to observe the whole line watching, with Argus eyes, the motions of a few men who knew the indications in the sand of those roots. The knowing one sprung, half a dozen followed, he who grabbed it ate the root instantly. Though hunger urged, it was far from me to contend in that way with powerful men, such as those were. Strokes often occurred.

During this day's march (about 10 or 11 A.M.) my shoe having given away again, we came to a fire, where were some of Captain Thayer or Topham's men. Simpson was in front; trudging after, slipshod and tired, I sat

down on the end of a long log, against which the fire
was built, absolutely fainting with hunger and fatigue,
my gun standing between my knees. Seating myself,
that very act gave a cast to the kettle which was placed
partly against the log, in such a way as to spill two-
thirds of its contents. At the moment a large man
sprung to his gun, and pointed it towards me, he threatened to shoot. It created no fear; his life was with
much more certainty in my power. Death would have
been a welcome visitor. Simpson soon made us friends.
Coming to their fire, they gave me a cup of their broth.
A table spoonful was all that was tasted. It had a
greenish hue, and was said to be that of a bear. This
was instantly known to be untrue, from the taste and
smell. It was that of a dog. He was a large black
Newfoundland dog, belonging to Thayer's[1] and very fat.
We left these merry fellows, for they were actually such,
maugre all their wants, and marching quickly, towards
evening encamped. We had a good fire, but no food.
To me the world had lost its charms. Gladly would
death have been received as an auspicious herald from
the divinity. My privations in every way were such as
to produce a willingness to die. Without food, without
clothing to keep me warm, without money, and in a
deep and devious wilderness, the idea occurred, and
the means were in my hands, of ending existence. The
God of all goodness inspired other thoughts. One principal cause of change (under the fostering hand of Providence) in my sentiments, was the jovial hilarity of my
friend Simpson. At night, warming our bodies at an
immense fire, our compatriots joined promiscuously
around — to animate the company, he would sing Plato;
his sonorous voice gave spirit to my heart, and the
morality of the song, consolation to my mind. In truth
the music, though not so correct as that of Handel,

---

[1] Said to have belonged to Dearborn, afterwards Maj. Gen. Henry
Dearborn, of the United States army.— *M.*

added strength and vigor to our nerves. This evening it was, that some of our companions, whose stomachs had not received food for the last forty-eight hours, adopted the notion that leather, though it had been manufactured, might be made palatable food, and would gratify the appetite. Observing their discourse, to me the experiment became a matter of curiosity. They washed their moccasins of moose-skin, in the first place, in the river, scraping away the dirt and sand, with great care. These were brought to the kettle and boiled a considerable time, under the vague but consolatory hope that a mucilage would take place. The boiling over, the poor fellows chewed the leather, but it was leather still ; not to be macerated. My teeth, though young and good, succeeded no better. Disconsolate and weary, we passed the night.

November 3d. We arose early, hunger impelling, and marched rapidly. After noon, on a point on the bank of the river, some one pretended he descried the first house, ten miles off. Not long after another discerned a boat coming towards us, and turning a point of land, presently all perceived cattle driving up the shore. These circumstances gave occasion to a feeble huzza of joy, from those who saw these cheerful and enlivening sights. We were now treading a wide and stony beach of the river. Smith, our captain, who at this moment happened to be in company, elated with the prospect of a supply of food, in the joy of his heart, perhaps thoughtlessly, said to me, " take this Henry." It was gladly received. Opening the paper, which had been neatly folded, there appeared a hand's breath and length of bacon-fat, of an inch thick ; thoughtlessly, it was eaten greedily, inattentive to all former rule, and thanks to God, did me no harm. Here it was that for the first time, Aaron Burr, a most amiable youth of twenty, came to my view. He then was a cadet. It will require a most cogent evidence to convince my mind, that he ever intended any ill to his country of late years,

by his various speculations.   Though differing in political opinion from him, no reason has as yet been laid before
me, to induce a belief that he was traitorous to his
country.   However, take this as the wayward ideas of a
person totally excluded from a knowledge of the secrets
of the cabinet ; who was somewhat attentive to its
operations, so far as newspaper information can elucidate.

We marched as hastily as our wearied and feeble
limbs could admit, hoping soon to share in something
like an abysinian feast.   The curvatures of the river
had deceived us in the calculation of distance.   It was
many hours ere we came to the place of slaughter.   We
found a fire, but no provision, except a small quantity
of oaten meal, resembling in grit, our chopped rye.
Simpson warmed some of this in water, and ate with
gout.   To me it was nauseous ; this may have been
owing to the luncheon from Smith's hoard.   The French
men told us, that those who preceded, had devoured the
very entrails of the cattle.   One of the eastern men, as
we came to the fire, was gorging the last bit of the colon,
half rinsed, half broiled.   It may be said, he ate with
pleasure, as he tore it as a hungry dog would tear a
haunch of meat.   We soon encamped for the night,
cheered by the hope of succor.

November 4th.   About two o'clock, P.M., we arrived
at a large stream coming from the east, which we ran
through, though more than mid-deep.   This was the
most chilling bath we had hitherto received ; the weather
was raw and cold.   It was the 17th, and the harshest
of my birthdays.   Within a few hundred yards of the
river, stood the first house in Canada ; we approached
it in ecstacy, sure of being relieved from death by the
means of famine.   Many of our compatriots were unaware of that death which arises from sudden repletion.
The active spirit of Arnold, with such able assistants as
John M. Taylor and Steele, had laid in a great stock of
provisions.   The men were furious, voracious, and insa-
tiable.   Three starvations had taught me wisdom.   My

friends took my advice. But, notwithstanding the irrefragable arguments the officers used to insure moderation, the men were outrageous upon the subject ; *they* had no comprehension of such reasoning. A Pennsylvanian German of our company, a good and orderly soldier, who, from my affection towards him, I watched like another Doctor Pedro Positive ; yet all representation and reasoning on my part, had no influence. Boiled beef, hot bread, potatoes, boiled and roasted, were gormandized without stint. He seemed to defy death, for the mere enjoyment of present gratification, and died two days after. Many of the men sickened. If not much mistaken, we lost three of our company by their imprudence on this occasion. The immediate extension of the stomach by food after a lengthy fast, operates a more sudden extinction of life, than the total absence of aliment. At this place we, for the first time, had the pleasure of seeing the worthy and respectable Indian, Natanis, and his brother Sabatis, with some others of their tribe, the Abenaquis. Lieutenant Steele told us that when he first arrived, Natanis came to him, in an abrupt but friendly manner, and gave him a cordial shake by the hand, intimating a previous personal knowledge of him. When we came, he approached Cunningham, Boyd, and myself, and shook hands in the way of an old acquaintance. We now learned from him, that on the evening when we first encamped on the Dead river (September 29th) in our first ascension, he lay within view of our camp, and so continued daily and nightly to attend our voyage, until the path presented which led directly into Canada. This he took ; to the question, " Why did you not speak to your friends ? He readily answered, and truly, " You would have killed me." This was most likely, as our prejudices against him had been most strongly excited, and we had no limit in our orders, as to this devoted person. He, his brother Sabatis, and seventeen other Indians, the nephews and friends of Natanis, marched with us to Quebec. In the attack of that place, on the morning of the first of January following, Natanis received a musket ball through his wrist. He adopted a chirurgery which seemed extraordinary at the time, and quite new, but which now seems to me to be that of nature itself. He drew a pledget of linen quite through the wound, the ends of which hung down on each side of the arm. He was taken prisoner, but General Carleton discharged him immediately with strong tokens of commiseration. This is the first instance in the course of our revolutionary war, of the employment of Indians in actual warfare against our enemies. To be sure it was the act of a junior commander, unwarranted, so far as has come to my knowledge, by the orders of his superiors ; yet it seemed to authorize, in a small degree, upon the part of our opponents, that horrible system of aggression which in a short time ensued, and astonished and disgusted the civilized world.

November 5th. Hunger, which neither knows governance or restraint, being now gratified, we turned our attention towards our friends, who were still in the wilderness. Smith and Simpson (for recollection does not serve to say how my friends Hendricks and Nichols were employed, but it was certainly in doing good), always active, procured two young Indians, nephews of Natanis, " Sweet fellows," as Simpson called them, to proceed on the following morning to the great fall, for the person of the invaluable M'Cleland. Before we started, it gave me pleasure to see these youths, excited by the reward obtained, pushing their birch-bark canoe against the strict current of the river. It seemed like an egg-shell to bound over the surface of the waves of every opposing ripple. To end at once this dolorous part of our story ; the young men, in despite of every impediment from the waters, and the solicitations of the starved wanderers in the rear, for food, hurried on to the fall, and on the evening of the third day, brought our dying friend to the first house. The following day he died, and his corpse received a due respect from the inhabitants of the vicinage. We were informed of this a month after. This real Catholicism towards the remains of one we loved, made a deep and wide breach upon my early prejudices, which since that period has caused no regret ; but has induced a more extended and paternal view of mankind, unbounded by sect or opinion.

November 6th. This morning we marched in straggling parties, through a flat and rich country, sprinkled, it might be said, decorated, by many low houses, all white washed, which appeared to be the warm abodes of a contented people. Every now and then, a chapel came in sight ; but more frequently the rude, but pious imitations of the sufferings of our Savior, and the image of the virgin. These things created surprise, at least, in my mind, for where I thought there could be little other than barbarity, we found civilized men, in a comfortable state, enjoying all the benefits arising from the institutions of civil society. The river, along which the road ran, in this day's march, became in the most part our guide. It now flowed in a deep and almost sightless current, where my opportunities gave me a view. Our abstemiousness was still adhered to. About noon of the next day, we arrived at the quarters of Arnold, a station he had taken for the purpose of halting and embodying the whole of our emaciated and straggling troops. We were now perhaps thirty miles from point Levi ; which is on the St. Lawrence, and nearly opposite to Quebec. Now our mess had " friends at court." Arnold, since we left the twelve-mile carrying place, the last time, had, deservedly, taken Steele as a guide, into his mess ; and he had become a kind of aid-de-camp — he was, to say no more, a confidential man. John M. Taylor, keen and bold as an Irish greyhound, was of our company, being a ready penman and excellent accountant. He was at once exalted, by the shrewd and discerning eye of Arnold, to the offices of purveyor and commissary. We had no distinctions of office, scarcely any of rank, in those days. Our squad,

in consequence, came boldly up to head-quarters, though
we came not now into their presence.   Steele, who was
in waiting, pointed to the slaughter-house, a hundred
yards distant.   Thither we went, determined to indulge.
Here we found our friend Taylor, worried almost to
death, in dealing out the sustenance of life to others.
Without hyperbole or circumlocution, he gave us as
many pounds of beef-steaks as we chose to carry.   Proceeding to the next house, a mile below, some one of
the party became cook.   Good bread and potatoes, with
the accompaniment of beef steak, produced a savory
meal.   Believing myself out of danger from any extraordinary indulgence of appetite, the due quantity was
exceeded, and yet, believe me, it was not more than an
anchorite might religiously take.   We soon became
sensible of this act of imprudence.   The march of the
afternoon was a dull and heavy one.   A fever attacked
me.   I became, according to my feelings, the most
miserable of human beings.   Determined not to lag behind, my eyes, at times, could scarcely discern the way,
nor my legs do their office.   We did not march far this
afternoon.   In this high latitude, a winter's day is very
short and fleeting.   The evening brought me no comfort, though we slept warmly in a farm house.

November 7th.   The army now formed into more
regular and compact order ; in the morning pretty
early we proceeded.   About noon my disorder had increased so intolerably, that I could not put a foot forward.
Seating myself upon a log at the way side, the troops
passed on.   In the rear came Arnold on horseback.   He
knew my name and character, and, good naturedly, inquired after my health.   Being informed, he dismounted,
ran down to the river side, and hailed the owner of the
house, which stood opposite across the water.   The
good Canadian, in his canoe, quickly arrived.   Deposit-
ing my gun and accoutrements in the hands of one of our
men, who attended upon me, and had been disarmed by
losing his rifle in some one of the wreckings above, and

Arnold putting two silver dollars into my hands, the Frenchman carried me to his house. Going to bed with a high fever upon me I lay all this and the following day without tasting food. *That had been the cause* of the disease, *its absence* became the *cure.*

November 10th. The morning of the third day brought me health. The mistress of the house, who had been very attentive and kind, asked me to breakfast. This humble, but generous meal, consisted of a bowl of milk, for the guest, with excellent bread. The fare of the family was this same bread, garlic, and salt — I had observed, that this was the usual morning's diet, for I lay in the stove-room, where the family ate and slept. This worthy family was composed of seven persons ; the parents in the prime of life, and five charming, ruddy children, all neatly and warmly clothed in woolen, apparently of their own manufacture. You might suppose, from the manner of their living, that these persons were poor. No such thing. They were in good circumstances. Their house, barn, stabling, etc., were warm and comfortable, and their diet such as is universal among the French peasantry of Canada. Proffering my two dollars to this honest man, he rejected them with something like disdain in his countenance, intimating to me that he had merely obeyed the dictates of religion and humanity. Tears filled my eyes when I took my leave of these amiable people. But they had not even yet done enough for me. The father insisted on attending me to the ferry some miles off, where the river takes a turn almost due north, to meet the St. Lawrence. Here my worthy host procured me a passage *scott free,* observing to me my money might be required before the army could be overtaken. Landing on the north bank of the river, the way could not be mistaken, the track of the army had strongly marked the route. To me it was a most gloomy and solitary march. Not a soul was to be seen in the course of ten miles. Being without arms, and in an unknown country, my inconse-

quence, and futileness lay heavy on my spirits. Here
and there was a farm-house, but the inhabitants were
either closely housed or absent from their homes. Afternoon, arriving at the quarters of our company, my gun
and accoutrements were reclaimed with ardor, and a
solemn resolution never to part with them again, unless
it happened by the compulsion of the foe. The house,
which the company possessed, lay some hundreds of
paces from head-quarters, but within view. Morgan's
quarters were nearer. Where Hendricks made his lodgment is not now recollected, but it was at no great
distance.

November 11th, on the following day, our guns in
order, a scene opened, which then and now seems to me
to have exhibited us in a disreputable point of view ; it
evinced, at least, the necessity of a staid and sober conduct of the officer, as well as a strict subordination and
obedience of the private. A hurried and boisterous report. came from head-quarters, that the British were
landing to our left at a mill, about a mile off. Each one
grasped his arms. Morgan and the Indians, who lay
nearest to the commander's quarters, were foremost.
The running was severe. The lagging Indians, and
a variety of the three companies were intermingled.
Coming to the brow of the precipice, but still unseen,
we perceived a boat landing, which came from a frigate
lying in the stream a mile below. The boat came
ashore. A youth sprung from it. The tide ebbing, the
boatswain thought it better to obtain a deeper landing-
place, nearer the mill, and drew off. Morgan, apprehensive of a discovery of our presence, fired at the boat's
crew. A volley ensued without harm, probably because
of the great space betweeen us. They pulled off shore,
until beyond the range of our guns, leaving the midshipman to our mercy. The hapless youth, confounded,
unknowing what to do, plunged into the river, hoping to
regain his boat. His friends flying from him, he waded,
he swam, yet could not reach the boat. At the distance,

perhaps of one hundred and fifty yards, nothing but his head above water, a shooting-match took place, and believe me, the balls of Morgan, Simpson, Humphreys, and others, played around, and within a few inches of his head. Even after a lapse of thirty years, it gives me pain to recollect that my gun was discharged at him. Such, however, was the savage ferocity engendered, in those ungracious times, by a devolution of the ministry of the mother-country from the true line of conduct towards her colonies.

M'Kensie (the name of the young man), seeing that his boat's crew had deserted him, showed a desire to surrender, by approaching the shore. The firing ceased. But a still more disgusting occurrence than the preceding, followed. The lad, coming towards the shore, evidently intending to submit, Sabatis, the Indian, the brother of Natanis, sprung forward, scalping knife in hand, seemingly intending to end the strife at a single blow. The humanity of Morgan and Humphreys, towards a succumbent foe, was excited. One or the other of them, it is not now recollected which, in particular, by his agility and amazing powers of body, was enabled to precede the Indian by several yards. This contest of athleticism was observed from the shore, where we were, with great interest. Morgan brought the boy (for he was really such), to land, and afterwards esteemed him, for he merited the good will of a hero. Wet and hungry, we returned to quarters. Running along the shore with our prey, the Hunter, sloop of war, having warped up for the purpose, pelted us all the way with ball and grape shot. It was no easy matter to ascend the bank, which was steep and craggy. Our prisoner was prudently loquacious, and very genteel. He had left the sloop, of which he was a midshipman, upon command, to procure spars and oars, which lay in the mill. He had ordered off the boat to procure a better landing, when our imprudent fire drove his people from him. He was the brother of Captain M'Kensie of the Pearl fri-

gate. In 1777, the young M'Kensie was again taken.
I saw him at Lancaster (Pennsylvania), active, lively,
and facetious as ever. During our stay at Point Levi,
Colonel Arnold was busily engaged. Being now discovered, it became us to pass the St. Lawrence as soon
as possible. The main difficulty consisted in the pro-
curement of boats or canoes. Those kinds of craft on
this part of the river had, previously to our arrival, been
secured by the vigilance of government, which it is
likely had some intimation of an inroad in the direction
we came. Twenty-five canoes, chiefly of birch bark,
were with difficulty procured. The command of these
was conferred upon Lieutenant Steele, who selected the
steersmen, of whom it came to me to be one. The
passage, if practicable, must be made in the night, and
that in the most silent manner, at a time the tide served.

Between the hours of ten and eleven o'clock, on the
night of the 13th of November, the troops paraded on
the beach, near the mill before mentioned, without noise
or bustle. One cargo was despatched — then a second :
upon making the traverse a third time, an accident
happened to my friend Steele, which you can scarcely
credit. Being at a considerable distance behind with his
canoe, I could not, at its occurring, observe the transaction, nor share in the danger, though my life would
have been willingly risked for his, and yet the relation of
this fact is most unquestionably true. These frequent
asseverations may appear somewhat awkward, and to
blur the detail of our story ; but our sufferings were so
extraordinary in their kinds, and so aggravated by the
nature of the severe services we underwent, that now-a-
days it will require a faith almost approaching to credulity,
to convince the mind of their truth. Steele steered a
birch-bark canoe, the weight, and it is likely the awkward-
ness of the men, when about the middle of the river
(which at this place is fully two miles wide), burst the
canoe. The men who were in it, swam to, or were
taken up, by the canoes nearest to them. It was other-

wise with Steele.   He was the last to get to a canoe
under the management of the worthy Wheeler: but it
was full of men.   There could be no admittance.   The
steersman advised, and Steele was compelled from necessity, to throw his arms over the stern — Wheeler, seating
himself upon them, so as to hold him securely, for it
was a bleak and numbing night.   Thus, in this manner
was this worthy and adventurous officer floated to the
shore at Wolf's cove.   Here there was an uninhabited
house.   A fire had been lighted in it, by some of our
people, who first landed.   It became a pole-star to us in
the rear, we steered for it.   Landing about half an hour
after Steele, we found him at the fire, seemingly chilled
to the heart ; but he was a man not to be dispirited by
slight matters.   Friction soon restored him to his usual
animation.   The moon, now about three o'clock, shone
brightly, and the tide run out rapidly, so that the passing
of the rest of the troops, about one hundred and fifty in
number, this night was given up.   This circumstance,
of the absence of so large a part of our force, was known
but to few.   They joined us on the following night.   It
had been the intention of our chief to storm the town
this night ; but the deficiency of our scaling ladders,
many of which were left beyond the river, now repressed
that design.

November 14th.   The troops easily ascended the hill,
by a good road cut in it slantingly.   This was not the
case in 1759, when the immortal Wolf mounted here,
it was then a steep declivity, enfiladed by a host of
savages, but was surmounted by the eager and gallant
spirit of our nation.

November 15th.   Arriving on the brow of the precipice, we found ourselves on the plains of Abraham, so
deservedly famous in story.   The morning was cold,
and we were thinly clad.   While an adventurous party
despatched by Arnold, under the command of one of
Morgan's lieutenants, were examining the walls of the
city, we were pacing the plains to and fro, in silence,

to keep ourselves warm. The winter had set in — a cold north-wester blew, with uncommon keenness. By the time the reconnoitering party returned, daylight was not very distant. The party found every thing towards the city, in a state of perfect quietness. This report *was delivered, in my presence, to Morgan,* however the contrary may have been represented since. Not even the cry of " All's well," was uttered, was a part of their report, yet we heard that cry from the walls, even where we were ; but this in a direct line, was nearer to us than the voices opposite to the party. This was the happy moment, but with our small and disjointed force, what could be done ? There was scarcely more than three hundred and fifty men, willing and determined to be sure, but too few to assail a fortress, such as Quebec is. If *that* had been known this night, which was evidenced in a few days by the fugitives from the city, Arnold would most assuredly have hazarded an attack. St. John's gate, which opens on Abraham's plains, and is a most important station, was unbarred, nay, unclosed: nothing but a single cannon under the care of a drowsy watch, was there as a defence ; we were not a mile distant, and might have entered unknown, and even unseen. These are uncertain opinions, resting on the vague reports of the moment, which might have been true, or untrue. My memory is, however, fresh in the recollection of the heart-burnings this failure caused among us. Providence, for wise purposes, would have it otherwise. Near daylight, requiring rest and refresh-ment, the troops moved a mile, to a farm-house of Lieutenant Governor Caldwell's. This was a great pile of wooden buildings, with numerous outhouses, which testified the agricultural spirit and taste of the owner. He, good soul, was then snug in Quebec. Those who came first, fared well, and as luck would have it, we were of the number: all within and without the house, became a prey. Adversity had destroyed in our minds, every decorous or delicate sensation. Guards were

stationed next the city. Wrapped in my blanket, fearless of events, casting my person on the floor of an elegant parlor, I slept sweetly and soundly, till two in the
afternoon, and then was roused solely by a cry, that the
enemy was advancing. We flew to arms, and rather in
a hurried manner run towards the city, which was nearly
two miles from us. We saw no enemy. It turned out
that a Mr. Ogden, a cadet from Jersey, a large and
handsome young man in favor with Arnold, had been
authorized to place the sentinels that day. He did place
them, most stupidly. George Merchant, of Morgan's,
a man who would at any time, give him fair play, have
sold his life dearly, he stationed in a thicket, within view
of the enemy ; at the time of placing him, when at his
post, he was out of sight of the garrison ; but the mis-
chief was (though *he* could not be seen), *he* could see
no one approach ; he was taken absolutely unaware of
danger. A sergeant of the seventh, who, from the
manner of the thing, must have been clever, accompanied by a few privates, slily creeping through the
streets of the suburbs of St. John, and then under cover
of the bushes, sprung upon the devoted Merchant, even
before he had time to cock his rifle. Merchant was a
tall and handsome Virginian. In a few days, he, hunting shirt and all, was sent to England, probably as a
finished specimen of the *riflemen* of the colonies. The
government there very liberally, sent him home in the
following year.

The capture of Merchant grieved us, and brought us
within a few hundred yards of the city. Arnold had the
boldness, you might say the audacity, or still more correctly, the folly, to draw us up in a line, in front and
opposite to the wall of the city. The parapet was lined
by hundreds of gaping citizens and soldiers, whom our
guns could not harm, because of the distance. They
gave us a huzza ! We returned it, and remained a considerable time huzzaing, and spending our powder against
the walls, for we harmed no one. Some of our men to

the right, under the cover of something like ancient ditches and hillocks, crept forward within two hundred yards of the works, but their firing was disregarded by the enemy as farcical. Febiger, who was a real and well instructed soldier, and engineer, did advance singly within a hundred paces, and pored with the eye of an adept. During all this, as my station in the line happened to be on a mound, a few feet higher than the common level of the plain, it was perceptible through the embrasures that there was a vast bustle within. In some minutes a thirty-six pounder was let loose upon us ; but so ill was the gun pointed, that the ball fell short, or passed high over our heads. Another, and another succeeded — to these salutes, we gave them all we could, another and another huzza. It must be confessed, that this ridiculous affair gave me a contemptible opinion of Arnold. This notion was by no means singular. Morgan, Febiger and other officers, who had seen service, did not hesitate to speak of it in that point of view. However, Arnold had a vain desire to gratify, of which we were then ignorant. He was well known at Quebec. Formerly, he had traded from this port to the West Indies, most particularly in the article of horses. Hence, he was despised by the principal people. The epithet *Horse jockey* was freely and universally bestowed upon him, by the British. Having now obtained power, he became anxious to display it in the faces of those, who had formerly despised and contemned him. The venerable Carleton, an Irishman of a most amiable and mild character, Colonel Maclean, a Scotchman, old in warfare, would not, in any shape, communicate with him. If Montgomery had originally been our commander, matters might have been more civilly conducted. This particularity in relating a most trivial and disgusting occurrence, arises from a desire to set before you a cautionary rule, which it will be prudent for you to observe in your historical reading. "Do not believe an author, unless the story he relates be probable, accompanied by

such circumstances as might reasonably attend the transaction, unless he is corroborated by others, who speak
on that subject." Many of our wisest men, within the
colonies, wrote and spoke of this bravading, as a matter
of moment, and with much applause. Even some of
our historians (Gordon), have given it celebrity. But a
more silly and boastful British historian (Amwell), says
there was a dreadful cannonade, by which many of the
rebels were destroyed. The truth is, that this day not
a drop of blood was shed, but that of Governor Caldwell's horned cattle, hogs and poultry, which run plenti-
fully. After this victory in huzzaing, which was boys'
play, and suited me to a hair, we returned to quarters to
partake of the good things of this world.

November 15, the next day, a scene of a different
kind opened, which let us into the true character of
Arnold. In the wilderness, the men had been stinted
to a pint of flour by the day. This scanty allowance of
flour had been continued since we had come into this
plentiful country. Morgan, Hendricks and Smith
waited upon the commander in chief, to represent the
grievance and obtain redress. Altercation and warm language took place. Smith, with his usual loquacity, told
us that Morgan seemed, at one time, upon the point of
striking Arnold. We fared the better for this interview.

November 16, on the following day, the rifle companies removed further from the city. About half a
mile from Caldwell's house, our company obtained excellent quarters, in the house of a French gentleman,
who seemed wealthy. He was pleasing in his manners,
but the rudeness our ungovernable men exhibited, created
in him an apparent disgust towards us. Here we remained near a week. During that time, we had constant and severe duty to perform. There was a large
building on the low grounds, near the river St. Charles,
which was occupied by a most respectable society of
ladies as a nunnery. In the front of this house, at the
distance of fifty yards, there was a spacious log building,

which seemed to be a school house, occupied by the priesthood attendant on the nunnery. This house we took possession of, as a guard-house, under an idea, as it stood directly between the town and the nunnery, which contained some precious deposits, that they had not had time to remove, that the enemy would not fire in this direction. The conjecture was just.

November 16. In the afternoon a distressing occurrence took place here, notwithstanding our vicinity to this holy place. Towards the evening the guard was relieved. Lieut. Simpson commanded it. This guard was composed of two-and-twenty fine fellows, of our company. When the relief guard came, a Frenchman, of a most villainous appearance, both as to person and visage, came to our lieutenant, with a written order from Colonel Arnold, commanding him to accompany the bearer, who would be our guide across the river St. Charles, to obtain some cattle feeding beyond it, on the account of government. The order in the first instance, because of its preposterousness, was doubted, but, upon a little reflection, obeyed. Knowing the danger, our worthy lieutenant also knew the best and only means of executing the enterprise. The call " come on lads," was uttered. We ran with speed from the guard-house some hundreds of yards, over the plain to the mouth of the St. Charles, where the ferry is. Near the ferry there was a large wind-mill, and near it stood a small house resembling a cooper's shop. Two carts of a large size were passing the ferry heavily laden with the household-stuff, and women and children of the townsmen flying from the suburbs of St. Roque, contiguous to palace-gate, to avoid the terrible and fatal effects of war. The carts were already in a large scow, or flat-bottomed boat, and the ferrymen, seeing us coming, were tugging hard at the ferry-rope, to get off the boat, which was aground, before we should arrive. It was no small matter, in exertion, to outdo people of our agility. Simpson, with his usual good humor, urged the race, from a hope that the garrison would not fire upon us, when in the boat with their flying townsmen. The weight of our bodies and arms put the boat aground in good earnest. Simpson vociferously urging the men to free the boat, directing them to place their guns in my arms, standing on the bow. He ordered me to watch the flashes of the cannon [1] of the city near palace gate. Jumping into the water mid-deep, all but Sergeant Dixon and myself, they were pushing, pulling, and with handspikes attempting to float the scow. One of the carts stood between Dixon and myself — he was tugging at the ferry rope. Presently a shot was called, it went wide of the boat, its mark. The exertions of the party were redoubled. Keeping an eye upon the town, the sun about setting, in a clear sky, the view was beautiful indeed, but somewhat terrific. Battlements like these had been unknown to me. Our boat lay like a rock in the water, and was a target at point blank shot, about three-fourths of a mile from palace gate, which issues into St. Roque. I would have adored all the saints in the calendar, if honor and their worships would have permitted the transportation of my person a few perches from the spot where it then stood, by the austere command of duty. It was plainly observable that many persons were engaged in preparing the guns for another discharge. Our brave men were straining every nerve to obtain success. "A shot," was all that could be said, when a thirty-six pound ball, touching the lower edge of the nob of the cart-wheel, descending a little, took the leg of my patriotic friend below the knee, and carried away the bones of that part entirely. "Oh! Simpson," he cried, "I am gone." Simpson, whose heart was tender and kind, leaped into the boat : calling to the men, the person of Dixon was borne to the wind-

---

[1] This was a ridiculous practice, universally adopted in the camp near Boston, and was now pursued at this place. It is merely designative of the raw soldier. Such indications of fear should now a-days be severely reprimanded.— *Henry.*

mill. Now a roar of triumph was heard from the city, accompanied by some tolerably well directed shots. The unfortunate was borne at a slow and solemn pace to the guard-house, the enemy, every now and then, sending us his majesty's compliments, in the shape of a twenty-four or thirty-six pound ball. When the procession came into a line with the town, the guard-house and nunnery, the firing ceased. At the time we were most busily engaged with Dixon, at the windmill, the vile Frenchman, aghast and horror stricken, fled from us to the city. If his desertion had been noticed in time, his fate had been sealed, but the rascal was unobserved till he had run several hundred yards along the beach of the bay of St. Charles. He turned out to be a spy, purposely sent by government to decoy and entrap us, and he succeeded but too easily with the vigilant Arnold. Dixon was now carried on a litter to the house of an English gentleman, about a mile off. An amputation took place — a tetanus followed, which, about nine o'clock of the ensuing day, ended in the dissolution of this honorable citizen and soldier. There are many reasons for detailing this affair so minutely to you. Among these are, to impress upon your minds an idea of the manners and spirit of those times : our means and rude methods of warfare : but more particularly for the purpose of introducing to your observation an anecdote of Dixon, which is characteristic of the ideas and feelings then entertained by the generality of his countrymen. Before we left our native homes, tea had, as it were, become an abomination even to the ladies. The taxation of it by the parliament of England, with design to draw from us a trifling revenue, was made the pretence with the great body of the people, for our opposition to government. The true ground, however, with the politically wise, was, that that law annihilated our rights as Englishmen. It is an axiom of the common law of our glorious ancestors, that taxation and representation must go hand in hand. This rule was now violated. Hence it was, that no one, male or female, knowing their rights, if possessed of the least spark of patriotism, would deign to taste of that delightful beverage. The lady of the house, though not one who approved of our principles of action, was very attentive to our wounded companion : she presented him a bowl of tea ; " No madam," said he, " it is the ruin of my country."

November 17th, uttering this noble sentiment, this invaluable citizen died, sincerely lamented by every one who had the opportunity of knowing his virtues. Dixon was a gentleman of good property and education, though no more than the first sergeant of our company. His estate lay in West Hanover township, in the county of Lancaster (now in Dauphin). He was an agriculturist, which, in the vagueness and uncertainty of our language, is called *a farmer*. In fact he was a freeholder, the possessor of an excellent tract of land, accompanied by all those agreeables which render the cultivator of the earth, in Pennsylvania, the most independent, and, with prudent economy, the most happy of human beings. The following morning, Simpson was the first to give me an account of Dixon's death, which affected us much; his corpse received the usual military honors. Duty compelled my absence elsewhere. The blood of Dixon was the first oblation made upon the altar of Liberty at Quebec, and Merchant was the first prisoner. The latter was a brave and determined soldier, fitted for subordinate station ; the former was intuitively a captain. The city and vicinity occupied the attention of the commander nearly a week.

November 18th. Not being fully in the secret, it does not become me to recount the causes of our retreat to Point Aux Tremble. We did, however, make this retrograde movement, rather in a slovenly style, accompanied, probably, by the maledictions of the clergy and nobility, but attended by the regrets of a host of well-wishers among the peasantry. Point Aux Tremble is at the distance of twenty, or more, miles from Quebec.

The route thither, though in a severe winter, was interesting. The woods were leafless, except as to those
trees of the fir-kind ; but numerous neat and handsomely
situated farm houses and many beautiful landscapes were
presented, and enlivened our march along this majestic
stream.   At Detroit, which is supposed to be little short
of nine hundred miles from Quebec — even there, it is
no contemptible river, but here the immense volume of
its waters, strikes the mind of the stranger with astonishment and rapture.   Our Susquehanna, which, from its
grandeur, attracts the European eye, stands in a low
grade when compared with the St. Lawrence.   Ascending the river at a distance of ten or fifteen miles, we observed the rapid passage, down stream, of a boat, and
soon afterwards of a ship, one or other of which con
tained the person of Sir Guy Carleton.   That it was the
governor of the province, flying from Montgomery, who
had by this time captured Montreal, we were informed
by a special kind of messenger, which was no other than
the report of the cannon, by way of feu-de-joie, upon
his arrival at the capital.   Water, in regard to the communication of sound, is nearly as good a conductor as
metals are, for the transmission of the electric fluid.
Though near to the place of our destination, we could
mark with precision the report of every gun.   Point
Aux Tremble, at this time, had assumed the appearance
of a straggling village.   There was a spacious chapel,
where the ceremonies of the Roman Catholic religion
were performed, with a pomp not seen in our churches
but by a fervency and zeal apparently very pious, which
became a severe and additional stroke at early prejudices.
Quarters were obtained in the village and farm houses,
dispersed over a space of some miles, up and down the
river.   We enjoyed as much comfort as tight houses,
warm fires, and our scantiness of clothing would admit.
Provisions were in plenty, and particularly beef, which,
though small in bulk, was of an excellent flavor.   Being
in a few days, as it were, domesticated in a respectable

farmer's house, we now had leisure to observe the economy of the family. Every crevice through which cold air could penetrate, was carefully pasted with strips of paper of every color. To permit the cold air to intrude is not the only evil which results ; but the smallest interstice with the air, also admits an almost impalpable snow, which is very inconvenient, particularly at night, when the winds blow most sharply. A stove of iron stood a small space from the wall of the kitchen chimney, but in such a way that it might be encompassed by the family or the guests. This stove was kept continually hot both by day and by night. Over the stove there is a rack so constructed as to serve for the drying of wet clothes, moccasins, etc., etc. When these people slaughter their beasts for winter use, they cut up the meat into small pieces, such as a half pound, two pounds, etc., according to the number of the family. In the evening before bedtime, the females of the house prepare the dinner of the following day. It may be particularly described, as it was done in our view for a number of days together, and during the time was never varied. This was the manner : a piece of pork or beef, or a portion of each kind, together with a sufficiency of cabbage, potatoes and turnips, seasoned with salt, and an adequate quantity of water, were put into a neat tin kettle with a close lid. The kettle thus replenished, was placed on the stove in the room where we all slept, and there it simmered till the time of rising, when it was taken to a small fire in the kitchen, where a stewing continued till near noon, when they dined. The contents were turned into a large basin. Each person had a plate, no knife was used, except one to cut the bread, but a five or six pronged fork answered the purposes of a spoon. The meat required no cutting, as it was reduced to a mucilage, or at least to shreds. This, you may say, is trifling information, and unworthy of your notice ; according to my mind, it is important to all of us, to know the habits, manners, and means of existence of that class of society,

which, in all nations, composes the bulk and strength of
the body politic.   Our dinner followed in a few hours.
The manner of our cookery excited astonishment in our
hosts.   As much beef was consumed at a single meal,
as would have served this family for a week.   Remember,
however, that the mess consisted of persons who were
entitled to double and treble rations.   Two rosy-cheeked
daughters of the house, soon contrived the means and
obtained the surplus.   This circumstance, most probably, made us agreeable to the family, for we had nothing
else to bestow.   The snow had now fallen in abundance,
and enlivened the country.   Sleighs and sleds were passing in every direction.   The farmers began to supply
themselves with a full stock of winter's fuel from the
forest.   No fowls were visible about the house ; a few
were kept alive for breeding in the ensuing summer, in
a close and warm coop in the upper story of the barn.
The rest of the fowls, intended for the market or winter's
use, had been slaughtered, early in autumn, at setting
in of the frost, and were hung up in the feathers in the
garret.   Thence they were taken as wanted.   Towards
March they become unsavory, but in no way tainted.
We became acquainted with this kind of economy, but
upon a much larger scale afterwards, when in a state of
affliction and sorrow.   The roads in this part of Canada
are kept in excellent order.   The corvee of European
France is maintained by the government in full effect,
as to its principles, but far less rigid in its practice.
The roads in low grounds, were ditched on the sides
and curved towards the centre.   Every forty or fifty
yards on each side of the road, throughout the extent of
it, young pines were stuck in the ground, to mark the
central and safest passage.   It is a law, that the land-
holder, whenever a snow falls, whether by day or night,
when it ceases, shall with his horses and cariole, retrace
the road, formed on the preceding snow, throughout the
extent of his grounds.   This is a laborious duty, but it was
discernible that it was performed with punctuality, if

not pleasure. In December, January and February, when the snow lays from three to five feet deep over the surface, there is no traveling in this country, but by ways thus formed, or upon snow shoes.

December 1. General Montgomery, who was anxiously expected, arrived. Arnold's corps was paraded in the front of the chapel. It was lowering and cold, but the appearance of the general here, gave us warmth and animation. He was well limbed, tall and handsome, though his face was much pockmarked. His air and manner designated the real soldier. He made us a short, but energetic and elegant speech, the burden of which was, an applause of our spirit in passing the wilderness ; a hope our perseverance in that spirit would continue ; and a promise of warm clothing ; the latter was a most comfortable assurance. A few huzzas from our freezing bodies were returned to this address of the gallant hero. Now new life was infused into the whole of the corps.

December 2d. The next day we retraced the route from Quebec. A snow had fallen during the night, and continued falling. To march on this snow, was a most fatiguing business. By this time, we had generally furnished ourselves with seal-skin moccasins, which are large, and, according to the usage of the country, stuffed with hay or leaves, to keep the feet dry and warm. Every step taken in the dry snow, the moccasin having no raised heel to support the position of the foot, it slipped back, and thus produced great weariness. On this march the use of the snow-shoe was very obvious, but we were destitute of that article. The evening brought up the riflemen at an extensive house, in the parish of St. Foix, about three miles from Quebec. It was inhabited by tenants. We took possession of a front parlor on the left, Morgan one upon the right, Hendricks, a back apartment, and the soldiery in the upper parts of the house, and some warm out-buildings.

December 3d. Morgan, not finding himself comforta-

ble, moved a short space nearer to the city.   Here, in
low and pretty country houses, he and his men were
neatly accommodated.   It seemed to me, that the Canadians in the vicinage of Quebec lived as comfortably,
in general, as the generality of the Pennsylvanians did,
at that time, in the county of Lancaster.   It may readily
occur to you, that some restriction ought to cramp this
latitude of expression ; take it, however, as a description
of our sensations, entertained in our minds by the con-
veniences we now enjoyed, in opposition to our late
privations.   We had just arrived from a dreary and inhospitable wild, half-starved and thinly clothed, in a land
of plenty, where we had full rations and warm quarters,
consequently, our present feelings contrasted with former
sufferings, might have appreciated in too high a degree,
the happiness of the Canadian.   What is now said,
ought not to be taken in anywise as an allusion to the
political rights, but be confined solely to the apparent
prosperity and economy of families.

December 12th.   We remained about ten days at
these quarters.   The tours of duty, to Arnold's party,
were peculiarly severe.   The officers and men still wore
nothing else than the remains of the summer clothing,
which, being on their back, had escaped destruction in
the disasters of the wilderness.   The snow lay three feet
deep over the face of the whole country, and there was
an addition to it almost daily.   Many impediments
occurred, to delay the transportation of the clothing,
which General Montgomery had procured for us at
Montreal.   Our miserable state, contrary to our principles, excited an illicit desire to be appareled more
comfortably.   This desire would probably have lain dor-
mant, but for a scoundrel Canadian, who in all likelihood
was an enemy of Lieutenant Governor Cromie's.   One
morning having returned from a cold night's duty, near
palace gate, the fellow addressed Simpson, who was the
only officer in quarters, and communicated the information : " That about two miles up the St. Lawrence, lay

a country seat of Governor Cromie's, stocked with many
things we wanted, and he would be our guide." Carioles were immediately procured. The house, a neat
box, was romantically situated on the steep bank of the
river, not very distant from a chapel. Though in the
midst of winter, the spot displayed the elegant taste and
abundant wealth of the owner. It must be a most delightful summer residence, in the months of July and
August, when the heat of this northern climate seems
greater to sensation, than that of our country, in the
same season. The house was closed; knocking, the
hall door was opened to us by an Irishwoman, who, of
the fair sex, was the largest and most brawny that ever
came under my notice. She was the stewardess of the
house. Our questions were answered with an apparent
affability and frankness. She introduced us into the
kitchen, a large apartment, well filled with those articles
which good livers think necessary to the happy enjoyment of life. Here we observed five or six Canadian
servants, huddled into a corner of the kitchen, trembling
with fear. Our prying eyes soon discovered a trap-
door leading into the cellar. In the country houses of
Canada, because of the frigidity of the climate, the cellars are usually under a warm room, and are principally intended for the preservation of vegetables. The cavity
in this instance, abounded with a great variety of eata-
bles, of which we were not in the immediate want.
The men entered it. Firkin after firkin of butter, lard,
tallow, beef, pork, fresh and salt, all became a prey.
While the men were rummaging below, the lieutenant
descended to cause more despatch. My duty was to
remain at the end of the trap door, with my back to the
wall, and rifle cocked, as a sentry, keeping a strict eye
on the servants. My good Irishwoman frequently
beckoned to me to descend; her drift was to catch us all
in the trap. Luckily she was comprehended. The
cellar and kitchen being thoroughly gutted, and the spoil
borne to the carriages, the party dispersed into other

apartments. Here was elegancy. The walls and partitions were beautifully papered and decorated, with large engravings, maps, etc., etc., of the most celebrated artists. A noble view of the city of Philadelphia, upon a large scale, taken from the neighborhood of Cooper's ferry, drew my attention, and raised some compunctive ideas; but war and the sciences always stand at arms length in the contests of mankind. The latter must succumb in the tumult. Our attention was much more attracted by the costly feather beds, counterpanes, and charming rose-blankets, which the house afforded. Of these there was good store, and we left not a jot behind us. The nooks and crevices in the carioles were filled with smaller articles; several dozens of admirably finished case-knives and forks; even a set of desert knives obtained the notice of our cupidity. Articles of lesser moment, not a thousandth part so useful, did not escape the all-grasping hands of the soldiery. In a back apartment there stood a mahogany couch, or settee in a highly finished style. The woodwork of the couch was raised on all sides by cushioning, and lastly, covered by a rich figured silk. This to us was lumber, besides our carioles were full. However, we grabbled the mattrass and pallets, all equally elegant as the couch. Having, as we thought, divested his excellency of all the articles of prime necessity, we departed, ostensibly and even audibly accompanied by the pious blessings of the stewardess for our moderation. No doubt she had her mental reservations; on such business as this, we regarded neither. Near the chapel we met a party of Morgan's men coming to do that which we had already done. The officer appeared chagrined when he saw the extent of our plunder. He went on, and finally ransacked the house, and yet a little more, the stables. The joy of our men, among whom the plunder was distributed in nearly equal portions, was extravagant. Now an operation of the human mind, which often takes place in society, and is every day discernible by persons of observation, became clearly

9

obvious. "Let a man once, with impunity, desert the strict rule of right, all subsequent aggression is not only increased in atrocity, but is done without qualm of conscience." Though our company was composed principally of freeholders, or the sons of such, bred at home under the strictures of religion and morality, yet when the reins of decorum were loosed, and the honorable feeling weakened, it became impossible to administer restraint. The person of a tory, or his property, became fair game, and this at the denunciation of some base domestic villain.

December 13th. On this morning the same audacious scoundrel again returned. By leading to the first affair, and his intercourse with the privates, he had so wormed himself into their good graces that nothing would do but a system of marauding upon our supposed enemies, the tories. In this new expedition, which was further than the former, the officers thought it prudent to accompany the men, in truth, to keep order and repress their ardency. We arrived at a farm said to belong to Gov. Cromie or some other inhabitant of Quebec. The farm house, though low, being but one story, was capacious, and tolerably neat. The barn built of logs, with a threshing-floor in the center, was from seventy to eighty feet in length. The tenant, his wife, and children, shuddered upon our approach. Assurances that they should be unharmed, relieved their fears. The tenant pointed out to us the horned-cattle, pigs and poultry of his landlord. These we shot down without mercy, or drove before us to our quarters. Thus we obtained a tolerable load for our caravan, which consisted of five or six carioles.

With this disreputable exploit, marauding ceased. A returning sense of decency and order, emanating from ourselves, produced a species of contrition. It is a solemn truth that we plundered none but those who were notoriously tories, and then within the walls of Quebec. The clergy, the nobles, and the peasantry, were respected and protected, especially the latter, with whom, to use a trite expression, we fraternized. The minuteness of this description of occurrences, of a trivial, yet disgraceful nature, is made the more strongly to impress your minds with the horrors attendant on civil wars. This species of war, more than any other, not only affects the great and the wealthy, but it intrudes itself into, and devastates the cottage. This the American people know, from the many melancholy scenes which succeeded the period spoken of.

Gracious and Almighty God! the shield and protector of the good, as well as thou art the scourge of the base and wicked nation, avert from my country this the most terrible of thy modes of temporal vengeance.

December 15th. In a short time, the rifle companies moved and occupied good quarters on the low grounds, near St. Charles river, and about two miles from Quebec. Our clothing was still of the flimsy kind, before noted, but our hearts were light, even to merriment. Individually, from our own funds, we supplied ourselves with arm-gloves, and renewed our moccasins. This was about the middle of December. During all this time, our daily duty was laborious in various ways, and every other night we mounted guard at St. Roque. A guard-house ere this, had been established at this place, in a very large stone house, which, though strong, being exposed to the enemy's fire, was soon battered about our ears, the distance scarcely more than three hundred yards. That position was changed for one more secure. A house which had been a tavern, was adopted in its stead. This house was peculiarly situated. It was comparatively small with the former in its dimensions, but the walls were strong, and the ceilings bomb-proof. It stood under the hill, so as to be out of the range of the shot from the ramparts contiguous to palace gate, which were elevated far above us. Simpson would say, Jack, let us have a shot at those fellows. Even at noon-day, we would creep along close to the houses, which ranged under the hill, but close in with it, till we came within forty yards of palace gate. Here was a smith-shop, formed of logs, through the crevices of which we would fire, at an angle of seventy, at the sentries above us. Many of them were killed, and it was said, several officers. This was dishonorable war, though authorized by the practices of those times. The distance from this guard-house to palace gate, may be three hundred and fifty yards. The hill, at the back of the house, seemed to make an angle of sixty or seventy degrees. This activity continued from the walls of the city, and around it by the lower town (where it is greatest), for many miles up the St. Lawrence and St. Charles, and forms the basis of Abraham's plains. It was about that time the York artillerists, under Captain Lamb, had constructed a battery on the Plains, at the distance of six hundred or seven hundred yards from the fortress. The earth was too difficult for the intrenching tools to pierce, the only method left was to raise a battery composed of ice and snow. The snow was made into ice by the addition of water. The work was done in the night time. Five or six nine-pounders, and a howitzer were placed in it ; it was scarcely completed, and our guns had opened on the city, before it was pierced through and through, by the weightier metal of the enemy. Several lives were lost on the first and second day. Yet the experiment was persisted in, till a single ball, piercing the battery, killed and wounded three persons. In the quarters last mentioned, we enjoyed some pleasant days. The winter in Canada, as with us, is the season of good humor and joy.

December 18th, 19th. Upon a secession from the out-post, or other military employments, we were agreeably received in the farm houses around. Our engagements near palace gate, still continued to be of the arduous kind; our numbers being few, every second watch was performed by the same persons who had made the guard the last but one. Between the guard-house, and the extreme end of the suburbs of St. Roque, which may be half a mile from the ramparts, there was a rising ground in the main street fairly in view of the enemy, and whilst we relieved in daylight, was raked even by grape shot. Some good men were lost here. This circumstance changed the time of relief, to nine o'clock in the evening. The rifle men were principally employed as guards at this dangerous station. It is but fair and honest to relate to you an anecdote concerning myself, which will convey to your minds some notion of that affection of the head or heart, which the military call a panic terror. Being one of the guard and having been relieved as a sentry, about twelve or one o'clock at night, upon returning to the guard house, in a dozing state, I cast myself on a bench next the back wall — young, my sleeps were deep and heavy; my youth obtained this grace from Simpson, the officer who commanded; about three o'clock I was roused by a horrible noise. The enemy, in casting their shells, usually began in the evening, and threw but a few, towards morning they became more alert. Our station being out of sight, it was so managed as to throw the shells on the side of the hill, directly back of us, so as they would trundle down against the wall of the guard house. This had frequently occurred before, but was not minded. A thirteen inch shell, thus thrown, came immediately opposite the place where my head lay; to be sure the three feet wall was between us. The bursting report was tremendous, but it was heard in a profound sleep. Starting instantly, though unconscious of the cause, and running probably fifty yards, through untrod snow, three feet deep, to a coal house, a place quite unknown to me before, it was ten or fifteen minutes before the extreme cold restored that kind of sensibility which enabled me to know my real situation. Knowing nothing of the cause, the probable effect, nor anything of the consequences which might follow from this involuntary exertion, it seemed to me to be a species of the panic which has been known to affect whole armies. The circumstance here related, caused a laugh against me; but it was soon discovered that those of the soldiery, though wide awake, were as much panic stricken as myself. The laugh rebounded upon them. During this period we had many bitter nights. To give you some idea of a Canada winter, allow me to relate an occurrence which is literally genuine.

December 24th. One night, at the time of relief, a confidential person came from Colonel Arnold, accompanied by an Irish gentleman named Craig, directing the relieved guard to escort him to his own house, which stood between twenty and thirty paces from palace gate. Craig was a merchant of considerable wealth, and what was more, an excellent whig. He was expelled from his habitation because of his whigism, and took refuge in Arnold's quarters. Montgomery, by this time, had furnished us with personal clothing suitable to the climate, but there were a thousand other things wanting for comfortable accommodation. Many of these Mr. Craig possessed, and Arnold's luxurious cupidity desired. Craig's house was an extensive building, three stories high, with back buildings of an equal height, running far in the rear along the foot of the hill. This last building consisted of stores which, as well as the house, was of brick work. We came to the back part of the house silently, and with the utmost caution. Mr. Craig by a slight knock brought a trusty old negro to the door, who was the sole guardian of the house. The objects of Mr. Craig were frying pans, skillets, and a great variety of other articles of ironmongery, together with cloths, flannels, linens, etc., etc., etc. The party with Craig entered the house. As a man of confidence and as a sentry, it became my business to watch the palace gate. There was a clear moonlight, but it was exceedingly bleak. My place of observation was under a brick arch, over which were stores of Mr. Craig, perhaps less than eighty feet from palace gate. My

gloves were good and well lined with fur, and my moccasins of the best kind, well stuffed.   Unseen, continually pacing the width of the arch, my companions
seemed to employ too much time.   Some Frenchmen,
of Colonel Livingston's regiment, without our knowledge, had been below palace gate marauding.   Repass-
ing the house we were at, like so many hell hounds,
they set up a yelling and horrid din, which not only
scared our party, but alarmed the garrison itself.   My
companions in the house (apprehensive of a sally from
palace gate), fled, carrying all they could.   Though I
heard the noise, the flight of my friends was unseen, as
they emerged from the cellars.   The noise and bustle
created by the Canadians attracted the attention of the
enemy.   Large and small shells were thrown in every
direction, wherever a noise was heard in St. Roque.
Having on a fine white blanket coat, and turning my cap,
or *bonnet rouge,* inside out, the inside being white, made
me, as it were, invisible in the snow.   Under the arch
the conversation of the sentries, as it were, almost over
my head, was very distinguishable.   In this cold region,
many reasons operate to induce the placing two sentries
at the same post — they enliven each other by conversing, and it prevents the fatal effects which follow from
standing still in one position.   Fifteen minutes, at this
time, was the term of the sentries standing.   The time
of my standing under the arch seemed to be several
hours, yet honor and duty required perseverance.   At
length, being wearied out, going to the back door of the
house and knocking, no whisper could be heard within,
the old negro was soundly asleep in his bomb-proof
shell.   At this moment those Canadians ran past the
gateway again, with their usual noisy jabber ; to me, in
my deserted state, it seemed a sally of the enemy.
There was no outlet but by the way we came, which
seemed hazardous.   Running gun in hand into a large
enclosure, which was a garden of Mr. Craig's, here was
a new dilemma.   There was no escape but by return-

ing to the house or climbing a palisade twenty feet high. The latter was preferred ; but my rifle was left within the enclosure, as no means could be fallen upon to get it over the stockade.   The guard house was soon reached.   One of the sergeants kindly returned with me to assist in bringing over my gun.   It was grasped in ecstasy.   Alas ! the determination never to part with it again, but with life, was futile.   While in the enclosure, going from and returning to it, we were assailed with grape-shot and shells, not by any means aimed at us, for the enemy knew not that we were there, but was intended to disperse those vociferous and vile Canadians, and it had the effect.   They were as cowardly as noisy. The cohorn shells were handsomely managed.   They usually burst at fifteen or twenty feet from the earth, so as to scatter their destructive effects more widely.   Again coming to the guard house, my immediate friends all gone, I ran thence to our quarters, about two miles, with great speed.   This was about three o'clock in the morning.   Coming to quarters, my feet and hands were numbed, without ever having, during those many dreary hours, been sensible of the cold.   It was soon discovered that they were frozen.   Pulling off my leggings, etc., and immerging my feet and legs knee deep in the snow at the door, rubbing with my hands a few minutes, soon caused a recirculation of the blood ; the hands were restored by the *act*.   For fifteen, and even twenty years afterwards, the intolerable effects of that night's frost were most sensibly felt.   The soles of my feet, particularly the prominences, were severely frostbitten and much inflamed ; so it was as to my hands.   But it was very remarkable that these subsequent annual painings uniformly attacked me in the same month of the year in which the cause occurred.

On the night of the 20th, or 21st of December, a snow-storm, driving fiercely from the north-east, induced the noble Montgomery to order an attack on the fortress. Our force, altogether, did not amount to more than

eleven hundred men, and many of these, by contrivances
of their own, were in the hospital, which, by this time,
was transferred to the nunnery. The storm abated —
the moon shone, and we retired to repose, truly unwill-
ingly. We had caught our commander's spirit, who
was anxious, after the capture of Chamblee, St. Johns
and Montreal, to add Quebec, as a prime trophy to the
laurels already won. Captain Smith,[1] the head of our
mess, as captain, had been invited to General Montgomery's council of officers (none under that grade
being called); like most of uninstructed men he was
talkative, and what is much worse, in military affairs,
very communicative. I believe blushing followed the
intelligence he gave me : the idea of impropriety of conduct in him, deeply impressed my mind. The whole
plan of the attack on the two following days was known
to the meanest man in the army. How it was disclosed,
is uncertain, unless by the fatuity of the captains. One
Singleton, a sergeant in the troops which accompanied
Montgomery, deserted from the guard at the suburbs of
St. Johns, and disclosed to our foes the purport of our

[1] Colonel Matthew Smith of Paxtang, who commanded the company in
which young Henry served in the Quebec campaign, was one of the war
eagles of the revolution. He was a native of Lancaster county, now Dauphin, born about 1730. He took a warm interest in the affair at Conestoga
and Lancaster in 1763-4, and was delegated by the Paxtang Boys to make
a proper representation to the provincial assembly who were bent on per-
secuting that band of heroes. He enlisted his company in June, 1775, and
with Hendricks was the first south of the Hudson river to reach the be-
leaguered city of Boston after the battle of Bunker hill. At the time of the
attack upon Quebec, Captain Smith was on detached duty, and not with
his company. He was, however, taken prisoner, released on parole and
exchanged the latter part of the year 1776, and subsequently promoted to
major. He served as a member of the supreme executive council of
Pa., in 1778-9, and was for a brief period vice-president of the state.
Early in 1780 he was appointed prothonotary of Northumberland county.
He died at Milton, July 21, 1794, and was buried at Warren Run burying
ground six miles distant. Col. Smith was a fine looking man, had the air
of a soldier, and was as ardent a patriot as ever breathed. Judge Henry,
on account of Capt. Smith's rigid discipline, took a dislike to him, and in
his narrative shows it prominently.— *Dr. Wm. H. Egle.*

schemes; his desertion caused much anxiety. The general prudently gave out that it was by command, he would return soon with intelligence. This was believed generally. The latter information came to my knowledge some months afterwards, when a prisoner. The relation of Smith to me is perfect on my memory. Youths seldom forget their juvenile impressions. It was this: " That we, of Arnold's corps, accompanied by Captain Lang's York artillerists, should assail the lower town, on the side of St. Roque : General Montgomery was to attack the lower town by the way of Cape Diamond, which is on the margin of the St. Lawrence. A false attack was to be made eastwardly of St. John's gate. When Montgomery and Arnold conjoined in the lower town, then the priests, the women and the children, were to be gathered and intermingled with the troops and an assault be made on the upper town." Visionary as this mode of attack was, from what ensued, it is sincerely my belief that Smith was correct in his information, as to the plan suggested by the general. In those turbulent times, men of gallantry, such as Montgomery, were imperiously necessitated, to keep up their own fame and the spirits of the people, to propose and to hazard measures, even to the confines of imprudence. There was another circumstance which induced our brave and worthy general to adopt active and dangerous means of conquest. Many of the New England troops had been engaged on very short enlistments, some of which were to expire on the first of January, 1776. The patriotism of the summer of seventy-five, seemed almost extinguished in the winter of seventy-six. The patriotic officers made every exertion to induce enlistments but to no purpose. We, of the rifle corps, readily assented to remain with the general, though he should be deserted by the eastern men, yet this example had no manner of influence on the generality. The majority were either farmers or sailors, and some had wives and children at home. These, and other reasons, perhaps the austerity of the winter, and the harshness of the service, caused an obstinacy of mind which would not submit to patriotic representation. Besides the smallpox, [1] which had been introduced into our cantonments by the indecorous, yet fascinating arts of the enemy, had already begun its ravages. This temper of the men was well known to the general.

It was not until the night of the thirty-first of December, 1775, that such kind of weather ensued as was considered favorable for the assault. The forepart of the night was admirably enlightened by a luminous moon. Many of us, officers as well as privates, had dispersed in various directions among the farm and tippling houses of the vicinity. We well knew the signal for rallying. This was no other than a snow-storm. About twelve o'clock P.M., the heaven was overcast. We repaired to quarters. By two o'clock we were accoutred and began our march. The storm was outrageous, and the cold wind extremely biting. In this northern country the snow is blown horizontally into the faces of travelers on most occasions — this was our case.

January 1st. When we came to Craig's house, near palace gate, a horrible roar of cannon took place, and a ringing of all the bells of the city, which are very numerous, and of all sizes. Arnold, heading the forlorn hope, advanced, perhaps, one hundred yards before the main body. After these, followed Lamb's artillerists. Morgan's company led in the secondary part of the column of infantry. Smith's followed, headed by Steele, the captain, from particular causes, being absent. Hendrick's company succeeded, and the eastern men, so far as known to me, followed in due order. The snow was

---

[1] In relation to the small-pox, the circumstance about to be related, is most assuredly true, as it is known to me of my own particular knowledge. A number of women loaded with the infection of the small-pox, came into our cantonments.— *Henry.*

deeper than in the fields, because of the nature of the
ground.   The path made by Arnold, Lamb and Morgan,
was almost imperceptible, because of the falling snow ;
covering the locks of our guns with the lappets of our
coats, holding down our heads (for it was impossible to
bear up our faces against the imperious storm of wind
and snow), we ran along the foot of the hill in single
file.   Along the first of our run, from palace gate, for
several hundred paces, there stood a range of insulated
buildings, which seemed to be store-houses ; we passed
these quickly in single file, pretty wide apart.   The
interstices were from thirty to fifty yards.   In these
intervals we received a tremendous fire of musketry
from the ramparts above us.   Here we lost some brave
men, when powerless to return the salutes we received,
as the enemy was covered by his impregnable defences.
They were even sightless to us, we could see nothing
but the blaze from the muzzles of their muskets.

A number of vessels of various sizes lay along the
beach, moored by their hawsers or cables to the houses.
Pacing after my leader, Lieutenant Steele, at a great rate,
one of those ropes took me under the chin, and cast me
headlong down a declivity of at least fifteen feet.   The
place appeared to be either a dry dock, or a sawpit.   My
descent was terrible ; gun and all was involved in a great
depth of snow.   Most unluckily, however, one of my
knees received a violent contusion on a piece of scraggy
ice, which was covered by the snow.   On like occasions,
we can scarce expect, in the hurry of attack, that our
intimates should attend to any other than their own
concerns.   Mine went from me, regardless of my fate.
Scrabbling out of the cavity, without assistance, divesting
my person and gun of the snow, and limping into the
line, it was attempted to assume a station, and preserve
it.   These were none of my friends — they knew me
not.   We had not gone twenty yards, in my hobbling
gait, before I was thrown out, and compelled to await
the arrival of a chasm in the line, where a new place

might be obtained. Men in affairs such as this, seem in the main to lose the compassionate feeling, and are averse from being dislodged from their original stations. We proceeded rapidly, exposed to a long line of fire from the garrison, for now we were unprotected by any buildings. The fire had slackened in a small degree. The enemy had been partly called off to resist the general, and strengthen the party opposed to Arnold in our front. Now we saw Colonel Arnold returning, wounded in the leg, and supported by two gentlemen, a Parson Spring was one, and in my belief, a Mr. Ogden the other. Arnold called to the troops, in a cheering voice, as we passed, urging us forward, yet it was observable among the soldiery, with whom it was my misfortune to be now placed, that the colonel's retiring damped their spirits. A cant term, " We are sold," was repeatedly heard in many parts throughout the line. Thus proceeding enfiladed by an animated but lessened fire, we came to the first barrier, where Arnold had been wounded in the onset. This contest had lasted but a few minutes, and was somewhat severe, but the energy of our men prevailed. The embrasures were entered when the enemy were discharging their guns. The guard, consisting of thirty persons, were either taken or fled, leaving their arms behind them. At this time it was discovered that our guns were useless, because of the dampness. The snow, which lodged in our fleecy coats, was melted by the warmth of our bodies. Thence came that disaster. Many of the party, knowing the circumstance, threw aside their own, and seized the British arms. These were not only elegant, but were such as befitted the hand of a real soldier. It was said that ten thousand stand of such arms had been received from England, in the previous summer for arming the Canadian militia. Those people were loath to bear them in opposition to our rights. From the first barrier to the second, there was a circular course along the sides of houses, and partly through a street, probably of three hundred yards,

10

or more. This second barrier was erected across and near the mouth of a narrow street, adjacent to the foot of the hill, which opened into a larger, leading soon into the main body of the lower town. Here it was, that the most serious contention took place ; this became the bone of strife. The admirable Montgomery, by this time (though it was unknown to us), was no more ; yet, we expected momentarily, to join him. The firing on that side of the fortress ceased, his division fell under the command of a Colonel Campbell, of the New York line, a worthless chief, who retreated without making an effort, in pursuance of the general's original plans. The inevitable consequence, was, that the whole of the forces on that side of the city, and those who were opposed to the dastardly persons employed to make the false attacks, embodied and came down to oppose our division. Here was sharp shooting. We were on the disadvantageous side of the barrier, for such a purpose. Confined in a narrow street hardly more than twenty feet wide, and on the lower ground, scarcely a ball, well aimed or otherwise, but must take effect upon us. Morgan, Hendricks, Steele, Humphreys, and a crowd of every class of the army, had gathered into the narrow pass, attempting to surmount the barrier, which was about twelve or more feet high, and so strongly constructed, that nothing but artillery could effectuate its destruction. There was a construction, fifteen or twenty yards within the barrier, upon a rising ground, the cannon of which much overtopped the height of the barrier, hence, we were assailed, by grape shot in abundance. This erection we called the platform. Again, within the barrier, and close in to it, were two ranges of musketeers, armed with musket and bayonet, ready to receive those who might venture the dangerous leap. Add to all this, that the enemy occupied the upper chambers of the houses, in the interior of the barrier, on both sides of the street, from the windows of which we became fair marks. The enemy, having the advantage of the ground in front, a vast superiority of numbers, dry and better arms, gave them an irresistible power, in so narrow a space. Humphrey's, upon a mound, which was speedily erected, attended by many brave men, attempted to scale the barrier, but was compelled to retreat, by the formidable phalanx of bayonets within, and the weight of fire from the platform and the buildings. Morgan, brave to temerity, stormed and raged, Hendricks, Steele, Nichols, Humphreys, equally brave, were sedate, though under a tremendous fire. The platform, which was within our view, was evacuated by the accuracy of our fire, and few persons dared venture there again. Now it was, that the necessity of the occupancy of the houses, on our side of the barrier, became apparent. Orders were given by Morgan, to that effect. We entered — this was near daylight. The houses were a shelter, from which we could fire with much accuracy. Yet, even here, some valuable lives were lost. Hendricks,[1] when aiming his rifle at some prominent person, died by a straggling ball, through his heart. He staggered a few feet backwards,

---

[1] The second company from Pennsylvania was commanded by Captain William Hendricks, a native of Cumberland county, born two miles west of the Susquehanna river at what was long known as Tobias Hendrick's place, and latterly as Oyster's point. He was killed at Quebec January 1, 1776, and buried in the same enclosure with General Montgomery, on the south side. The Rev. Dr. Smith, in his oration on the death of the gallant officer last named, makes this allusion to the former : " I must not, however, omit the name of the brave Captain Hendricks, who commanded one of the Pennsylvania Rifle companies and was known to me from his infancy. He was, indeed, prodigal of his life and counted danger out of his tour of duty. The command of the guard belonged to him on the morning of the attack ; but he solicited and obtained leave to take a more conspicuous part ; and having led his men through the barrier, where his commanding officer, General Arnold was wounded, he long sustained the fire of the garrison with unshaken firmness, till at last, receiving a shot in his breast, he immediately expired. These particulars were certified by Gen. Thompson and Col. Magaw, his commanders in the Pennsylvania Rifle Regiment, and they give me this further character of him in their letter : 'No fatigues of duty ever discouraged him ; he paid the strictest attention to his company and was ambitious that they should excel in discipline, sobriety and order. His social and domestic virtues you are well acquainted with.' "—*Dr. W. H. Egle.*

and fell upon a bed, where he instantly expired. He was an ornament of our little society. The amiable Humphreys died by a like kind of wound, but it was in the street, before we entered the buildings. Many other brave men fell at this place, among these were Lieutenant Cooper, of Connecticut, and perhaps fifty or sixty non-commissioned officers, and privates. The wounded were numerous, and many of them dangerously so. Captain Lamb, of the York artillerists, had nearly one half of his face carried away by a grape or canister shot. My friend Steele lost three of his fingers, as he was presenting his gun to fire; Captain Hubbard and Lieutenant Fisdle, were also among the wounded. When we reflect upon the whole of the dangers at this barricade, and the formidable force that came to " annoy us, it is a matter of surprise, that so many should escape death and wounding, as did."[1] All hope of success having vanished, a retreat was contemplated, but hesitation, uncertainty, and a lassitude of mind, which generally takes place in the affairs of men, when we fail in a project, upon which we have attached much expectation, now followed. That moment was foolishly lost, when such a movement might have been made with tolerable success. Captain Laws, at the head of two hundred men, issuing from palace gate, most fairly and handsomely cooped us up. Many of the men, aware of the consequences, and all our Indians and Canadians (except Natanis and another), escaped across the ice which covered the bay of St. Charles, before the arrival of Captain Laws. This was a dangerous and desperate adventure, but worth while the undertaking, in avoidance of our subsequent sufferings. Its desperate-

---

Of the other company officers Lt. John McClellan, who resided on the Juniata died on the march to Quebec. Lt. Francis Nichols was captured at Quebec; after the war he was commissioned brigadier general in the Pennsylvania forces. Dr. Thomas Gibson of Carlisle was also captured. He died at Valley Forge in the memorable winter of 1778.— *Ibid.*

[1] See General Nichols's letter.— *Henry.*

ness consisted in running two miles across shoal ice, thrown up by the high tides of this latitude — and its danger, in the meeting with air holes, deceptively covered by the bed of snow.

Speaking circumspectly, yet it must be admitted conjecturally, it seems to me, that in the whole of the attack of commissioned officers, we had six killed, five wounded, and of non-commissioned and privates, at least one hundred and fifty killed, and fifty or sixty wounded. Of the enemy, many were killed and many more wounded, comparatively, than on our side, taking into view the disadvantages we labored under; and that but two occasions happened when we could return their fire, that is, at the first and second barriers. Neither the American account of this affair, as published by congress, nor that of Sir Guy Carleton, admit the loss of either side to be so great as it really was, in my estimation. It seems to be an universal practice among belligerents of all nations, to lessen the number of the slain of the side of the party which reports the event, and to increase it on the part of the enemy. Having had pretty good opportunities of forming a just opinion on the subject, it is hoped that gentlemen who have thought or written differently, will not disdain to listen to my argument. As to the British, on the platform they were fair objects to us. They were soon driven thence by the acuteness of our shooting, which in our apprehension must have destroyed many. Perhaps there never was a body of men associated, who better understood the use and manner of employing a rifle, than our corps, which by this time of the attack, had their guns in good order. When we took possession of the houses, we had a greater range. Our opportunities to kill were enlarged. Within one hundred yards every man must die. The British, however, were at home — they could easily drag their dead out of sight, and bear their wounded to the hospital. It was the reverse with us. Captain Prentis, who commanded the provost guards, would tell me of

seven or eight killed, and fifteen or twenty wounded.
Opposed to this, the sentries (who were generally
Irishmen that guarded us with much simplicity, if not
honesty), frequently admitted of forty or fifty killed, and
many more wounded. The latter assertions accorded
with my opinion. The reasons for this belief are these :
when the dead, on the following days, were transported
on the carioles, passed our habitation for deposition in
the *dead house* we observed many bodies of which
none of us had any knowledge ; and again when our
wounded were returned to us from the hospital, they
uniformly spoke of being surrounded there, in its many
chambers, by many of the wounded of the enemy. To
the great honor of General Carleton they were all,
whether friends or enemies, treated with like attention
and humanity. The reason why the wounded of our
side bore so small a proportion to the dead, seems to be
this : in the long course we ran from palace gate to the
first barrier, we lost many men who were killed out-
right, but many more died, who were merely wounded,
yet in such a manner as in a milder region to make the
case a curable one. A blow from a ball so large as that
of a musket, staggers a man, whether the wound be in
the arm, leg, or elsewhere ; if in staggering he falls, he
comes down into a deep bed of snow, from which a hale
man finds it very difficult to extricate himself. Five or
ten minutes struggling in such a bed, benumbs the
strongest man, as frequent experience has taught me ;
if the party be wounded, though but slightly, twenty or
thirty minutes will kill him, not because of the severity
of the wound, but by the intensity of the frost. These
are my opinions, grounded on a tolerably distinct and
accurate knowledge of particular cases which occurred
in the first part of the attack, and a variety of information obtained afterwards from individual sufferers, who
were persons of credibility, rescued from death by the
humane activity of Governor Carleton. About nine
o'clock, A.M., it was apparent to all of us that we must

surrender. It was done. On this occasion, my friend
General F. Nichols, by his own native spirit, perseverance and determined bravery, obtained an honorable
distinction, and acknowledgment from a brave and dis-
tinguished enemy. It enhances his merit and the boon
(when we reflect that that enemy was no other than
General Carleton), an ornament such as would grace
any nation, whether in the worst or best of times. Some
privates came to Lieutenant Nichols, and demanded his
sword; the requisition was peremptorily denied, though
there was great risk in the refusal. He retained his
sword till meeting with Captain Endesly of the enemy,
to whom it was surrendered; but with the exaction of
a promise that it should be returned when he, the cap-
tive, should be released. In the August following,
before our embarkation for New York, Captain Endesly
waited on Lieutenant Nichols, and in the presence of
all the American officers, redelivered the sword, under
the assurance that it was by the permission and command of General Carleton. This trait in the character
of Carleton adds to the celebrity of his derivation, and
manner of thinking, and casts into a dark ground the
characters of most of the principal British officers, particularly the Scotch, who had much influence in those
days and bore towards us an intemperate hatred.

The commissioned officers, and some of the cadets
were conducted to the seminary, a respectable building.
It became my lot, in one way or other, to be lost in the
crowd, and to be associated with the non-commissioned
officers, in the company of some of whom ardent and
perilous duties had been undergone. These men are
by no means to be lessened in character, by contrasting
them with the levies made in Europe, or those made
since that time in our own country. Many of our
sergeants, and even of our privates, were, with good
educations, substantial freeholders in our own country.
Upon a former occasion you were told the story of the
respectable Dixon. He possessed (if sordid **wealth**

makes the man), two-fold the riches of his captain; and if it be permitted me to decide upon the characters of men, five-fold his understanding, activity and spirit. Amiable Dixon! Many of these men, in the progress of the bloody scenes which ensued, became props of our glorious cause, in defence of our sacred liberties. All could be named. Let a few suffice. Thomas Boyd, so often spoken of in the wilderness for his good humor, his activity and the intensity of his sufferings; struggled gloriously for his life as a captain, and died a dreadful death by the hands of the savages in 1779, in the expedition conducted by General Sullivan against the Six-nation Indians.[1]   Charles Porterfield, who lost his life in the

---

[1] The death of my friend Boyd was to me as a thunderbolt; painful in an excessive degree; many a tear has since been shed to his manes. In the autumn of 1779, he commanded a company of rifle-men of the first Pennsylvania regiment. When Sullivan had penetrated into the Seneca country, in the neighborhood of the Genesee river, Boyd, as my information is from various gentlemen, was ordered with a band of twenty choice men, before daylight to make an excursion towards an Indian village, on the river Genesee (which flows north into Lake Ontario), at a distance of eight miles, for the purpose of making discoveries. In his return, arriving at a rising ground, a knoll, he heard a rustling of the leaves in his front: an enemy was suspected; he gathered his men around him, each taking his tree. The enemy was sightless to Boyd and his party, yet the approach around him was sensible to every one. Boyd, not knowing the number of his assailants, it is said, considered them as a small body of observation. This party of Indians, probably one thousand, encompassed Boyd and his men, gradually: a defence worthy of the character of Boyd took place. Every man he had was killed, except three, who broke through the Indians, and brought the doleful tidings to our camp. Boyd was taken, and carried alive to the Indiantown, where he was tortured after their savage custom, and his body mangled in the most horrible manner. General Simpson. who was then with the army, assures me that on the following day, when the troops arrived at the town, in the wigwams, they found a number of fresh scalps stretched in the usual manner on small hoops, and painted. The head of Boyd lay in one of the cabins, newly dissevered. His scalp was still moist and hooped and painted. Simpson knew it by its long brown and silky hair: it is now preserved as a relic of our friend. An officer (Captain A. Henderson), lately, in describing this unequal but arduous fight, upon the part of Boyd, told me, "that the hands of the dead men, in many instances, were fast closed upon the hair of Indians."

To give you a more perfect idea of the brutality of savage torture, and of heart-rending sensations, I can do no better than to lay before you the

battle of Camden, when in the station of a colonel. Joseph Aston, of Lamb's, who served his country throughout the war, and was promoted to a majority. Doetor Thomas Gibson, of Hendricks', who died in the performance of his duty, at the Valley Forge, in the winter of 1778. Robert Cunningham, a wealthy free-holder of Smith's, who here imbibed the seeds of that disorder, which, at too early an age, hurried him to the grave. He was a younger brother of that excellent

---

letter of the Honorable Thomas Campbell, of the senate, who himself has been a martyr in our cause. He saw the corpse of the unfortunate Boyd on the following day, and interred it. Since the death of Colonel Craw-ford we know nothing like the present martyrdom, in the cause of liberty ; and it is to be hoped, from the prudence and strength of the federal go-vernment, nothing of the kind will again occur in our future wars with the aborigines of our country.

" SENATE CHAMBER, LANCASTER,

" *January* 30*th,* 1809.

"SIR,

" Captain Lieutenant Thomas Boyd, belonging to the riffemen of the state of Pennsylvania, was most inhumanly murdered by the Indians. His death occurred on the 13th day of September, 1779, at the Genesee Castle, on General Sullivan's expedition to the northwestward, against the Six-nation Indians."

" He was sent on the night of the 12th of September, from the camp, near a lake called ' Conesus,' with a party of men, consisting of twenty soldiers, five volunteers and an Indian chief, named Han-Jost, belonging to the Oneida nation : in all twenty-seven in number. They were sent by General Sullivan to reconnoitre an Indian town, supposed to be about six miles distant from the camp. On the morning of the 12th of September, the army took up the line of march before sunrise, but marching a short distance, was obliged to halt, till the pioneers made a bridge over a morass, otherwise the cannon could not have been brought up. The town that Captain Boyd was taken to, was evacuated by all except two Indians, one was on horseback, the other was leading a cow. James Elliot and Timothy Murphy were sent to stop them, they both discharged their guns at the same time, the one that led the cow was killed, the other, though severely wounded, escaped. Boyd returning slowly, expecting to meet the army, saw an Indian start up and run off. It was with great difficulty that Boyd stopped the men from pursuit, at the request of Han-Jost, who said the Indian was only a runner, sent to draw them into an ambuscade. Eighteen of the soldiers were killed, and Han-Jost the Oneida chief, was made a greater sacrifice than any of the white men who fell or were taken at that place.

" Captain Boyd and Michael Parker were made prisoners, and taken to the Genesee Castle, and there most inhumanly murdered. Boyd's head

citizen, and frequent representative of the people of the
county of Lancaster, James Cunningham. In short,
many others might be mentioned in the general, as worthy
and well informed as their superiors, without in anywise,
imputing to the latter, in so saying, the slightest degree
of disparagement. This will always be the case, when
the great body of a nation rises in its strength to defend
its rights. Those who understand the point in question,
in a national dispute, and are most strongly impressed

---

was taken off and totally skinned, his right eye was taken out, as also his
tongue. His right foot, from the ball of the heel to the toes, was laid
open as if with a knife. He was cut open across the bottom of his belly,
and his bowels were taken out, and a very long knife was sticking in between his shoulders, descending to the vital parts. This seems to have
been the *coup de grace.*

"General Simpson and myself, were sent to see the corpse of Boyd interred. I spread a blanket on the ground beside him, we then turned the
corpse over on it. I took the head of the deceased, and put it as near the
neck as possible. I procured a needle and thread from one of the tailors,
and sewed the corpse up as well as I could. As to the head of Michael
Parker, it could not be found. All the flesh was cut out from his shoulders
downward, and otherwise his body was most inhumanly mangled.

"We interred the corpses of both, near the Genesee Castle, in separate
graves, on the 14th day of September, 1779.

"I am Sir,
Your humble servant
Thomas Campbell.
*Late a captain of the fourth
Pennsylvania regiment.*"

"To the Hon. John Jos. Henry."

Though we have no account from an eye witness, of the barbarous manner
in which Captain Boyd was tortured, yet we may conceive from the appearance of his body, that the most malignant and hellish pains were exercised upon it. The being emboweled, conveys an idea of a known mode
of Indian torment : the fixing an end of the entrails to the stake, and
compelling the prisoner by fire and blows to run till the conglomerated
mass is expended. Upon the subject of these tortures, look at Dr.
Colden's *History of the Mohawks,* and Judge Smith's *History of New York.*

Colonel Campbell is of opinion, that the wound along the sole of Captain
Boyd's foot, was made before the savages brought him to their (castle) or
village. His reason is, that the wound was filled with bits of rotten
branches of wood, and small pieces of leaves. The conjecture may be
true, as Indian punishment, at its acme, is to give the greatest degree of
pain.— *Henry.*

with its importance, will be the first to arm. This has been, and ever will be, the disposition of men in all ages, past or to come, whenever their privileges are invaded. Offices of prime importance cannot be obtained by all. Men of talents, of genius and courage must step into subordinate stations. Socrates, Alcibiades and Demosthenes fought in the ranks.

God in his great goodness grant, in the future vicissitudes of the world, that our countrymen, whenever their essential rights shall be attacked, will divest themselves of all party prejudice, and devote their lives and properties in defence of the sacred liberties of their country, without any view to emolument, but that which springs from glorious and honorable actions. Pardon me for frequent digression, upon this subject particularly, as my whole soul was bound up in our cause, you *must* forgive me. The real apology is, we were, all of us, enthusiastic whigs.

When under guard, in the morning of the first of January, Colonel M'Dougal, a Scotch gentleman, near noon, came to review us ; his person was known to me at Detroit, as an intimate of an uncle, three years before this time. The colonel was naturally polite and kindhearted. When it came to my turn to be examined, as to name, place of birth, etc., besides making the proper answers to his inquiries, I was emboldened to declare that he was known to me. He seemed surprised, but not displeased ; a request was immediately added " that he would order me to be transferred to the quarters of the officers." " No, my dear boy," said he, " you had better remain where you are ; the officers, as you are in rebellion, may be sent to England, and there be tried for treason." The advice of this venerable veteran made an impression on my mind, which was then agitated by a thousand vagrant thoughts, and involved in doubt and uncertainty as to our destination. We then well knew of the voyage of Colonel Ethan Allen to England, and the manner of it ;[1] and that of George Merchant,

---

[1] Of the treatment of Ethan Allen, at the time spoken of, we know nothing but from report, which we then thought well grounded, and the truth of which, at this day, there is no reason to doubt. He was a man of much peculiarity of character. Large, powerful of body, a most ferocious temper (fearing neither God nor man), of a most daring courage, and a pertinacity of disposition, which was unconquerable, and very astonishing in all his undertakings : withal he had the art of making himself beloved, and revered by all his followers. When he was taken in the Isle of Montreal, in 1775, the government found it necessary to confine him in a cage, as one would a wild beast, and thus aboard ship, he was transported to Quebec. What his treatment was during this voyage to England, is unknown to me.

This, however, is known, that for many years he was a prisoner in England, returning from his captivity to America, he brought with him a manuscript, which he afterwards entitled *The Oracle of Reason.* My beloved children, it is the farthest from my thought to confine your knowledge to narrow bounds ; when you dip into scriptural history, dip deep, do not skim the surface of the subject, as many fools have done of late days. Upon a thorough inquiry, your hearts will be animated by a conviction that there came a Saviour to redeem you from eternal perdition, and to provide for you an eternal salvation and state of happiness.

That book was most certainly the composition of Ethan Allen. He was very illiterate ; he did not know the orthography of our language. The extent of his learning, probably bounded by some historic chronicles, and a few other books of little account, did not go beyond the scriptures. The gentleman who gave me the above information, was an elegant scholar, bred at Harvard college. Going to New York in the summer of 1786, a friend, from mere curiosity, requested me to purchase the book for him. Being detained at New York six weeks by business, I frequently looked into the detestable volume. The argument if so diabolical a work can be said to contain argument, was in general arranged, and conducted in the same manner as the *Age of Reason,* but in a coarser, and yet a more energetic language, than that of the latter work. On my return to Philadelphia, in a conversation with the Vermontese gentleman, who was still there, *Ethan Allen's Bible,* became a topic of discourse. He gave me this curious anecdote which he averred upon his honor to be true. A young gentleman, either a scholar of Harvard or Yale college, had come into Vermont, and there taught a school. Allen labored under the want of an amanuensis and transcriber of knowledge and learning. The scholar, to increase his emoluments, became such. Allen attended him daily, standing, staff in hand, at the back of the young man's chair. "Sir," he would say to Allen, "this word is misspelled." "Amend it." Again, "this word is misplaced, the sense is incorrect," etc. Allen, who was most profane, would swear (sometimes raising his staff) "By G** sir, you shall insert it ; you shall not alter it." Thus the *Oracle of Reason* came into the world ; which, of all books,

our fellow soldier, but the consequences were unknown.
It became my determination to take the fatherly advice

---

is the most bluntly vicious, as regards the well-being of society ; the salvation of souls ; and the happiness of those who have faith in the redemption
by the blood of our Saviour.   But that which is very remarkable, is, that
long after the publication of Allen's book, which had fallen into oblivion,
even with its readers, that vile reprobate, Thomas Paine, loaded with every
crime which stains and dishonors the Christian and the gentleman (in addition to his shameful practices in life, Paine, as an author, superadded
plagiarism), filched from Ethan Allen the great body of his deistical and
atheistical opinions, which from the time of Celsus, down to the age of
Chubb, Tindal and others, have been so often refuted by men of the utmost
respectability of character and fame.   When we reflect upon the vicissitudes
of this world, its immense revolutions in temporal affairs, the awful persecutions which occurred in early times, the collisions of opinion and party
rage, in the article of religious belief; and the vast body of martyrs who
devoted their lives in support of their faith, *we must* believe that there is
something more than ordinary ; something really divine in the system of
our religion, springing from God himself.   In the last ages, we know of
many of both sexes, of the soundest and best instructed minds, whom it is
almost needless to name, unless it be merely for the purpose of opposing
their virtues and characters to persons of a different mode of thinking.
All of them possessed a firm and solid credence in the celestial origin of
our holy faith, and some of them sealed their creed with their blood.
When such men suffer because of principle, some reliance should be placed
on their good sense and knowledge.   The terms enthusiasm and madness,
have been too often coupled, as conveying the same idea.   George Fox,
Captain Meade, and William Penn, have been called enthusiastic madmen,
but we now know that they acted through the course of the religious parts
of their lives, from a conviction of the principles of the gospel, being
genuine and absolutely true.   However, on this subject, but a few names
need be repeated to convey to your minds its importance and solemnity.
Many of the greatest men, as it concerns worldly things, were Christians.
John Huss, Jerome of Prague, Martin Luther, John Calvin, Cranmer,
Hooker, Tillotson, of the clergy ; of the laity, Sir Thomas Moore, Sir
Matthew Hale, Spangenberg, Mosheim, Joseph Addison, Richard Steele,
Lord Henry Littleton, Soame Jenyns, and thousands of others, all men of
profound learning, have testified by their lives and writings, a reliance on
the merits of the redemption by the blood of Christ Jesus.   But when we
find those men supported and reinforced by two of the strongest minded
men that ever lived, Sir Isaac Newton and John Locke, who can doubt ?
When we contrast their opinions with those of Hobbs, Chubb, Henry St.
John, Voltaire, J. J. Rousseau, Beringer, the great Frederick of Prussia,
or Mr. Gibbon, how deeply do the last not sink, by the weight of reason
and argument ?   Allen and Paine are paltry wretches, mere scribblers, if
classed with the men last named.   Those were beautiful writers, whose
language fascinates, but corrupts the youthful mind, these are dull plodders,

of Colonel M'Dougal, for it was really delivered in the parental style, and to adhere to it. He brought one of

---

who knew not the principles of their mother tongue; but it is perhaps from the circumstance of illiterateness, that Allen and Paine have attacked Christianity in so gross and indecorous a manner. The maniac Paine, when confined in the prison, Conciergerie, at Paris, seems to boast "that he kept no bible." This may be true. But the expression shows that his proper place, instead of a common jail, should have been a mad-house.

It shows, however, a vanity of mind beyond the bearing of men of understanding. Indeed he was inflated by a supercilious pride, and an imaginary importance, which made his society undesirable. He was one of that class of men who, with a small spice of learning, in company, domineered as if he had been a Johnson. He was almost unbearable to many men, who patronized him because of the good effect of his works during the revolution. To give you a few instances; the late David Rittenhouse, Esq., one of the most amiable, most ingenious and best of men, treasurer of the state, George Bryan, Esq., the vice-president of the council, a man of great reading and much good sense, Jonathan Sergeant, the attorney general of Pennsylvania, whose oratorical powers could scarcely be surpassed, and your grand-father, and many other gentlemen of character, during the course of the years '77, '78 and '79, were in habits of intimacy with him, but his dogmatic disposition and obstinacy of mind, frequently caused great disgust. Again, Colonel Samuel John Attlee, an excellent patriot, and a man of note among us, both in the military and civil capacities of a citizen, gave this anecdote to me, a few months after the occurrence happened. Though all the gentlemen present, approved of the writings of Paine, as they concerned our political state, for they were all of them to a man, good whigs, yet they abhorred him, because of his personal aberrations from virtue, and the decencies of social life. A Mr. Mease of Philadelphia, who was clothier general, had invited a number of gentlemen of the army, then in the city, to dine with him. Among whom were Colonel Attlee, Colonel Francis Johnson, General Nichols, and many members of the legislature of whom there was Matthias Slough of Lancaster. You may readily suppose, that the excellent wine of Mr. Mease exhilerated the company. When returning to their lodgings, Colonel Attlee observed Paine coming towards them down Market-street. There comes "Common Sense," says Attlee to the company. "Damn him," says Slough, "I shall common sense him." As he approached the party, they took the wall. Mr. Slough tripped him, and threw him on his back into a gutter, which at that time was very offensive and filthy.

This is told, to communicate a trait to you, in the character of Thomas Paine, who did some good, but a vast deal of harm to mankind, "that the very people who were most benefited by his literary labors, hated him." The company I have spoken of, were all men of eminence in the state; men who staked their *all* on the issue of the revolution. The writings of Paine as concerns *us*, are many of them handsomely worded, have pith and much strength of argument, and are in general correct, yet his domestic

his sons, whom I had formerly known, to see me on the
following day.   About mid-day we were escorted to a

---

life and manners were so very incorrect, that a disgust, which was perhaps
right, destroyed every favorable personal feeling towards him.   His indelicacy was intolerable.   His numbers of Common Sense, the Crisis, and
some other of his fugitive pieces, every American who recollects those
" trying times," must acknowledge to have been extremely beneficial to
our cause.   This has often been admitted by our Generals Washington,
Gates, Greene, etc., but he was compensated, and had the secretaryship
for foreign affairs.   Like all men of bad principles, he betrayed his trust,
and a virtuous congress displaced him, yet the different states more than
remunerated him for all his writings.

So it is, that that man who was without virtue, a disturber of society,
an ill husband, an unworthy citizen, cloaked by every vice, would now by
his *Age of Reason,* which he stole from the ignorant Ethan Allen,
who was as iniquitous as himself, destroy the peace of mind, and all the
hope of happiness in futurity, of those who rely on the redemption of their
souls by the blood of Christ; and that, without substituting, or even sug-
gesting, any other manner of faith, tending to quiet the minds of sinners.
I knew Paine well, and that personally, for he lodged in the house of my
father, during the time that Generals Howe and Clinton were in Philadelphia.   His host often regretted the entertainment he gave him.   His
manners were in opposition and hostile to the observances of the proprieties
and due ordinances of social life.   Many who approved of his political
writings abominated his detestable mode of living and acting.

[I am justified in using these expressions, by an occurrence in 1794,
with my own mother.   She was a woman of strong understanding, and of
unfeigned and rigid belief in the truths of gospel-history, yet a dispassionate,
placid and mild religionist.   Her heart was so free from thinking ill of any
one, that of a truth of her it might be said " she knew no guile."   One
day going to a bookseller's in Lancaster, I met with an extract in the shape
of a pamphlet of Doctor Joseph Priestley's *History of the Corruption of
Christianity.*   Never having seen any of that gentleman's polemic works,
it was purchased.   My mother as usual came in in the evening, to sit and
converse with my family.   I was reading the pamphlet.   " What have you
got ? "   " A work of Doctor Priestley's on religion."   I was then at the
chapter of the " Doctrine of the Atonement of Christ," for the sins of the
world.   The title of the chapter excited the attention of my mother.
Before she came in the passage had been partly perused, and she eagerly
asked me " to read the whole of it to her."   I began, but had scarcely proceeded through two or three pages, when she rapped the book from my
hands, and threw it into the fire, where it was most deservedly burned.
Smilingly, I said " mother, why do you destroy my book ? "   The reply was
with an observable degree of anger : " Because your book would destroy my
happiness, in this and the world to come ! I know that I have a Savior,
who redeemed me, whose blood was shed upon the cross for me : of this,
I am convinced.   Your book goes to make me doubt of the merits of the

ruinous monastery of the order of St. Francis, called the
Reguliers. It was an immense quadrangular building,

---

sufferings of that Savior. The book would deprive me of the only staff
upon which my hope of salvation rests, and gives me none other, upon
which I can lean." These notions of my beloved mother, which accorded
fully with my own, on that topic, were submitted to with a juvenile frankness which pleased her, and of all the world I knew none whom I so
much wished to oblige, as that dear, amiable and instructive mother. My
father had been a mechanic of much respectability, and great skill.
During the war usually called " Braddock's war," and afterwards in Forbes's
campaign (in 1758), he was at the head of the armory, which in those
days was no mean station, and required talents of a superior grade.
Afterwards, having made a tolerable fortune, he entered into trade, but
his inclinations led him into chemical experiments. His evenings and
mornings were devoted to the laboratory. This gave rise to my mother's
acquaintance with Mr. Priestley, as an experimental philosopher. For the
instruction of his children, my father would discourse upon the subjects of
science and particularly of chemistry, which was his favorite theme, and in
which the names of Franklin and Priestley were sure to stand foremost.
My beloved parent's manner showed me that she was stung to the quick.
My apology to her, had the desired effect, as her curiosity and mine
sprung from similar motives, " a desire to know the religious opinions of a
man of whom we had had superlative ideas," because of his acquirements
in many other branches of knowledge.

The position wished to be proved to you, by this relation which is true,
is " that for the sake of public and private comfort and genial happiness, it
is better not to disturb the devout mind by fanciful and newfangled schemes
of belief, and that those should be open only to the eyes of the learned."
My mother was a person of extensive reading; her religious tenets and
faith were solely grounded on the scriptures of the Old and New Testa-
ments, as these, in her mind, were considered as clearly correct, but
nevertheless she was fearful of a disturbance of her mind by the quirks
and quibbles of deistical scribblers. Therefore to interfere with her
devotional principles, in so rude and heterodox a manner, tended to derange
her charming mind, and devastate those elegant maxims of Christian belief,
which the excellency of her maternal education had infused into her heart ;
in short, to destroy that firmness with which she relied on the merits and
sufferings of our Lord and Savior Jesus Christ.

Such men as Hobbs, Chubb, etc., seem not to have reflected on the
dreadful ills and calamities their writings would create, if their books came
into general circulation. If they did reflect, posterity ought to consider
them to have been the tigers and hyenas of human society, opposed to the
well being of the human race. Voltaire and John James Rousseau, in my
humble opinion, intended well to the people of France, but when speaking
of those gentlemen, we should recollect that they, as well as the virtuous
and celebrated Montesquieu, were the subjects of a prince who might, if he
pleased, be despotic : but that which was still worse, was, that the people

containing, within its interior bounds, half an acre or
more, of an area, which seemed to be like a garden or

---

were abandoned to the control of a theological aristocracy — bigoted,
wealthy, imperious and scandalously subjected to vices, in many instances,
greater than those of laymen, insomuch that in the reign of Louis XIV,
because of the infamous lives, and the oppressions of all classes of the
nation by the clergy, there was scarcely a gentleman in the kingdom, who
was not deistically inclined.   For when the ministers of a religion of so
high sanctity, as that of our Holy Faith, demean themselves in a manner
which evinces to laymen their want of confidence in the religion (which
they had been consecrated to propagate and enforce), by an unholy life and
conduct, particularly in their cruel exactions from devotees; in the latter
instance, of enormous fees, and various demands of tithes of a most
exorbitant nature, which from time to time, they wickedly usurped.
Hence, it arose that Montesquieu, Voltaire, Diderot, Rousseau, and
hundreds of others, of the learned men of France (considering the state of
that government), formed a phalanx of historic knowledge, genuine
reasoning, true wit, and an inexhaustible fund of humor, which slurred
their opponents to such a degree, as in the minds of the generality of Europe
gave them a deserved victory even over the government, which supported
the theocracy, with its vast power.   It also, most probably, came from
thence, that those men under the clerical persecutions raised against them
(for many were confined in the dungeons), in the heat of controversy,
emitted opinions and ideas inconsistent with our pure, simple and holy
religion, according to the Augsburg creed, which we know has been adopted,
either in the whole or in part, by all the reformed churches.   In polemic
disputes, and perhaps more particularly in those which happened in
monarchies, there is an acrimony and irascibility of temper, inflaming the
minds of men generally, greater than is the case in democracies.   The
cause seems to be, that in monarchies the priesthood becomes a machine
of government, in democracies it is the vehicle by which the people
simply adore God.
    Those controversies, between the so styled philosophers of France and
the clergy, were conducted with such hatred and obloquy towards each
other, that they elicited sparks which enkindled that nation in a dreadful
flame of internal destruction; and the brand has not only communicated
itself to all Europe, but in general to the world at large.   Since the time
of Julius Cæsar, nothing has occurred equal in barbarity, irruption, bloodshed,
murder, by public or domestic treason, as that which has happened in
Europe, since the year 1789.   Gracious and omnipotent God, restore the
peace of the world ! ! !]
    Such is the man who, upon his slight intercourse with the American
people, pluming himself with the well-earned celebrity of his political pieces,
that now presumes to become a reformer of our morals, our religious opinions and thinkings on Divine subjects.   He himself a reprobate, cloaked by
every vice, would dictate to a great and independent Christian people, their
formulary of belief.   Such insolence and presumption was never before

shrubbery. The monks, priests or what not, who inhabited the house, must have been few in number, as

---

witnessed unless it was in the instance of Mahomet, or in those of the im-
postures (such as Sabbati Sevi), who frequently as Messias, appeared to de-
ceive the remnant of the Jewish people. Paine with all his other vices had
a foible injurious to our country. To keep up the spirits of the people it
was requisite that there should be a series of patriotic publications. Paine
was the most indolent of men; if he was inspired by a muse, the
goddess most certainly made him but few visits. The office of secretary
of foreign affairs, was conferred upon him, because of the merit of his
Common Sense, or what are called the *Crisis,* under the signature to
Common Sense. It was to him personally a sinecure. He never went
to York (Penn.), where congress then sat, but occasionally, and stayed but
a day or two. His true employment was that of a political writer. In
the summer and winter of 1777, and 1778, he was an inmate of my
father's house, as were the late David Rittenhouse, the state-treasurer, and
John Hart, a member of the then executive council.

Paine would walk of a morning until twelve o'clock; come in and make
an inordinate dinner. The rising from table was between two and three
o'clock. He would then retire to his bed-chamber, wrap a blanket around
him, and in a large arm-chair, take a nap, of two or three hours — rise and
walk. These walks, and his indolence, surprised my parents; they knew
him as the author of *Common Sense,* who had written patriotically, and
in those writings, promulged some moral and religious ideas, which induced
them to believe he was an orthodox Christian. Indeed Paine, during the
revolution, was careful to emit no irreligious dogmas, or any of his late dia-
bolic ideas; if he had, the good sense of the American people, their virtue,
and unfeigned worship of the Deity, would have, in those days, banished
him from their country. Your grandfather's feelings a few months before
his death (which occurred on the 15th of December, 1786), when speaking of the unbeliever (Paine), were truly poignant; for now the wretch's
true character had began to open on the world. He lamented with tears
that he had ever admitted him into his house, or had a personal acquaintance and intercourse with him. He was, from conviction, a sincere Christian, converted by the scriptures; of a strong mind, and of a most tender
conscience.

Do not permit anything now said, to induce you to undervalue the saga-
city of my father, for he was wise; but of so benevolent a mind, that in
the common affairs of life he held a principle in morality as true, which
is by no mean generally received; to wit, "That we should consider every
one as possessing probity, until we discover him to be otherwise." Other
gentlemen think differently. However, it may well be maintained that
the side my father took on this topic, which I have often heard argued,
accords with the true spirit of the gospel, the other side is stoicism. From
these last observations, you will readily perceive how easy it was to impose
on my father. This is the reason for his entertaining Paine. I have said
that Paine was in indolent. Take this as an instance; the *Crisis,* No. **V,**

for my part, not more than half a dozen of distinct faces
came into my view while we staid here. We entered
by the ground floor (that is by the cellar), the building
on that side being built on the declination of the hill,
which in this part of the city is very uneven. The
apartments on our right, as we entered, seemed to be
filled with governmental stores, and of provisions of all
kinds. They made us ascend a large staircase into an
upper story, where we were complimented with two
sides, or rather a part of each of the two sides of the
quadrangle. The whole building would have accommodated four thousand men. Monkish spirit must have

---

is but a short political essay, to be sure of great skill in the composition, of
much eloquent invective, strong reasoning, some historic anecdote, and a
fund of ridicule which fitted the passions of the times. But recollect
that this piece, to Paine, was a labor of three months in the inditing. It
was written in my father's house. Mr. Rittenhouse inhabited the front
room, in the upper story, where was the library. There he kept the
office of the treasury of Pennsylvania. The room of Mr. Hart and Paine,
was to the left hand as you come to the stair-head entering the library.

When my wound in 1778 was so far mended, that hobbling on crutches,
or by creeping up stairs (as you may have seen me of late years do), my
greatest recreation in my distressed state of mind was to get into the chamber of Mr. Rittenhouse where the books were. There, his conversation,
(for he was most affable), enlivened my mind, and the books would so
amuse it, that it became calm, and some desperate resolutions were dissolved. While that excellent man was employing his hours in the duties
of his office, for the benefit of the people, Paine would be snoring away his
precious time in his easy chair, regardless of those injunctions imposed upon
him by congress, in relation to his political compositions. His remissness,
indolence or vacuity of thought, caused great heart-burning among many
primary characters in those days. I have heard the late George Bryan,
Esq., then vice-president of the council, speak of his gross neglects with
remarkable harshness. I would sometimes go into Paine's room, and sit
with him. His *Crisis*, No. V, lay on his table, dusted ; to-day three or
four lines would be added, in the course of a week, a dozen more, and so
on. No. V, is dated 21st March, 1778, but it was not published until some
months after that date, and it was generally thought by good whigs, that
it had been too long delayed. For my own part, I was so passionately engaged at heart, in the principles of our cause, that Paine's manner of living
and acting, gave me a high disgust towards him. No idea could enter my
mind, that any one in that noble struggle could be idle or disengaged. As
to myself, my sensations were such, that the example of a Decius might
have been renewed.—*Henry.*

been in high vogue, when so great a pile could be erected merely from the alms of the people, and that too, for so egregiously absurd a purpose. The ranges of the rooms, though extensive in the length of the galleries, were small in their size, being scarcely more than ten by twelve or fourteen feet. The galleries were about twelve feet wide; many rooms were comfortable, others were dilapidated. Ten or a dozen of our poor fellows were compressed into one of these small rooms. So much the better, as it served to keep them the warmer. Boyd, Cunningham and a few of our intimates, took possession of a room near a large stove. The first week we slept most uncomfortably. Gracious God! what did we not suffer.

It was now that we fully learnt the destinies of our dear and revered general and his companions in death. But allow me before the detail of that sad story, to give you an anecdote. The merchants of Quebec, like those of England and our country, are a spirited and generous sect in society; they applied to Governor Carleton, and obtained leave to make us a " New Year's gift." This turned out to be no other than a large butt of porter, attended by a proportionate quantity of bread and cheese. It was a present which exhilerated our hearts and drew from us much thankfulness. We shared more than a pint per man.

General Montgomery had marched at the precise time stipulated, and had arrived at his destined place of attack, nearly about the time we attacked the first barrier. He was not one that would loiter. Colonel Campbell,[1] of the New-York troops, a large good-looking man, who was second in command of that party, and was deemed a veteran, accompanied the army to the assault; his station was rearward, General Montgomery with his aids, were at the point of the column.

---

[1] This was not my friend Col. Thomas Campbell of York (Penn.). He was fighting the battles of our country at Boston.— *Henry.*

It is impossible to give you a fair and complete idea of the nature and situation of the place solely with the pen, the pencil is required.   As by the special permission of government, obtained by the good offices of Captain Prentis, in the summer following, Boyd, a few others and myself reviewed the causes of our disaster, it is therefore in my power, so far as my abilities will permit, to give you a tolerable notion of the spot.   Cape Diamond nearly resembles the great jutting rock which is in the narrows at Hunter's falls, on the Susquehanna. The rock, at the latter place, shoots out as steeply as that at Quebec, but by no mean forms so great an angle on the margin of the river ; but is more craggy.   There is a stronger and more obvious difference in the comparison.   When you surmount the hill at St. Charles, or the St. Lawrence side, which, to the eye are equally high and steep, you find on Abraham's plains, and upon an extensive champaign country.   The birds-eye view around Quebec bears a striking conformity to the sites of Northumberland and Pittsburg, in Pennsylvania ; but the former is on a more gigantic scale, and each of the latter want the steepness and craggyness of the back ground, and a depth of rivers.   This detail is to instruct you in the geographical situation of Quebec, and for the sole purpose of explaining the manner of General Montgomery's death, and the reasons of our failure.   From Wolf's cove there is a good beach down to, and around " Cape Diamond."   The bulwarks of the city came to the edge of the hill above that place.   Thence down the side of the precipice slantingly to the brink of the river there was a stockade of strong posts, fifteen or twenty feet high, knit together by a stout railing at bottom and top with pins.   This was no mean defence, and was at the distance of one hundred yards from the point of the rock.   Within this palisade, and at a few yards from the very point itself, there was a like palisade, though it did not run so high up the hill.   Again, within Cape Diamond, and probably at a distance of fifty yards, there stood a block-house, which seemed to take up the space between the foot of the hill and the precipitous bank of the river leaving a cart way or passage on each side of it.   When heights and distances are spoken of you must recollect that the description of Cape Diamond and its vicinity is merely that of the eye, made as it were running, under the inspection of an officer.   The review of the ground our army had acted upon was accorded us as a particular favor.   Even to have stepped the spaces in a formal manner would have been dishonorable if not a species of treason.   A block-house if well constructed, is an admirable method of defence which in the process of the war to our cost was fully experienced.   In the instance now before us (though the house was not built upon the most approved principles), yet it was a formidable object.   It was a square of perhaps forty or fifty feet.   The large logs neatly squared were tightly bound together by dove-tail work.   If not much mistaken the lower story contained loop-holes for musketry, so narrow that those within could not be harmed from without. The upper story had four or more port holes for cannon of a large calibre.   These guns were charged with grape or canister shot, and were pointed with exactness towards the avenue at Cape Diamond.   The hero Montgomery came.   The drowsy or drunken guard did not hear the sawing of the posts of the first palisade.   Here, if not very erroneous, four posts were sawed and thrown aside so as to admit four men abreast.   The column entered with a manly fortitude.   Montgomery, accompanied by his aids, M'Pherson and Cheeseman, advanced in front. Arriving at the second palisade, the general with *his own hands* sawed down two of the pickets, in such a manner as to admit two men abreast.   These sawed pickets were close under the hill and but a few yards from the very point of the rock out of the view and fire of the enemy from the block-house.   Until our troops advanced to the point, no harm could ensue but by stones thrown from above.   Even now, there had been but an imperfect discovery of the advancing of an enemy, and that only by the intoxicated guard. The guard fled, the general advanced a few paces. A drunken sailor returned to his gun, swearing he would not forsake it while undischarged. This fact is related from the testimony of the guard on the morning of our capture, some of those sailors being our guard. Applying the match, this single discharge deprived us of our excellent commander.[1]

Examining the spot, the officer who escorted us, professing to be one of those who first came to the place, after the death of the general, showed the position in which the general's body was found. It lay two paces from the brink of the river, on the back, the arms extended — Cheeseman lay on the left, and M'Pherson on the right, in a triangular position. Two other brave men lay near them. The ground above described, was visited by an inquisitive eye, so that you may rely with some implicitness on the truth of the picture. As all danger from without had vanished, the government had not only permitted the mutilated palisades to remain, without renewing the enclosure, but the very sticks, sawed by the hand of our commander, still lay strewed about the spot.

Colonel Campbell, appalled by the death of the general, retreated a little way from Cape Diamond, out of the reach of the cannon of the block house, and pretendedly called a council of officers, who, it was said, justified his receding from the attack. If rushing on, as military duty required, and a brave man would have done, the block-house might have been occupied by a small number, and was unassailable from without, but by cannon. From the block-house to the centre of the lower town, where we were, there was no obstacle to impede a force so powerful as that under Colonel Campbell.

---

[1] I have related this as I received it — from my own knowledge, I can say nothing — I leave to the world to determine the credibility the story is entitled to.— *Henry.*

Cowardice, or a want of good will towards our cause, left us to our miserable fate. A junction, though we might not conquer the fortress, would enable us to make an honorable retreat, though with the loss of many valuable lives. Campbell, who was ever after considered as a poltroon in grain, retreated, leaving the bodies of the general, M'Pherson and Cheeseman, to be devoured by the dogs. The disgust caused among us, as to Campbell, was so great as to create the unchristian wish that he might be hanged. In that desultory period, though he was tried, he was acquitted; that was also the case of Colonel Enos, who deserted us on the Kennebec. There never were two men more worthy of punishment of the most exemplary kind.

On the third or fourth of January, being as it were domesticated in the sergeant's mess, in the *reguliers*, a file of men headed by an officer, called to conduct me to the seminary. Adhering to the advice of Colonel M'Dougal, the invitation was declined, though the hero Morgan had solicited this grace from Governor Carleton, and had sent me a kind and pressing message. My reasons, which were explained to Morgan, in addition to the one already given, operated forcibly on my mind. Having lost all my clothes in the wilderness, except those on my back, and those acquired by the provident and gratuitous spirit of General Montgomery, having remained at our quarters, and become a prey to the women and invalids of the army; nothing remained fitting me to appear in company anywhere. Additionally, it had become a resolution, when leaving Lancaster, as my absence would go near to break the hearts of my parents, never to break upon my worthy father's purse. Dire necessity compelled me to rescind this resolution in part, in the wilderness, but that circumstance made me the more determined to adhere to the resolve afterwards. Again, my intimate friends were not in the seminary. Steele was in the hospital, and Simpson, by previous command, on the charming Isle of Orleans, which, from its fruitfulness had become, as it were, our store-house.[1]   Add to all these reasons; it could not be said of the gentlemen in the seminary " they are my intimates," except as to Captain Morgan, and Lieutenant F. Nichols of Hendrick's.   Besides my leather small-

---

[1] In former times, as now, lying was in vogue, but methinks within the last thirty years there has been vast improvements in the art.   Receive information of two instances, which were somewhat remarkable in those days.   Simpson, one of the most spirited and active of officers — always alert — always on duty, was traduced and vilified for a want of courage, because he was not taken a prisoner at Quebec.   This small canton (Paxton), was bursting with the falsehoods propagated on this subject.   On the other hand, Captain M. Smith, our commander, was applauded for his immense bravery shown in the attack of that place, when in fact, he was on the isle of Orleans, many miles distant from the city.   Simpson had been commanded to that place by a regular order from Colonel Arnold.   Captain Smith skulked thither illicitly.   Here is a fac-simile, as to orthography of Arnold's order to Lieut. Simpson, which I took from the original now in his possession.   On my part, it seems to be a duty to make it known to you in justification of an exçellent patriot, one of my friends from early youth.

" LIEUT. SIMPSON,

"SIR : — You are to proceed to Orleans, and take charge of the men there, and keep all provisions from going to town; you will be assiduous in gaining the esteem of the inhabitants, who are now complaining that they have been treated in a rigorous manner ; for provisions or assistance you receive from them, you will pay them the value, or give orders on me *for the* same.   I make no doubt but you will endeavor to cultivate the friendship of the people as far as is consistent with your duty.   You will be careful to keep your men under strict discipline, and not suffer them to have too much liquor.   I am told there has been open house kept there.   You will use as much economy as is consistent with our circumstances.

" I am, Sir, Your humble servant,

" B. ARNOLD, *Col.*"

" December 29, 1775."

[This rigor was administered by a William Cross, our third lieutenant, with as free a hand as he was lax in his principles of morality.   Cross was a handsome little Irishman, always neatly dressed, and commanded a detachment of about twenty men.   The Canadian gentlemen who came as agents from the islanders on this occasion, stated that Cross had extorted from them their wines and other liquors, and all kinds of provisions, which he lavished on worthless people ; making no compensation for his exactions.   This was rigor indeed ! for the people of the isle were our friends.   In short, this unworthy officer kept " open house," and had a short, but a luxurious and merry reign over that charming spot.   He was not with us at the attack of the city, but gaily danced his way to quarters.]

clothes, all in fritters, had been cast away, and a savage covering adopted, until more auspicious times came. But even now, an idea of escape and vengeance inflamed the breasts of many, and we were here in a much superior situation for such a purpose, than that of the seminary. More of this hereafter. All these facts and circumstances, induced an evasion of the friendly solicitation of the kind-hearted Morgan.

On the third day of our capture, the generous Carleton despatched a flag to Arnold, to obtain what trifling baggage we had left at our quarters; mine was either forgotten, or miserable as it was, had been plundered; but as good luck would have it, the knapsack of one Alexander Nelson of our company, who was killed when running to the first barrier, was disclaimed by all of our men. Your father in consequence, laid violent hands upon the spoil. It furnished Boyd and myself, with a large, but course blue blanket, called a *stroud* and a drummer's regimental coat. The blanket became a real comfort, the coat an article of barter. It was on this day that my heart was ready to burst with grief, at viewing the funeral of our beloved general. Carleton had, in our former wars with the French, been the friend and fellow-soldier of Montgomery. Though political opinion, perhaps ambition or interest, had thrown these worthies on different sides of the great question, yet the former could not but honor the remains of his quondam friend. About noon, the procession passed our quarters. It was most solemn. The coffin covered with a pall, surmounted by transverse swords — was borne by men.

Smith wrote, but Simpson acted. A letter from Smith to a worthy and patriotic clergyman, the Rev. Mr. Elder, of Paxton, which was filled with bombast and trash, and stuffed with the most flagrant untruths; that he was in the " midst of the battle, covered by smoke; bullets of all sizes playing around him, etc, etc.," every word of which was fabulous. This person was among the last of those savage men who murdered the innocent and unoffending Indians in the jail of the town we now live in. They have all died miserably; but a few remaining to relate the anecdote of the occurrence of that horrible massacre. —*Henry.*

The regular troops, particularly that fine body of men, the seventh regiment, with reversed arms, and scarfs on the left elbow, accompanied the corpse to the grave. The funerals of the other officers, both friends and enemies, were performed this day. From many of us it drew tears of affection for the defunct, and speaking for myself, tears of greeting and thankfulness, towards General Carleton. The soldiery and inhabitants appeared affected by the loss of this invaluable man, though he was their enemy. If such men as Washington, Carleton and Montgomery, had had the entire direction of the adverse war, the contention in the event might have happily terminated to the advantage of both sections of the nation. M'Pherson, Cheeseman, Hendricks, Humphreys, were all dignified by the manner of burial.

On the same, or the following day, we were compelled (if we would look), to a more disgusting and torturing sight. Many carioles, repeatedly one after the others, passed our dwelling loaded with the dead, whether of the assailants or of the garrison, to a place, emphatically called the *dead-house.* Here the bodies were heaped in monstrous piles. The horror of the sight to us southern men, principally consisted in seeing our companions borne to interment uncoffined, and in the very clothes they had worn in battle ; their limbs distorted in various directions, such as would ensue in the moment of death. Many of our friends and acquaintances were apparent. Poor Nelson lay on the top of half a dozen other bodies — his arms extended beyond his head, as if in the act of prayer, and one knee crooked and raised, seemingly, when he last gasped in the agonies of death. Curse on these civil wars which extinguish the sociabilities of mankind, and annihilate the strength of nations. A flood of tears was consequent. Though Montgomery was beloved because of his manliness of soul, heroic bravery and suavity of manners ; Hendricks and Humphreys, for the same admirable qualities, and especially for the endurances we underwent in conjunction, which enforced many a tear; still my unhappy and lost brethren, though in humble station, with whom that dreadful wild was penetrated, and from whom came many attentions towards me, forced melancholy sensations. From what is said relative to the *dead-house* you might conclude that General Carleton was inhumane or hard-hearted. No such thing. In this northern latitude, at this season of the year, according to my feelings (we had no thermometer), the weather was so cold, as usually to be many degrees below zero. A wound, if mortal, on even otherwise, casts the party wounded in the snow; if death should follow, it throws the sufferer into various attitudes, which was assumed in the extreme pain accompanying death. The moment death takes place, the frost fixes the limbs in whatever situation they may then happen to be, and which cannot be reduced to decent order, until they are thawed. In this state, the bodies of the slain are deposited in the *dead-house* hard as ice. At this season of the year, the earth is frozen from two to five feet deep, impenetrable to the best pick-axe, in the hands of the stoutest man. Hence you may perceive a justification of the *dead-house*. It is no new observation, that " climates form the manners and habitudes of the people."

January 4th, on the next day, we were visited by Colonel Maclean, an old man, attended by other officers, for a peculiar purpose, that is, to ascertain who among us were born in Europe. We had many Irishmen, and some Englishmen. The question was put to each; those who admitted a British birth, were told they must serve his majesty in Colonel Maclean's regiment, a new corps, called the *emigrants*. Our poor fellows, under the fearful penalty of being carried to Britain, there to be tried for treason, were compelled by necessity, and many of them did enlist. Two of them, very brave men, Edward Cavenaugh and Timothy Conner, deserve to be named, because of a particular occurrence which happened shortly afterwards. These two men, among others, called upon me for my advice how to act. Being, at that time, neither a lawyer nor a casuist, they had my opinion according to the dictates of nature, and some slight reading. That is, that they should enlist, for a constrained oath, as theirs would be, could not be binding on the conscience : and by all means to join our army as soon as practicable. They enlisted under the notion that the oath was non-obligatory, and a hope of a speedy return to their sweet-hearts and wives. Allow me here to recount, by anticipation, the residue of the adventures of " honest Ned." It is due to him, for he saved my life, and that of Simpson, on the Dead river. Towards the end of January, Cavenaugh and Conner happened to compose a part of the same guard at palace gate, where the walls are from thirty to forty feet high, independently of the declivity of the hill. Cavenaugh was stationed as a sentry in conjunction with one of the British party. Conner had procured a bottle of rum ; coming to the station, he drank himself, and presented the bottle to the British sentry. While the latter was in the act of drinking, Cavenaugh gave him a push with the butt of his musket, which stunned and brought him to the earth. Taking his arms, they sprung over the wall into a bed of snow, perhaps twenty-five feet deep. This averment concerning the depth of the snow, may appear problematical, as we know nothing like it in our climate. Form no definitive opinion until you have heard the reasons why it does happen. As you may recollect several instances in this memoir, where the asperity of a Quebec winter is intimated, and a description of its effects attempted — such as frequent snow storms and fierce winds. In the month of January, particularly, when the snow has increased to a depth of seven feet over the face of the country, notwithstanding the shining of the sun, the cold is so great, that those winds drive the snow daily against the high ramparts of the city, where it forms a compact mass — the last stratum being light and dry, as the finest sand, which may be whirled by the wind. Cavenaugh and Conner leaped mid-deep into such a soft bed. Their disadvantage consisted in sinking too deep; the height of the leap, plunging them deeper than ordinary walking would do, made it difficult for them to extricate themselves. The relief guard came in time to give them a volley, as they were scampering away. Thanks to God, my worthy Irishmen escaped unharmed, though as they passed through St. Roque, they were complimented by several discharges of cannister and grape shot. This was the first notice we had of the escape of our daring friends. We heard next morning, all the minutiæ from those who guarded us. Cavenaugh is still alive — is laborious, and has a large family of children, who are respectable in their way. You cannot conceive the joyousness of my heart, when hearing of him in my peregrinations a few years since, in the mountainous parts of York county. The pittance then spared him, it is hoped, will make you never the poorer. The assembly of Pennsylvania have granted him a pension for which that honorable body have my most fervent blessings. Old age and decrepitude, by the extremity of our sufferings, is brought upon us long before the ordinary allotments of nature. We served our country faithfully, and at this late day it is really pleasant to observe the spirit of the public, inclined to compensate the veterans of 1775 and 1776. So much for my preserver "honest Ned," which epithet he still bears among his neighbors, by whom, bating a venial vice, he is esteemed. Timothy Conner, on the contrary, possessing the art of acquiring wealth, married, had a competency, but lost it subsequently by his vices, which bore a strong affinity to gross criminality.

By the middle of January, we were settled down into a state something like household order: those who could economize, fared tolerably well, though they could have used more. Our daily provision consisted of a biscuit made of a coarse meal, from something like our chopped rye; very often chaff or straw, half an inch in length,

was found in this species of bread. A biscuit of the
size of a cake of gingerbread, now sold with us for a
cent, was the daily allowance of this article ; half a pound
of pork, or three-quarters of a pound of beef, though
these were much salted, even so as to be uncomfortable — they were of Irish preparation, perhaps for the
sea-service : a competent allowance of butter, originally
fine, yet now rancid ; candles, molasses, and even
vinegar : this last article, so long as it could be afforded
us, was a preservative from the disorders which un-
wittingly we were imbibing daily. Knowing the difficulties under which the garrison lay — foes at the gates,
and an uncertainty of succor ; the governor was thought
of by me, with similar allowances, that ought to be
made to our own generals, in circumstances of such
pinching necessity. From all information attainable on
our part, we were as well treated as those of the garrison,
who lived on the same kinds of food, except as to liquor,
which deprivation was more beneficial than injurious to
our men. It is grateful to my heart, now to remember
and repeat, the benevolent sensations this mildness and
humanity created in my mind, towards the virtuous, the
amiable and venerable Carleton. He was a genuine
representative of the gentility of the Irish nation, which
is so deservedly famous for the production of real heroes,
patriotic statesmen, and a generosity and suavity of
manners. He was of great candor, uprightness and
honor, and full of the spirit of philanthropy, which marks
the real gentleman. He made us several visits, in all
of which he seemed merely to have a solicitude for our
welfare, without any sinister view, such as a seduction
from our principles, etc. That he granted us every
accommodation his trying situation authorized, there
can be no doubt. Shortly after the time now spoken of,
we were conducted to the Dauphin jail. Before we quit
the *Reguliers,* admit me to state to you something more,
relating to our manner of living there. My youthful
appetite required and demanded a greater quantity of

food than we then enjoyed. We wanted spoons, not only in our own mess, but throughout the whole corps. There was no money among us to purchase such an implement, and if there had been, and opportunity had offered, it is likely the jealousy of government would have deprived us of them, if formed of metal of any kind.

One day being at the unloading a cord of wood, a birch stick, the only piece of hard wood in the load, was eagerly laid hold of, and borne to the mess-room ; from this, a wooden spoon was soon formed for my own use. Lobscouse made a part of our diurnal food. This term, though vulgar, conveys to one, who, when hungry, has tasted the dish, some agreeable ideas. Among soldiers and sailors, it is esteemed equal to the *olla podrida* of the Spaniards, and nearly so to the *speck and oyer*[1] of the Germans ; it is certainly more nourishing than what the latter call *water soup*, and even *meal soup*. We put our vile biscuit into a tin vessel, with a sufficient quantity of water, and permitted it to stew on the stove, until there was a perfect mucilage, some thin slices of bacon fat (the reserve of the last meal), were then added ; or some of the skimmings of the boilers, but most usually the rancid butter (which was thus made palatable) : when these substances were well incorporated with the biscuit; a few spoon-fulls of molasses finished the dish. This was the ordinary breakfast, and a good one, when we could spoon it into our mouths. My spoon therefore, was an article in great demand, and of prime necessity. The production of one spoon, created a desire for more ; they were manufactured in abundance, by the means of two knives — a great and a small, but always disposed of for biscuit. Spoons were made as large as small ladles, some with a deer at full stretch, a hound pursuing — an Indian sitting — a beaver — and twenty other devices were in-

---

[1] Spek en eijeren, ham and eggs, or eggs and bacon.— *M.*

vented, and tolerably well carved.   Some came to five
biscuits, some to ten, and one in particular at twenty,
which my friends thought worthy of the acceptance of
the governor, but care was taken not to present it.
Boyd and Cunningham carefully furnished the wood.
Thus we could exist pretty well on our slender diet.
But we had other resources, which were by no means
neglected.   Henry Crone, a well bred young man,
descended from a worthy and respectable family of York
county, Pennsylvania, much my senior, but who was
known to me during his apprenticeship at Lancaster, had
dissipated a good fortune at the gaming-tables ; he was
a sergeant of Hendricks'.   Miserable as was our predicament, the demon of play had intruded itself among us,
though there was neither money nor clothing but that
upon our backs, and our daily provisions to sport with.
The play was for biscuit, and most usually at a game
called *all-fours*, in which Crone was a real adept.
He was a droll dog, and much inclined to play with and
beat the Yankees, as he termed them.   Many mornings,
being compelled by the inclemency of the season to
leave our uncomfortable beds, pacing the avenues in front
of our cells for exercise and warmth, drawing aside the
curtain of the gambling room door, which was no other
than a thread-bare blanket, Crone was seen and heard,
with bleared eyes and a vociferous voice, after a night's
sitting, contending for a biscuit, with as much spirit and
heat, as most probably he had done in former times for
fifty or a hundred dollars.   The passion of gaming, is
almost an inexplicable trait in the human character, the
poor, the rich, the savage and the civilized, are equally
its devotees.   The greatest and the least are alike
subject to its fascinations.   Crone, poor dog, was one
of the devoted.

Montgomery, in his care for Arnold's party, besides
an excellent blanket coat, had assigned to each man a
new red regimental coat of the seventh, or some other
regiment, stationed in the upper country.   This clothing

had been seized at Montreal. Crone, in the division, had fared well. He had obtained a large superfine broad-cloth coat, such as is worn by the sergeant-major of the British army, which "fitted him like a shirt." He was so totally devoid of care, that he never once applied to the tailors of the army, who were employed by the pub-lic, to fit the coat to his back, and to sew it regularly. What was still more laughable, he had no pockets to this coat, unless you may call the flannel such, which interiorly lined the lappets, and bore the appearance of large bags dangling about his heels. Crone was facetious and clever ; he had an affection for me. Often about daylight he would come to my blanket and waken me, and shake the lappets of his coat. He would say " Damme Jack, here's something for you," and would force upon me ten, fifteen, and several times, even thirty biscuits. With all his vices he bore a great share of my esteem, for the goodness of his heart. When ill-luck occurred, there was a refunding on my part, but it seldom hap-pened. Our other resource was William M'Coy, a sergeant of Hendricks' an excellent clerk, who came into favor of the governor, by giving to Major Murray, of the garrison, a genuine copy of his journal of the route through the wilderness into Canada. He was a sedate and sensible man. He was installed clerk of the kitchen, and put me much in mind of Gil Blas' clerk. The cook, whom M'Coy patronized was a very Boni-face in accomplishments and a Sancho Panza in rotundity. He was of Thayer's or Dearborn's company. Believe me that these two men were courted by our hungry wights among the soldiery, with as much eagerness and solicitude, and often sycophancy, as would have been the case had they been the ministers of a great state. What could you suppose to be the object of such ser-vility ? To explain — the boiling utensils were two very large coppers. A boiling of pork, produced a great quantity of liquid fat, which the men called *slush*. The skimmings constituted the importance of the cook, who

made a profit from it by selling it to certain tradesmen
of the city.   A half pint of this slush was a good succedaneum for better food, to a mess of six stout men.
It, with the molasses, formed an excellent lobscouse.
Oleaginous matter, next to bread, is, however, the
great support of the animal functions, and even superior to bread, to sustain life, and gratify the palate.
Here you see the real ground of the causes of distinctions
in society.   The cook possessing this perquisite, commanded his applicants for additional food, with an un-
warrantable austerity.   As to our mess, it was strong in
habits of intimacy with M'Coy, *who* was one of *us*.   The
cook was far below our notice.   Friend M'Coy gave
us every advantage our melancholy situation afforded
him.   This minute information is given to you, to in-
spire you with a disgust towards war of any kind.   As
to my sons, if the liberties of our country ever be invaded,
it is humbly hoped, under the protecting hand of Providence, that they will always be ready and active to rally
round the standard of Freedom, the principles of which
we derived from our forefathers, whose blood freely
flowed in its defence.

Coming to the Dauphin jail, escorted by the military,
we found it well accommodated for our lodgment.
There were four rooms below, and as many above
stairs, all capacious and well supplied with berths or
bulks, in the common method of barracks.   Our company taking the right our precedency in the procession
gave us, assumed the possession of a room in the third
story, which was in truth the very best.   Morgan's
took a room immediately below us ; Hendrick's one
adjoining ; but remember that at this time we were reduced most lamentably by killed, wounded and missing.
Many were in the hospital.   Out of sixty-five who
came on Abraham's plains in November, we had
scarcely more than thirty left with us in prison.   The
fire of the enemy and disease had so thinned us.   Morgan's gallant men fared worse.   Like the eastern people

before and at that period, they detested the introduction
of the small-pox into their country by inoculation.   Now
they were its victims.   Less than twenty-five of the
privates of that company regained their native homes.
They were originally as elegant a body of men as ever
came within my view.[1]   To use the style of my friend
Simpson, " they were beautiful boys, who knew how to
handle and aim the rifle."   Indeed many of them, adroit
young men, courageous and thorough going, became
the subjects of death by that virulent disease, both without and within the city.   We of Pennsylvania had no
fears from that source.   This disease had visited us in
youth, either naturally or by inoculation.   This observation which is a serious one, should convey to your
minds the immensity of the discovery of the inoculation
of the kine pock, by Doctor Jenner.   The discovery of
the causes of lightning, its dreadful effects, the means of
avoiding its power by the celebrated Franklin, our
countryman, is (as it concerns the happiness of man,
speaking diffidently), perhaps inferior in importance to
that of Jenner.   The Jennerian discovery tends to save
the lives of millions, the Franklinian of hundreds.   But
all lovers of natural philosophy are compellable to acknowledge that the identity of the electric fluid, obtained
artificially, with that of the clouds, has given a wider
scope to human thought than the recency of the Jennerian discovery has as yet afforded.   There can be little
doubt, that in a succession of years, some gigantic gen-
iuses of the medical profession, will improve and extend
the benefits of the happy disclosure.

At the Dauphin jail our notions of escape were

---

[1] In the spring of the year 1776, our army was reduced by decease of
men, or debilitation of body, so that they could not act effectively, and in
the eyes of the world, a disreputable retreat took place, which it was not
then quite prudent to explain.   Now it may be safely asserted, that great
numbers of the soldiers inoculated themselves for the small-pox, by lacerat-
ing under the finger nails, by means of pins or needles, either to obtain an
avoidance of duty, or to get over that horrible disorder in an easy and
speedy way.— *Henry.*

strengthened. The prison may be three huudred yards from St. John's gate, the interval at that time was free from buildings. From without the building appeared formidable. The courtyard was very contracted for so large a house, and was encompassed by a strong stone wall at least twenty feet high. The windows and doors were seemingly by their bars impenetrable. But what cannot men of true spirit effect when made the subjects of oppression? Opposite to the jail, across the street leading to St. John's gate, at a distance of forty yards there stood a house which became the station of the guard who superintended us. In the first of our imprisonment we were attended by the regular troops, or sailors, who were embodied by government as soldiers, but now the guard (as our force without had made a firm stand), was replaced by the militia, who were the most inert and despicable of military men. The sentries were stationed on the outside of the jail; we had no witnesses of our conduct within, except the captain of the provost, who did not pry with a suspicious eye. He was a generous and open-hearted enemy — had no guile himself, nor imputed it to others. The principal defence on this side of the city, as it regarded our attempt at evasion, lay at and near St. John's gate. The guard here was most usually composed of thirty men of the regular troops or sailors. They would have given us a hustle but of a certainty we should have overpowered them by the force of numbers as stout and as able bodied men as themselves whose courage was not to be questioned, though there was a great difference in the nature of our respective arms. Having examined the jail carefully, its imbecility to restrain us was apparent. It was an old French building in the Bastile style. The walls of stone, and more than three feet thick, were impenetrable by any of our means. Upon examining the bars of the windows, which were originally ill-constructed, many were found so much corroded as to move up and down in the sockets. These could be taken out. The mildness of Governor

13

Carleton's reign seemed not to require a strict inspection into places of this kind. About this time a selected council was called, of which your father had the honor to be one, and was chiefly composed of the sergeants. The present Major Joseph Aston, of Lamb's artillerists, then a sergeant-major had the presidency. Our discoveries were disclosed, the means of escape considered, and a consultation of the men recommended. This was done, and there was not a dissentient voice. At the stair head there was a small room lighted by a small window; the door was locked. Peeping through the keyhole large iron hoops were discovered; the spring of the lock kindly gave way to our efforts, the room was ransacked; and as neatly closed. The room furnished us with a large number of strong iron-hoops, two and three inches broad, and a considerable quantity of other iron, of different shapes and sizes deposited there as lumber. From the first of these articles we formed a rough, but weighty species of sword with a wooden handle, a blow from which, in the hands of one of our stout men would have brought down one of the stoutest of the enemy. The residue of the iron was applied to formation of spear-heads. These were affixed to splits of fir-plank, about ten feet in length, which had formed in part, the bottoms of the lower berths. These weapons, it is true, were of the coarsest make, yet in the hands of men determined to sacrifice their lives for freedom, they would have had a considerable sway. Our long knives, which many of us secreted when captured, also became spear-points. These weapons were concealed under the lower range of berths, which were raised a foot from the floor. The planks were neatly raised, the nails were extracted, and the nail-head with a part of its shank, placed in its former position. Over these lay our blankets and bundles. It was a standing rule to have two sentries constantly on the watch, one at each end of the interior of the jail. Their duty consisted in giving a signal of the approach of the officers of the garrison, who were in the habit of visiting us daily, as there were shoemakers and tailors among us, who worked cheaper than those of the city, merely for the purpose of bettering their condition.   There was policy in this watchfulness. When the signal was given the inner doors were thrown open, those appointed for the purpose laid upon the berth which hid our arms, as if in a drowsy state.   The officers were accosted with assumed confidence, and much complaisance.   The council met daily, sometimes in small squads, and when anything of much consequence was to be considered in larger ; but at all times secretly, or at least not obviously as a council, from a fear of traitors, or some indiscretion of the young men.   Our arrangements, so far as my judgment could discern, were judicious. Aston was to act as general, M'Coy and some others became colonels.   Boyd and others of the most spirit became majors, captains, lieutenants, etc.   That which cheered me much was that the council assigned me a first lieutenancy under my friend Boyd, whose vigor and courage were unquestionable.

The plan of the escape was thus : Aston, who was an excellent engineer, was to have the particular superintendency of Lamb's company, which to a man was well informed in their duty, active and spirited.   These were to be increased to a band of one hundred and fifty men, whose duty it was to attack the guard at St. John's gate. The attack of the guard opposite the jail was assigned to the discretion of Boyd, Cunningham and myself ; the council generously giving us the authority of a first selection of twenty two persons, from the whole body of our men.   The residue of our force was so disposed of as to act as a body of reserve to Aston, under the command of M'Coy, and another smaller body was reserved to support Boyd, particularly by way of setting fire to the jail, the guard house, and the buildings in its neighborhood, to amuse or employ the enemy, while we were running to St. John's gate.   It was expected we could arrive there by the time Aston and his party would be victorious. Our particular duty was of the desperate kind, something of the nature of the "forlorn hope." Nothing but the virtue and bravery of our comrades could ensure the safety of our lives; for if they should arrive at St. John's gate, and discomfit the guard, and if then seeking safety by flight, they would leave us to the mercy of an enraged enemy, who would sacrifice us to their fury. But there has been too much precipitation in the relation. Previously to the last observations, besides being told of our force, our weapons, and our military plans, you should have been informed also, of the real site of the jail, of its internal structure, from which the sally was to be made. The Dauphin jail is built on a plain, pretty much declined towards the street. It follows that the front of the lower story, that is the cellars, was on a level with the street. The back ground was ten or twelve feet higher. In the cellar, near the foot of the stairway, there was a plenteous fountain of water, which supplied the house. The conduits leading from the spring, by the severity of the weather, were impeded by ice, so that the water, in great quantity remained in the cellar, which with the additional carelessness of our people, who cast the rinsing of their buckets on the floor of the apartment, formed a bed of ice a foot thick, and very firm and solid. This cellar had a door newly made of strong pine plank, five feet in width, which opened inwards, the sill was level with the street. The door was hung upon H hinges of a large size, fixed on the inside, exposed to our view and operations. But what was still more absurd, the door was hasped within and secured by a large pad lock. Close inspection and thoughtfulness had made the members of the council, by the means they enjoyed, perfect masters of those hinges and the lock; they would not have stood a second of time. The principal obstacle was the ice which was raised fully a foot against the door. Even this would have given way to our ingenuity. The whole of our plan was well laid, and thoroughly

digested.   That door was to be our sally port.   Boyd
preceding with our division, Aston and M'Coy following,
they turning rapidly to the left for St. John's gate.   The
dislocation of the iron bars of the windows, was to
ensue : all those which could be removed being known,
were to become issues for our bravest men.   Every
man knew his station.   It is an old and a trite observation, that it is a difficult thing to describe a battle, so as
to give a clear idea of all the causes and effects of each
movement, without overloading and confusing the picture.   The same may be said of a conspiracy such as
ours.   Going through the entry from the front door
into the jail yard, near the back door but still within the
prison, there are two cavities opposite to each other,
strongly walled and arched.   We called them the black
holes.   On the outside of the building in the yard, these
cavities assumed the forms of banks, ten or eleven feet
high, and as wide ; and well sodded.   With some address
and agility a sprightly man could surpass either of them.
The wall above those banks was probably ten feet
higher.   In the daytime we often climbed up the wall,
by means of its interstices, from which the mortar had
fallen in the course of time, to take a peep at the city,
merely putting our eyes above the level of the top of it.

A Mr. Martin, a hardy, daring and active young man,
of Lamb's company, I think a sergeant, proposed to
bear intelligence of our projects, to the American commander without the walls.   His plan was approved.   A
time for irruption was named, though the day was not
particularized.   The signals to invite the advance of our
army to St. John's gate, were the burning of the houses,
and the firing of the guns of the ramparts towards the
city.   As yet, we were unprepared to move.   This expedition of Martin's was profoundly a secret among those
of the council, from a fear that some bungler might attempt the same path, fail, and by his being taken, unveil
our plots.   Permit me a short episode on the escape of
Martin.   It was singularly adventurous, and the neatness

of its execution renders it worthy of remark. I had the pleasure of hearing it recounted, in more happy times, at New York. Martin was dressed in warm clothing, with good gloves; a white cap, shirt and overalls were prepared for him. He appeared in the jail yard among the prisoners, in his daily dress. The time of locking up, and calling the roll generally happened about sundown. It was the business of the captain of the provost, who was accompanied by a file of men. The prisoners, instigated by those in the secret, employed themselves out of doors, until late in the evening, in play, as if to keep their bodies warm. It was a blowing and dreary evening, which was purposely chosen. At locking up, those in the secret lagged behind, tardily, pushing the uninformed before, yet so slowly, as effectually to crowd the gangway; Martin remaining in the rear. The operation took place at the clanging of the lock of the great front door. This measure was imagined and effected on purpose to procure to Martin a sufficiency of leisure to get to his hiding place, which was no other than a nook formed by the projection of the door way, and on the top of one of the banks before spoken of. Here he had time to put on his cap, shirt, etc. The officer who examined the yard, could not perceive him, unless he went out of the door, several paces to the left, and most probably, not even then, for Martin would be covered in the snow, and imperceptible. Happily the officer went no further than the threshold, and made but a slight survey of the yard. This account, so far, is derived from my own knowledge; what follows, is from Martin himself. " Martin tarried there until seven or eight o'clock. The dilemma he was in, could only be surpassed in imminence of danger, by his extreme activity, skill and courage. There were four sentries stationed around the jail — two at each corner in front, and the like number at the corners of the yard in the rear. Those sentries, though relieved every quarter of an hour, were soon driven into the sentry boxes, by the cold and keenness of the whistling winds. If they had paced the spaces allotted them by duty, the escape of Martin must have been impossible. Watching the true time, he slipped down the wall into the deep snow underneath unobserved. Hence, he made a sudden excursion to the left of St. John's gate, at a part of the wall where he well knew no sentry was placed. Leaping the wall, into the snow, he received the fire of a distant sentry. Martin was unharmed. The soldier fired, as it were, at a phantom, for when Martin's body came into contact with the snow it was undiscernible — the desired information was given;" but of this, we could merely make surmises until the May following. That which is very remarkable is, that the absence of Martin was unknown to government, until the explosion of our plot.

Our next solicitude was the acquisition of powder. This article could be obtained but by sheer address and shrewd management. But we had to do with men who were not of the military cast. We began first to enter into familiarity with the sentries, joking with them and pretending to learn French from them. The guard, usually of Canadians, consisted of many old men, and young boys, who were very "*coming*." A few small gun-carriages were constructed, not more than six inches in length, and mounted with cannon, or howitzers, which were made of many folds of paper, and were bound tightly around with thread. These were shown to the sentries from time to time, and a little powder was requested, with which to charge them. Our berths formed an angle of the room. The upper berths, as well as the lower, had a ledge of several inches in height, in which embrasures were formed with the knife. Two parties were raised in opposition to each other, each of which took possession of one side of the angle. The blaze and report, which was nearly as great and as loud as that of small pistols, created much laughter and merriment. This sport, the child of a seeming folly, served us as a pretence and justification for soliciting

powder.   The apparent joy prevailing among us pleased
the Canadians, both old and young, and did not alarm
the government.   We obtained many cartridges in the
course of a few weeks, two-thirds of which came to the
hands of Aston and his corps, for the purpose of manu-
facturing matches, etc., etc.   Fire arms of any kind
could not, by any finesse, be procured.   The commerce
of cartridges, accompanied by a suavity and deference
of manners towards our young friends, procured us
many quarters of pounds of powder, which they bought
secretly out of funds, some of which were procured in
a ludicrous way.   We had many sick in the hospital,
for when any one appeared to be disordered in the least
degree, he was hurried to the infirmary, when cured,
he was returned to us.   Some of the men went so far
as to feign sickness to get to that place, where they
lived in a more sumptuous style than that of the jail.
The frequent removals caused the propagation of a report that the prison was unhealthy.   Many pious matrons
came to see us, and never empty handed.   Some
elderly nuns, of respectable families, were of the number,
and generally brought money, truly not great in quantity,
but not the less acceptable to the sick and convalescent,
as these alms procured them some slight comforts, such
as tea, etc.   These were the religious and humane collections of the sisterhood, and mostly consisted of the
smallest change.   There was a beautiful countenanced
youth, Thomas Gibson, first sergeant of Hendricks,
who had studied physic at Carlisle, Pennsylvania, allied
to me by affinity, who had, probably from a knowledge
he had of his profession, sustained his health hitherto ;
his cheeks were blooming as roses.   He was one of the
council.   As young men, we cared little about the
means, so that we obtained the end, which was powder.
We lived above stairs, and never shared in the gratuities
of the ladies, which were rapaciously awaited at the
entrance of the prison.   Gibson and myself were
standing at a window near the great door, and opposite

to M'Coy's room, a neat little box which had been knocked up for his purposes. Looking into the street, a lady with a thick vail, was observed to take the path through the snow to our habitation. "Zounds, Gibson, there's a nun," was scarcely expressed, before he was hurried into M'Coy's apartment and put to bed, though dressed. Several of us waited respectfully at the door, till the officer of the guard unlocked it. The nun entered — she seemed, from her manners, to be genteel and respectable. We were most sedulous in our attentions to the lady, and so prevailed, as to induce her to come into M'Coy's room. Here lay Gibson, covered to the chin with the bed-clothes, nothing exposed but his beautiful hair and red cheeks, the latter indicating a high fever. It was well the lady was no physician. The nun crossing herself, and whispering a pater-noster, poured the contents of her little purse into the hand of the patient, which he held gently, without the blanketing, and left us. What should the donation be, but twenty-four coppers, equal at that time to two shillings of our money. The latter circumstance added much to the humor, and extreme merriment of the transaction. This money was solely appropriated for powder. Thus, careless of every thing but the means of escaping, we enjoyed many merry, and even happy hours. Aston, who was provident of time, by the middle of March (I have no note of the precise period), had all his matters of arrangement in good order.

The council assigned a day for the irruption. As we dared not touch the door in the cellar, from a fear of discovery by inspection (and it was examined almost daily), it was determined to postpone the unloosing the hinges and lock, which were under our command, until the moment of escape. It became a main question how to remove the ice at the foot of the door. Here lay the great difficulty, as it was universally agreed that the door must be dragged down suddenly, so that we might march over it. Remember also, that a sentry was posted not more than from fifteen to twenty feet from the outside of the door. Many propositions were made in council, how to effect the removal of the body of ice without exposure to detection. One was lightly to pick it away with hatchets, a few of which had been secretly retained by the prisoners, and brought into the jail. To this, there were several insuperable objections; the softest stroke of the lightest tomahawk upon the ice would be heard by a sentry so near; or an unlucky stroke might touch the door which would resound and inevitably cause a discovery. Others proposed to wear away the ice by boiling water; two most obvious objections lay here; the steam would search for a vent through the crevices of the door and window, and develop our measures; besides the extreme cold would have congealed the hot water the moment it fell, so as to add to our difficulties. Another idea was suggested that was " with knives to cut the door across on the surface of the ice;" to this plan there was a fatal exception, the ice had risen on the lower cross-piece of the door nearly an inch, so that we must cut through the cross-piece lengthwise, and through the thick plank crosswise. Though this labor might have been accomplished by industry and perseverance, yet the time it would necessarily take would cause a discovery by the searchers. The last and only method to avoid discovery was adopted. This was to embody sixteen or eighteen of the most prudent men who knew the value of silence, who should, two and two, relieve each other, and with our long knives gently pare away the ice next the sill of the door, so as to make a groove of four or six inches wide, parallel with, and deep as the sill. The persons were named and appointed to this service. Now the capability of the execution of our plot, infused comfort and joy into all hearts. It was intended immediately after locking up, on the night of the irruption, that those prudent men, should descend into the vault by pairs, and by incessant labor have the work finished by three o'clock in the morning, when the sally should be made.

We had carefully noticed from the walls of the jail, and the ridge of the house where there is a trap-door, the placing of the guards, the numbers and stationing of the sentries. We were safe therefore, in the measures we had taken for the attack of the guard of St. John's gate. Our own guard was perfectly scrutinized. The opportunities were of the most commodious kind. The guard-house was directly in our front, where we could see and be seen. Their windows had no shutters. They had lights all the night through; we, the better to observe them, kept none. This latter circumstance, enabled us distinctly to see that the arms with fixed bayonets were placed in the right hand corner of the room, as we would enter from the stairhead, and that the guard towards morning to a man were lying asleep on the floor. The sentries as they were relieved, did the like. This guard, as was before said, in ordinary consisted of thirty persons. Boyd's party, from a perfect knowledge of their method of conducting, esteemed it no great hardiness to undertake the overwhelming them. Subsequently our danger must appear. The nights were piercingly cold — the sentries soon housed themselves in their boxes. As the sally, to succeed, must be most silent and quick, it was hoped to quiet all of them before any alarm could spread. Besides Boyd's division (the first rank of which, were to despatch the nearest sentry by the spear), others of the succeeding corps, were assigned to assail the rest of the sentries, immediately around the prison. The getting up the stairs of *our* guard-house so quickly as to create no alarm was not only feasible, but in my mind (with the force delegated to us), of absolute certainty of success. The front door was always open by night and by day, we knew the precise number of steps the stairs contained. An agile man would mount at three strides. A light was continually in the passage. Entering the room and turning to the right the arms in the corner were ours. The bayonet, from necessity, would become the lot of the guard. In this part of the enterprise profound silence was all important ; the section was to rely on the spear and tomahawk.   Aston on the other hand, being victorious at St. John's gate, was instantly to turn the cannon upon the city ; his fuses, portfire, etc., were prepared and ready as substitutes for those of the enemy, if *they* were extinguished or taken from the guns.   It was known to us, that all the cannon of the ramparts were charged and primed, and boxes of ammunition and piles of balls in the vicinity of each gun, it was calculated that the execution of the business of our section, might be effected in at least fifteen minutes, together with the firing of the houses.   Then running to support Aston and if he was victorious, to maintain our position on the walls, under a hope of the arrival of the American army from without.   In that event St. John's gate, as a first measure, was to be opened.   But if Aston should unfortunately be beaten (which was most improbable,) then we were to fly in all directions, and make the adventurous leap.   It was supposed that in the latter case the hurry and bustle created by so sudden, unforseen and daring an attack, would throw the garrison into consternation and disorder, to so great a degree, as to admit the escape of many.   Sluggards might expect to be massacred.

The particularity of the foregoing details are purposely made to impress on your minds a single truth : " That the best imagined schemes and thoroughly digested designs, whether in military or civil life, may be defeated by a thoughtless boy, the interference of an idiot or a treacherous knave."   Two lads from Connecticut or Massachusetts, whose names are now lost to my memory, prisoners with us, but who had no manner of connection or intercourse with the chiefs, nor knew the minute, yet essential parts of the measures of the council, but probably having overheard a whisper of the time and manner of the evasion ; those young men, without consultation, without authority from their superiors, in the thoughtless ardor of their minds, on the eve of the sally, descended into the cellar, and with hatchets, picked at the ice at the door-sill. The operation was heard. The sentry threatened to fire. The guard was instantly alarmed and immediately doubled, and all our long labored schemes and well digested plans, annihilated in a moment. You cannot form an adequate idea of the pangs we endured. My heart was nearly broken by the excess of surprise and burning anger, to be thus fatuitously deprived of the gladdening hope of a speedy return to our friends and country. It became us, however, to put the best face upon it. It was suddenly resolved by the chiefs to kill the person who should disclose the general plot, and to wait upon the officers on the ensuing morning, with our usual attentions. When morning came, it found us afoot. About sunrise, the formidable inquisition took place. Major Murray, Captain Prentis, the officer of the guard, and a dozen musketeers came,— we awaited their approach undismayed. They accosted us very coolly. The cellar was visited, and the work of those fools was apparent. Reascending, we could assure the gentlemen that this effort to escape, was without the knowledge of any of us. This, to be sure, was said in the jesuitical style, but those who made the assertion, did not then know either the persons or the names of the silly adventurers. The officers and the guard were departing, fully persuaded that it was no more than the attempt of one or two persons to escape. Major Murray was the last to recede. An Englishman of whom we knew not that he was a deserter from our enemies at Boston, had posted himself close to the right jamb of the door, which was more than half opened for the passage of the major. Those of us who were determined to execute our last night's resolution, armed with our long knives, had formed a half circle around the door, without observing the intrusion and presence of the deserter. Major Murray was standing on the threshold, speaking in a kindly manner to us, when the villain sprung past the major, even jostling him. The spring he made, was so sudden and so entirely unsus-

14

pected, that he screened himself from our just vengeance. Touching Major Murray's shoulder, "Sir," says he, "I have something to disclose." The guards encompassed the traitor, and hurried him away to the governor's palace. We instantaneously perceived the extent and consequences of this disaster. The prisoners immediately destroyed such of the arms as were too bulky to hide, if destructible, and secreted the rest. In an hour or two, a file of men with an officer, demanded Boyd, Cunningham and others, represented by the vile informer, as lukewarm in the plot. They were escorted to the governor's council. Here they found that the wretch had evidenced all our proceedings minutely, naming every one who was prominent. Our worthy compatriots were examined on oath, and as men of honor could not conceal the truth. The questions of the council (furnished by the informer), did not admit of equivocation or evasion, if the examinants had been so inclined, and besides all tergiversation, when the outline was marked, was nugatory. They boldly admitted and justified the attempt. We did not fare the worse in our provisions nor in the estimation of our enemy. Returning to the jail, my dear Boyd shed the tears of excruciating anguish in my bosom, deploring our adverse fate. We had vowed to each other to be free or die, and to be thus foolishly baulked caused the most heart rending grief. Towards two o'clock P.M. were seen several heavy cart loads, consisting of long and weighty irons, such as bilboes, foot-hobbles and hand-cuffs, arrive. The prisoners were ordered to their rooms. The ironing began below stairs with Morgan's company. Here the bilboes were expended. If not much mistaken, ten or twelve persons were secured, each by a foot to a bar twelve feet long, and two inches in diameter. The heavy bolts were exhausted in the story below us. When they came to our range of rooms, they turned to the left, instead of coming to the right where we were. By the time the officers came to us, even the handcuffs were nearly out.   Each of us was obliged to take to his berth, which contained five men each.   When they had shackled those of the lower berths, they commenced at one the most distant from ours.   Slipping in the rear of my companions, bent down in apparent trepidation, the blacksmith ironed my messmates, and then called to me to descend and submit to his office.   Coming — " Never mind that lad," said my friend Captain Prentis.   They had but three or four pair of handcuffs left, which were clapped on the elderly and robust.   Besides M'Coy, our Boniface the cook, Doctor Gibson, two others and myself, who were unhampered, all the rest were, in appearance, tightly and firmly secured.   Though M'Coy and Boniface were adepts at insurrection, yet their services were of too much importance to government to be dispensed with.   The others of the unfettered remained so from the exhaustion of the shackles.   A new species of interesting occurrences, mingled with much fun and sportive humor, now occurred, which was succeeded by a series of horrible anguish.   The doors were scarcely closed, before we began to assay the unshackling. Those who had small hands, by compressing the palms, could easily divest the irons from their wrist.   Of these there were many, who became the assistants of their friends, whose hands were larger.   Here there was a necessity for ingenuity.   Knives notched as saws, were the principal means.   The head of the rivet, at the end of the bar, was sawed off, it was lengthened and a screw formed upon it, to cap which a false head was made, either of iron or of lead, resembling as much as possible the true head.   Again new rivets were formed, from the iron we had preserved in our secret hoards, from the vigilance of the searchers.   These new rivets being made to bear a strong likeness to the old, were then cut into two parts — one part was driven into the bolt tightly, became stationary, the other part was movable.   It behoved the wearer of the manacle to look to it, that he did not lose the loose part, and when the searchers came to examine, that it should stand firm in the orifice. Some poor fellow, perhaps from a defect of ingenuity, the hardness of the iron, or the want of the requisite tools, could not discharge the bilboes. This was particularly the melancholy predicament of three of Morgan's men, whose heels were too long to slip through the iron, which encompassed the small of the leg. It was truly painful to see three persons attached to a monstrous bar, the weight of which was above their strength to carry. It added to the poignancy of their sufferings, in such frigid weather, that their colleagues at the bar, having shorter heels, could withdraw the foot and perambulate the jail ; where their companions left them, there they must remain, seated on the floor, unless some kind hands assisted them to remove.

There was a droll dog from the eastward who was doubly unfortunate ; in the attack of the city he had received a spent ball in the pit of the stomach, which had nearly ended him ; now it became his lot to have an immense foot bolt fastened to his leg, without a companion to bear him company and cheer his lonely hours. This victim of persecution and sorrow would sometimes come among us in the yard, bearing up his bolt, slung by a cord hitched over his shoulder. Nothing could damp his spirits. He talked, laughed and sung incessantly. Some others besides those, were similarly situated. Those who were so lucky as to have light hand cuffs, bore them about with them. The greatest danger of discovery arose from those who could free themselves from the heavy irons. The usual visitations were increased from twice to thrice a day, in the first and last the smith searched the bolts of each person. But there were other intrusions intermediately, by officers evidently despatched by the suspicions of government, for the purpose of discovery. To counteract these new measures of caution and jealousy, we were well prepared. Sentries, on our part, were regularly stationed at certain windows of the jail, to descry the

approach of any one in the garb of an officer.   The
view from these windows was pretty extensive down two
of the streets, particularly that leading to the palace.
Notwithstanding every caution to avoid detection, yet
the clang of the lock of the great door, was upon some
occasions the only warning given us of the impending
danger.   The scamperings at those times were truly
diverting, and having always escaped discovery, gave us
much amusement.   The clanking of the fetters followed,
and was terrible ; such as the imagination forms in childhood, of the condition of the souls in Tartarus ; even
this was sport.   Happily our real situation was never
known to any of the government officers ; unless the
good blacksmith (a worthy Irishman, of a feeling heart),
might be called such, and he was silent.

Towards the middle of April the scurvy, which we had
been imbibing during the winter, now made its appearance in its most virulent and deadly forms, preceded and
accompanied by a violent diarrhœa.   Many of those
who were first affected were taken to the hospital.   But
the disease soon became general among us.   We were
attended several times by Doctor Maybin, the physician-
general, who, by his tender attentions, and amiable manners, won our affections : he recommended a cleansing
of the stomach, by ipecacuanha and mild cathartics,
such as rhubarb, together with due exercise.   Those
who were young, active and sensible of the doctor's
salutary advice, kept afoot, and practiced every kind of
athletic sport we could devise.   On the contrary, those
who were supinely indolent, and adhered to their blankets,
became objects of real commiseration — their limbs contracted, as one of mine is now ; large blue and even
black blotches appeared on their bodies and limbs — the
gums became black — the morbid flesh fell away — the
teeth loosened, and in several instances fell out.   Our minds
were now really depressed.   That hilarity and fun which
supported our spirits in the greatest misfortunes, gave
way to wailings, groanings and death.   I know, from

dire experience, that when the body suffers pain, the
mind, for the time, is deprived of all its exhilarations —
in short, almost of the power of thinking. The elbow
joints, the hips, the knees and ancles were most severely
pained. It was soon observed (though the doctor's
mate attended us almost daily, and very carefully), there
was little or no mitigation of our diseases, except that
the diarrhœa, which was derived from another cause
than that which produced the scurvy, was somewhat
abated ; and that our remedy lay elsewhere in the materia
medica which was beyond the grasp of the physician. The
diarrhœa came from the nature of the water we used
daily. In the month of April the snows begin to melt,
not by the heat of the sun, but most probably by the
warmth of the earth beneath the snows. The ground,
saturated with the snow-water, naturally increased the
fountain-head in the cellar. Literally, we drank the
melted snow. The scurvy had another origin. The
diet — salt pork, infamous biscuit — damp and close con-
finement in a narrow space, together with the severity
of the climate, were the true causes of the scurvy.

There was no doubt in any reflective mind among us,
but that the virtuous and beneficent Carleton, taking
into view his perilous predicament, did every thing for
us, which an honest man and a good Christian could.

An observation may be made in this place with propriety, that is, that in the climates of all high southern
or northern regions, the soil is very rich and prolific.
This beneficial operation of nature, is, in all likelihood attributable to the nitrous qualities which the snow deposits.
Of the fact that nitre is the principal ingredient which
causes fertility in the earth, no man of observation can
at this day reasonably doubt. The earth is replete of
it. Wherever earth and shade unite, it is engendered
and becomes apparent. This idea is proved by the circumstance that nitre may be procured from caves, the
earth of cellars, outhouses, and even from common earth,
if kept under cover. During the late revolution, when

powder was so necessary, we every where experienced the good effects of this mineralogical discovery ; it gives me pleasure to say that it is most fairly ascribable to our German ancestors.   The snows which usually fall in Canada about the middle of November, and generally cover the ground until the end of April, in my opinion, fill the soil with those vegetative salts, which forward the growth of plants.   This idea was evinced to me by my vague and inconsiderate mind, from observations then made, and which were more firmly established by assurances from Captain Prentis, that muck or manure, which we employ in southern climates, is *there* never used.   In that country, the moment the ground is freed from snow, the grass and every species of plant, spring forward in the most luxuriant manner.   Captain Prentis, besides the continuation of his care and friendship to Gibson and myself, did not restrain his generosity to individuals, but procured for us a permission from government, to send out an old Irishman, of the New York line, an excellent catholic, to collect for us vegetable food.   The first specimen of this good old man's attention and industry, was the production of a large basket-full of the ordinary blue grass of our country ; this grass, by those who got at it, was devoured ravenously at the basket, if so happy as to be able to come near it.   Scurvy grass, in many varieties, eschalots, small onions, onion-tops and garlic, succeeded, and were welcomed by all of us for several months afterwards.   This voracious appetite for vegetables, seems to be an incident always concurring in that terrible disease, the scurvy ; nature seems to instil into the patient, a desire of such food, and of acids, which are the only specific, with a due attention to cleanliness, hitherto discovered, that do eradicate the stamina of the disease.   From my contracted knowledge, it is imperceptible that there is any material discrepancy between the sea-scurvy and the land-scurvy of high southern and northern latitudes.   The descriptions given by Robins (or if you please, the Rev. Mr. Walter), and other voyagers, of the causes, the symptoms and the effects of that disorder, seem to concur in every particular with our various experience at Quebec. Recollect it is not a physician who speaks.[1]

About the time above spoke of Governor Carleton directed that we should be supplied with fresh beef. This was no other than that which had been brought into the city when we lay at Aux-Tremble, in the foregoing autumn, and in aid of the stores of the garrison. It had lain in a frozen state during the winter, without salting, but now as warm weather was approaching, it began to thaw and was liberally disposed of to the garrison and prisoners. The beef was sweet, though here and there a little blueish, like the mould of stale bread, very tender, but somewhat mawkish. It was palatable and nutritive to men afflicted as we were. This beef, connected with vegetables, soon animated us with an idea of returning health and vigor ; yet, though it mitigated the pains we endured, it did not totally expel the scurvy.

The seventh of May arrived. Two ships came to the aid of the garrison, beating through a body of ice, which perhaps was impervious to any other than the intrepid sailor. This relief of men and stores, created great joy in the town. Our army began their disorderly retreat. My friend Simpson, with his party, were much misused, from a neglect of giving him information of the intended flight of our army. Some few of the men under his authority, straggled and were taken in the retreat. They came to inhabit our house. Now, for the first time, we heard an account of the occurrences during the winter's blockade, which to us, though of

---

[1] The late Captain Thomas Boyd, the strongest and largest man among us, when coming to the air, frequently fainted ; one Rothrock, of Morgan's, had so fetid a breath that it was disgusting to enter the room he inhabited ; one of Lamb's company lost his gums and some of his teeth, all were loose, of which I am certain as his mouth was examined by me.— *Henry.*

trivial import, were immensely interesting. The sally of this day, produced to the prisoners additional comfort. Though the troops took a severe revenge upon our friends without, by burning and destroying their properties. The next day, more ships and troops arrived; a pursuit took place, the effect of which was of no consequence, except so far as it tended to expel the colonial troops from Canada. To the prisoners, this retreat had pleasing consequences; fresh bread, beef newly slaughtered, and a superabundance of vegetables, was a salutary diet to our reduced and scorbutic bodies. Still freedom, that greatest of blessings, and exercise were required to bring back to us genuine health. About this time an incident occurred, which threw us into ecstasy, as it relieved our minds and faculties from a most torturing piece of preservative duty; this was no other than an authoritative divestment of the irons. One day, perhaps the fifteenth or eighteenth of May, Colonel Maclean, attended by Major Carleton, a younger brother of the general's, Major Maibaum,[1] a German officer, both of whom had just arrived from Europe, together with Captain Prentis, and other officers, entered the jail about mid-day. The prisoners paraded in the jail-yard completely ironed. Captain Prentis, by the direction of

---

[1] This gentleman was six feet and four or five inches high and as well proportioned. His disposition was a kindly one. He spoke his own language admirably, and French fluently, but no English. Knowing from his military dress and manners, that he was a German, I was induced to address him in that language. He appeared astonished, yet pleased at hearing his own tongue from an American lad, inquired concerning Pennsylvania, our way to Quebec, etc., but seemed apprehensive of the jealousy of the English officials, who did not understand us. The Baron Knyphausen wanted an interpreter. Captain Prentis, who was really my friend, made me the proposition, as from the Baron, and used various arguments to induce a compliance, all of which were spurned. In 1778 or 1779, I had again the pleasure of seeing the major at Lancaster, in the company of my father, but he was then a prisoner. — *Henry.*

This is supposed to have been Major Juste Christoph von Maibom, who was taken prisoner at Bennington, and died at Wolfenbuttel, duchy of Brunswick, in Germany, 17 Feb., 1804.— *M.*

Colonel Maclean, pointed out to the other officers:
" This is general such-a-one, — that is colonel such-a-
one," and in this, manner proceeded to name all the
leading characters. Happening to be very near the
amiable, it might be said, admirable Major Carleton,
he was overheard to say, " Colonel, ambition is laudable ;
cannot the irons of these men be struck off ? " This
the colonel ordered to be done immediately. Our
kind-hearted blacksmith was not distant : he came and
the officers remained to see some of the largest bolts
divested, and then left us. " Come, come, gentlemen,"
said the blacksmith, " you can put off your irons." In
a minute, the vast pile lay before him. Being now at
full bodily liberty, we completed a ball court, which had
been originally formed, as it were, by stealth. Here a
singular phenomenon which attends the scurvy, discovered itself. The venerable and respectable Maybin
had recommended to us exercise, not only as a mean of
cure, but as a preventive of the scorbutic humors operat-
ing. Four of the most active would engage at a game
of *fives*. Having played some games in continuation, if
a party incautiously sat down, he was seized by the
most violent pains in the hips and knees, which incapa-
citated him from play for many hours, and from rising
from the earth, where the patient had seated himself.
These pains taught us to keep afoot all day, and even to
eat our food in an erect posture. Going to bed in the
evening, after a hard day's play, those sensations of
pain upon, lying down, immediately attacked us. The
pain would continue half an hour, and often longer.
My own experience will authorize me to say two hours.
In the morning, we rose free from pain, and the routine
of play and fatigue ensued, but always attended by the
same effects, particularly to the stubborn and incautious,
who would not adhere to the wholesome advice of Doctor
Maybin. Those who were inactive, retained those excruciating pains to the last, together with their distorted,
bloated, and blackened limbs. Upon our return from

Canada, in the autumn of 1776, I saw five or six of my crippled compatriots hobbling through the streets of Lancaster on their way home. It cost a tear — all that could be given. By the month of August, the active were relieved from those pains.

Towards the end of May, Governor Carleton ordered each of the prisoners a linen shirt. This gift, to me, was most agreeable, as linen next the skin, for some months past, was unfelt, and few persons who have not felt the extremity of such endurances as ours, can form a full conception of the gratification we enjoyed. Having had but one shirt on at the time of our capture, it was soon destroyed by the wearing, and the repeated washings it required. Delicacy forbids a dilation upon the cause and effects. You would laugh at the description of one of our washing parties. Rising early, the prime object was to make a strong ley of wood ashes, of which we had plenty, into which the linen was plunged, and concocted for an hour or more, under a hope of putting an end to certain vagrants, of a genera with which most of us are acquainted. During the boiling, the votaries of cleanliness, cloaked in a blanket, or blanket coat, watched the ebullitions of the kettle. The boiling done, the linen was borne to the yard, where each one washed his own, and watched it during the drying, almost in a state of nature. Captain Prentis, pitying my sad condition, pressed upon me often to accept from him, money to purchase a suit of clothes, and he would trust to the honor and integrity of my father for payment, whose character he knew. Adhering to my first determination, this polite and generous proposal of my amiable and deserving friend was as often, yet most thankfully declined, maugre the advice of my bosom friends Boyd and Cunningham to the contrary. He however forced upon me a half johannes. This small sum was applied to the solace of my heart. In the first place, to an article still more necessary than a shirt. The residue was expended upon matters which cheered the hearts of my messmates, whom I dearly loved ; cheese, sugar, tea, coffee, etc., spirits was detested, as we knew it to be a poison to scorbutic persons.   What pleased me much more, and gave me pure delight, was the following occurrence : Of my own accord, no one knowing of the intention, the good old Irishman was delegated to purchase three or four pounds of tobacco.   It was secretly brought, and as secretly borne to our room.   A pound was produced and fairly parted among our tobacco chewers. You cannot conceive their joy.   When the first paroxysm was over, the remainder was disposed of in the same way.   The thankfulness of those brave, but destitute men, arose towards me, nearly to adoration.   You will ask why ?   Hear the reason.   From your small knowlege of mankind, you can have little conception of the force habit has on the human race.   One who chews, smokes or snuffs tobacco, is as little able to abstain from that enjoyment, as you would be, if compelled to refrain from your usual meals.   This particular is spoken of, to persuade you by no mean to use tobacco in any shape. It is a poison, of the most inveterate kind, which like opium, arsenic, and several other medicaments, may be applied to healthful purposes, yet, if employed in an extreme degree, produces instantaneous death.   These ideas are not visionary, but are supportable by the authority of some of the best physicians.   You are at full liberty to put your own constructions upon these observations. But to return to my fellow-prisoners.

In the wilderness where the army soon run out the article of tobacco, the men had many valuable succedaneums.   The barks of the different kinds of firs, the cedar, the red willow,[1] and the leaves of many astrin-

---

[1] Red willow (*Salix purpurea*).   This shrub, which is a native of the United States, is spread throughout our climates.   The outer bark of a deep red color, peels in a very thin scale, the inner is scraped off with a knife, and is dried either in the sun or over the fire.   The scent when burning, is delightful.   To increase the flavor, the Indians pluck the current year's branches of the upland sumach, and dry it in bunches over the smoke of

gent or bitter plants supplied the place; but within the bare walls of our jail there was no substitute for this dear and inebriating vegetable. Thus was all my money expended and much to my satisfaction and to the heart-felt pleasure of my brave and worthy companions, whose sufferings in certain points, were greater than my own. The table of the virtuous and generous Prentis had often furnished me liberally with wholesome viands. With convalescency, though pennyless, we again became merry and lighthearted.

In the beginning of August we were told by Captain Prentis, that the governor had concluded to send us by sea to New York upon parole for the purpose of being exchanged; that the transports which had brought the late reinforcements from Europe, were cleansing and preparing for the voyage. Now there was exultation. On the seventh of August we subscribed our written

---

a fire. A half part of red-willow bark, added to as much of the dryed sumach forms the killiknick. Those ingredients added to a third part of leaf tobacco, and the mass rubbed finely together in the palm of the hand, makes that delicious fume, so fascinating to the red, and also to the white men. Care must be taken by the consumer, not to use the swamp sumach (*Rhus vernix*) for the upland (*Rhus glabrum*) as the former is most poisonous, and resembles the latter, in the bark and leaf so much, that an incurious eye might be deceived. The difference to a stranger may be distinctively marked by observing that the bunch of berries of the upland sumach, is a cone closely attached to each other, and when ripe of a reddish color. The berries of the swamp sumach hang loosely pendant, from a lengthy foot-stalk, and when ripe, are of a greenish-gray : at least I never saw the berry in any other state. The unhappy person who would employ the swamp sumach in smoking, would forfeit his eyesight. This truth I had from Natanis in Canada, and it has since, many years ago, been confirmed to me by the celebrated Seneca, The Cornplanter. You know the experience of our own family, when clearing the swamp, as to the deleterious qualities of the wood as fuel : your mother suffered greatly from its poisonous vapors. The moose-deer prefer the red-willow as food ; we most frequently observed them in its neighborhood. The vanilla of South America, has been applied by the Spanish manufactors of tobacco, in various ways : it is strange, that we have never assayed the killikinick.— *Henry.*

15

paroles.[1] Captain Prentis procured me permission from government with a few friends to traverse the city. An officer of the garrison attended us. Our first desire was to see the grave of our general, and those of his aids, as well as those of the beloved Hendricks and Humphreys. The graves were within a small place of interment, neatly walled with stone. The coffins of Montgomery, Cheeseman and M'Pherson, were well arranged side by side. Those of Hendricks, Humphreys, Cooper, etc., were arranged on the south side of the inclosure, but as the burials of these heroes took place in a dreary winter, and the earth impenetrable, there was but little soil on the coffins, the snow and ice which had been the principal covering being now dissolved, the foot of the general's coffin was exposed to the air and view. The coffin was well formed of fir plank. Captain Prentis assured me that the graves should be deepened and the bodies duly deposited ; for he also knew Montgomery as a fellow soldier, and lamented his untimely fate. Thence we proceeded past the citadel, along the ramparts to Cape Diamond, descended the declivity slantingly, and examined the stockades and block house. It is this little tour which enabled me to describe to you the site and defences of that formidable pass. Proceeding thence through a part of the lower town, we came to a narrow street which led us to an immense stair way, one of the ascents into the upper town. Ascending here we came to the main passage, which curvatured down the hill into the lower town,

---

[1] It will perhaps be proper to give you an idea of the parole exacted at that time. " We whose names are hereunder written, do solemnly promise and engage, to his Excellency General Carleton, not to say or do any thing against his majesty's person or government ; and to repair, whenever required so to do by his excellency, or any of his majesty's commanders in chief in America, doth please to direct, in testimony of which, we have hereunto set our hands this day at Quebec. August 7th, 1776.

J. J. H. &c."

I received the original paper in 1778, in consequence of an exchange of the St. John's prisoners for us.— *Henry.*

and which was to lead us in our supposed attack upon
the upper town ; this we pursued and came to the place
of the second barrier, which had been lately demolished.
The houses on both sides of the street in which we had
taken our stand, were now in ruins, having been burnt
by the garrison as were the suburbs of St. Roque and
St. Johns.   This was done to render them unfit for the
shelter of future assailants.   Thus it is that war destroys
the wealth and robs the individual of happiness.   We
had no time to make observations but such as could be
done in passing hastily.   Returning to the upper town
by the principal and winding road, we were strongly impressed with the opinion that if our whole force, as was
intended, had formed a junction in the lower town, that
it was utterly impracticable, either from our numbers or
our means, to mount by a road such as this was.   Suppose it not to have been barricaded and enfiladed by
cannon, it must be assailed by the bayonet, of which
weapon we had very few and the enemy was fully supplied.   But when we reflect that across the road at the
centre of the arc of each curve there was a barricade,
and cannon placed to rake the intervals between the
different barricades, the difficulties of the ascent, which
is very steep, would be increased even to insurmounta-
bility.   The road is very narrow and lined next the hill
by a stupendous precipice ; on the other hand there were
some houses romantically perched on the side of the
declivity, and some rocks.   The declivity of itself was
an excellent defence if the besieged could maintain the
position in front, for in a short time, in so confined a
space, the assailants must either die, retreat, or be thrown
down the hill from the road.   But suppose all these
defences overcome, and we had arrived at the brow of
the hill at the entrance of the upper town, here a still
more formidable obstacle presented itself than those
which could be formed by art in the lower parts of the
road.   At this place there is a hollow way, which in the
hurry we were in and the slight view we dared take, ap-

peared as if cut out of the solid rock, of a depth of thirty or forty feet. Athwart this way there was a strong stockade of a height nearly equal with the perpendicular sides of the way or gulley. From the surface above we might have been stoned to death by the defenders of the fortress without a probability of their receiving harm from us below, though ever so well armed. But the stockade itself, from its structure and abundant strength, would have resisted a force manifold our numbers, and much better supplied and accoutred. From these observations (those of an uninstructed youth to be sure), there was no hesitation in telling my intimate friends, then and since, that the scheme of the conquest of the upper town was visionary and groundless ; not the result of our dear general's reflections, but forced upon him by the nature and necessities of the times and his disagreeable predicament. If a coalition of our forces in the lower town had taken effect, the general would then most probably have developed his latent and real plans. The reasons given in council may have been promulgated merely to induce a more spirited exertion upon the part of the officers and soldiery, who were not in the secret, to excite a factitious valor. Getting into serious action and warmed by the opposition of the enemy, the troops might have been induced to persevere in any apparently sudden design of the general. The cupidity of the soldiers had been played upon. This latter fact is known to me of my own particular knowledge. Some weeks before the attack the soldiers in their common conversations, spoke of the conquest of the city as a certainty ; and exultingly of the plunder they should win by their bravery. It was not my business to contradict, but to urge them on. Perhaps the setting fire to the lower town on the side of Cape Diamond, considering the prevailing wind which was at southeast, but afterwards changed to north and northwest, such a design might have been effected. The shipping also ice-bound, numerous and valuable, moored around the point, would have been consumable. All this destruction would have been a victory of no mean kind ; but adding *eclat* to the known gallantry and prowess of the general. The Almighty willed that we should never know the pith or marrow of his projects ; whatever they were, my mind is assured that they were considerately and well designed. He was not a man to act incautiously and without motive, and too honest and brave to adopt a sinister part. No doubt we could have escaped by the way of St. Roque, protected by the smoke of the conflagration, and the terror and bustle which would consequently be created in the town. Though this pass is too narrow for the operation of a large body of men in an extended front, still we should have been too numerous (under the circumstances supposed), for the enemy to afford a force issuing from palace gate, adequate to oppose us. In the next instance if we should happen to be so very fortunate in such a retreat, as to bat the foes, they *must retreat* into the city by the way of palace gate, and we should have entered pell-mell, and should thus have achieved the possession of that important place, the upper town, which was the primary view and last hope of the general and the army. These were the crude notions of a youth formed upon the spot, but in a maturation of thirty years, are still retained.

The general did not want for information. Many persons, male and female (unnecessary mouths), were expelled the city, to wander for subsistence among their friends in the country. His own knowledge of Quebec, where he had served, would enable him by interrogation to extort from those emigrants a full stock of information of all the new defences erected by Governor Carleton since. Consequently, knowing the practicability of Cape Diamond (*Aunce de mere*, which must be provincial, and I do not understand), as an entrance to the lower town (but a most dangerous one), and that of St. Roque, with which and its barriers, he was particularfy acquainted, from his own, and the observations of others ; if so, he would most assuredly be informed of the defensive obstructions on the slope of the hill, and the encloyment of the troops, which would in consequence attend ; and he would also know that this place, to the garrison, would be a perfect Thermopylæ, impassable by ten times our numbers, if we had been veterans and were better furnished. From these reasons, there was an inducement for my mind, at all times since the attack, to conclude that it was never General Montgomery's real design to conquer the upper town, by an invasion from the lower town, but his hidden and true plan was, by a consolidation of our whole force, to burn the lower town, and the shipping, and to retreat by the way of palace gate and St. Roque. If a sally was made at palace gate, the event, as was observed before, might be fatal to the enemy. The comprehensive mind of Montgomery would not only appreciate to the full extent the peculiar advantages of the enemy, but estimate to its true value the means he possessed, and the merits of his own army. Presuming the colonists to be successful in the lower town, where there was much wealth, and the avaricious among us be in some degree gratified, it would have created a spirit of hope and enterprise in the men, tending to induce them to remain with us. Afterwards, combining our whole force, with the reinforcements we had a prospect of receiving, an attack upon the upper town might have succeeded. In a word the destruction of the lower town, in my apprehension, should be considered merely as preparatory to a general assailment of the upper town, notwithstanding all that has been said in the memoirs of those days. A contrary opinion went abroad " that the general, if he had lived, by this assault would have conquered Quebec." No idea could be more fallacious. It was politically right to keep up that opinion among the people in those trying times, but its accomplishment, with our accompaniment of men and defective arms, was ideal. Our walk from the great gate and palisade, was considerable, ere we reached our detestable dwelling ; as we had enjoyed a few hours of fleeting liberty, the *locking-up* became the more horrible to our feelings. The next day, however, we had the ineffable pleasure of marching in a body to the water side, and embarked on board five transports. On the following day a new joy was in store for me. General William Thompson (of whom it might well be said, " *this is a man* "), who had commanded our regiment at Prospect hill, as its colonel: he had been taken prisoner at the Three rivers, with several other officers, in the preceding month of June. He was now aboard of our little fleet, destined to New York. Thompson came to our ship, to visit the miserable remnant of a part of his gallant corps. The general had a special message to me, from my father, with whom he was intimate. Coming through Lancaster in his way to his command in Canada, he was authorized by my father, if he saw me in that country, to furnish me with money. The good man proffered me four half-johannes, one only was accepted. What was nearer and dearer to my heart, was the information that my parents, relatives and friends were well. That money was applied to the use of my messmates, in the way of sea-stores. Permission being obtained, Boyd and myself went ashore ; our purchases consisted of a very large Cheshire cheese, coffee, tea and sugar, together with a large roll of tobacco for the men. Again pennyless, jollity and mirth did not forsake us.

We sailed on the tenth of August, convoyed by the Pearl frigate, Captain M'Kenzie. Passing the delightful island of Orleans, much in shore, we observed the farmers reaping their wheat, which, as we run along, we could observe the haum, in many instances, was green towards the foot of the stalk. From this circumstance it was concluded, that frequently, particularly in cold or wet seasons the grain must be kiln-dried, as it is done in the north of England, and in Scotland, before it is housed and threshed. The wheat, though sown between the fifteenth and twentieth of May, and probably sometimes earlier or later, is weighty, and produces a very fine white flour. The voyage down the river, except a few boisterous days, was pleasant. We had some noble views, interspersed here and there with something like villages, chapels, and farm-houses. Afterwards, we had in prospect a bleak and dreary coast and country, whose craggedness inspired disagreeable sensations. The greatest curiosities were the seals, whose history and manners were then known to me, but whose living form excited attention, as they were creeping up or basking on the rocks. The porpoises, perfectly white, in vast droves played before and around us, and drew my attention and surprise, as none but the black southern porpoise had before come under my view. To become a naturalist, it is necessary a man should travel; it was many years before books could persuade me of the existence of a green-haired monkey; but these were diminutive objects indeed in nature's scale, of comparative imagery, when contrasted with the immense river Cadaracqua, or as it is now called St. Lawrence, second to no river in the world, unless it be the La Plata, of South America. Making this observation, you must understand me to include within it, the Lake Superior, and the waters which feed that lake. Off Gaspy Point, where we soon arrived, in a due north line, across the island of Anticosta, the river is about ninety miles wide. Steering with favorable weather, the island of St. Johns came in view; passing it, and the Gut of Canceaux, experiencing some stormy weather upon the ocean, and a few difficulties, we happily arrived at New York on the eleventh of September, 1776, and anchored three miles south of Governor's island. Now it was, for the first time, that we heard of the dilemma in which our country stood.

The battle of Long Island, on the twenty-seventh of August, had been unsuccessfully fought by our troops, many of whom were prisoners.   In such hurrying times, intercourses between hostile armies in the way of nego- tiation upon any point, are effected with difficulty.   We had waited patiently several weeks, to be disembarked on our own friendly shore; yet tantalized every day with reports that to-morrow we should be put on shore; some, and in a little while all, began to fear it was the intention of General Howe to detain us as prisoners in opposition to the good will of Sir Guy Carleton.   This notion had so strongly impressed the minds of my friend Doctor Thomas Gibson, and a young man called John Blair, of Hendricks, that they determined to escape from the ship.   They were, both of them, athletic and able bodied men, and most adroit.   Gibson planned the manner of escape; its ingeniousness, hazard, boldness of execution and eventual success, received the applause of all, but was disapproved, upon the principle that it trenched upon their honor, and would impede our release. The story is this: Gibson and Blair, in the evening, dressed in shirts and trowsers, were upon the main deck with their customary flapped hats on their heads.   Gib- son gave me a squeeze of the hand in token of farewell; he was greeted kindly, for he was the brother of my soul.   He and his companion went to the forecastle, where there were two large New Foundland dogs, each of which had his party, or rather his partizans among the crew.   These, the adventurers hissed at each other. The dogs being engaged with their usual fury, attracted the attention of the sailors and many of the prisoners; they took this opportunity of stripping and letting them- selves down at the bow into the water.   Leaning over the sides of the ship, in company of some friends in the secret, and unregardful of the dogs, we awaited the management of the flight.   The last lighted cloud ap- peared low in the west.   Something extraordinary passed along the side, a foolish fellow asked, " what is that ?" " a wave, you fool — a mere deception of sight," was answered.   It was the head of Gibson, covered by his

large black hat. Within a few yards of Gibson came
Blair, but with a smaller hat, he was obvious ; his white
skin discovered him, but luckily the attention of the
ignoramus was engaged another way. These daring
men swam to the barge at the stern, entered it, and
slipped the rope. They had rowed a thousand yards
before the boat was missed. The other boats of our
ship, and of those near us, were despatched after the
runaways ; it was too late, the fugitives had too much of
a start to be easily overtaken. They landed (having
rowed about five miles), naked, in our own country,
somewhere in the vicinity of Bergen-neck, and bartered
the boat for some ordinary clothing. They waited on
General Washington, who disapproved of their demeanor.

A short time after the foregoing occurrence, a most
beautiful and luminous, but baleful sight occurred to us,
that is, the city of New York on fire. One night
(Sept. 22), the watch on deck gave a loud notice of this
disaster. Running upon deck we could perceive a light,
which at the distance we were from it (four miles), was
apparently of the size of the flame of a candle. This
light to me, appeared to be the burning of an old and
noted tavern, called the *Fighting Cock* (where, ere this
I had lodged), to the east of the battery, and near the
wharf. The wind was southwardly, and blew a fresh
gale the flames at this place, because of the wind, increased rapidly. In a moment we saw another light at
a great distance from the first, up the North river. The
latter light seemed to be an original, distinct and new
formed fire, near a celebrated tavern in the Broadway
called *White Hall.* Our anxiety for the fate of so fine
a city, caused much solicitude, as we harbored suspicions
that the enemy had fired it. The flames were fanned
by the briskness of the breeze, and drove the destructive
effects of the element on all sides. When the fire reached
the spire of a large steeple, south of the tavern, which
was attached to a large church, the effect upon the eye
was astonishingly grand. If we could have divested

ourselves of the knowledge that it was the property of
our fellow-citizens which was consuming, the view might
have been esteemed sublime, if not pleasing. The deck
of our ship for many hours was lighted as at noon day.
In the commencement of the conflagration we observed
many boats putting off from the fleet, rowing speedily
towards the city ; our boat was of the number. This
circumstance repelled the idea that our enemies were
the incendiaries, for indeed they professedly went in aid
of the inhabitants. The boat returned about daylight,
and from the relation of the officer and the crew, we
clearly discerned that the burning of New York was the
act of some mad-cap Americans. The sailors told us
in their blunt manner, that they had seen one American
hanging by the heels dead, having a bayonet wound
through his breast. They named him by his Christian
and surname, which they saw imprinted on his arm ; they
averred he was caught in the fact of firing the houses.
They told us, also, that they had seen one person who
was taken in the fact, tossed into the fire, and that
several who were stealing, and suspected as incendiaries,
were bayonetted. Summary justice is at no time laudable, but in this instance it may have been correct. If
the Greeks could have been resisted at Persepolis, every
soul of them ought to have been massacred. The testimony we received from the sailors, my own view of the
distinct beginnings of the fire, in various spots, remote
from each other, and the manner of its spreading, im
pressed my mind with the belief that the burning of the
city was the doings of the most low and vile of persons,
for the purposes, not only of thieving, but of devastation.
This seemed, too, the general sense, not only of the
British, but that of the prisoners then aboard the transports. Laying directly south of the city, and in a range
with Broadway, we had a fair and full view of the whole
process. The persons in the ships nearer to the town
than we were, uniformly held the same opinion. It was
not until some years afterwards, that a doubt was created ;

but for the honor of our country and its good name, an ascription was made of the firing of the city, to accidental circumstances. It may be well, that a nation, in the heat and turbulence of war, should endeavor to promote its interests, by the propagating reports of its own innocency and prowess, and accusing its enemy of flagrant enormity and dastardliness (as was done in this particular case), but when peace comes, let us in God's name do justice to them and ourselves. Baseness and villainy are the growth of all climes, and of all nations. Without the most. numerous, and the most cogent testimony, as the fact occurred within my own view, the eloquence of Cicero could not convince me that the firing was accidental. Some time after the burning of the city, we understood that we were to be embarked in shallops, and landed at Elizabethtown point.

The intelligence caused a sparkling in every eye. On the next day about noon, we were in the boats; adverse winds retarded us. It was ten or eleven at night, before we landed; the moon shone beautifully. Morgan stood in the bow of the boat ; making a spring not easily surpassed, and falling on the earth, as it were to grasp it — cried "Oh my country." We that were near him pursued his example. Now a race commenced which in quickness, could scarcely be exceeded, and soon brought us to Elizabethtown. Here, those of us who were drowsy, spent an uneasy night. Being unexpected guests, and the town full of troops, no quarters were provided for us. Joy rendered beds useless, we did not close our eyes till daylight. Singing, dancing, the Indian halloo, in short, every species of vociferousness was adopted by the men, and many of the most respectable sergeants, to express their extreme pleasure. A stranger coming among them, would have pronounced them mad, or at last intoxicated ; though since noon, neither food nor liquor had passed our lips ; thus the passions may at times have an influence on the human frame, as inebriating as wine or any other liquor. The

morning brought us plenty, in the form of rations of
beef and bread.   Hunger allayed, my only desire was
to proceed homewards.   Money was wanting.   How to
obtain it in a place where all my friends and acquaintances
were alike poor and destitute, gave me great anxiety and
pain.   Walking up the street very melancholy, unknowing what to do, I observed a wagon built in the Lancaster
county fashion (which at that time was peculiar in Jersey), unloading stores for the troops come or coming.
The owner seeing me, grasping my hand with fervor,
told me every one believed me to be dead.   Telling
him our story in a compendious manner, the good old
man, without solicitation, presented me two silver dollars
to be repaid at Lancaster.   They were gladly received.[1]
My heart became easy.   The next day, in company
with the late Colonel Febiger and the present General
Nichols, and some other gentlemen, we procured a light
return wagon which gave us a cast as far as Princeton.
Here we had the pleasure of conversing with Dr. With-
erspoon, who was the first that informed us of a resolution of congress to augment the army.   It gave u
pleasure, as we had devoted ourselves individually, tc
the service of our country.   The next day, if not incorrect, we proceeded on foot, no carriage of any kind
being procurable.   Night brought us up at a farm-house
somewhere near Bristol.   The owner was *one of us*, that
is, a genuine whig.   He requested us to tarry all night,
which we declined.   He presented us a supper that was
gratefully received.   Hearing our story, he was much
affected.   We then tried to prevail on him to take us to
Philadelphia in his light wagon.   It was objected that it
stood loaded with hay in the barn floor ; his sons were
asleep or abroad.   We removed these objections by
unloading the hay while this good citizen prepared the

---

[1] Who do you think this was ?   Why Stephen Lutz, of Lancaster —
poor but industrious.   I have thanked him a thousand times since, and
have had the pleasure of obliging him. — *Henry.*

16

horses. Mounting, we arrived at the *Harp and Crown* about two o'clock in the morning. To us it was most agreeable that we passed through the streets of Philadelphia in the night time, as our clothing was not only threadbare but shabby. Here we had friends and funds. A gentleman advanced me a sum sufficient to enable me to exchange my leggins and moccasins, for a pair of stockings and shoes, and to bear my expenses home. A day and a half brought me to the arms of my beloved parents.

At Philadelphia, I waited upon a cousin of my mother's, Mr. Owen Biddle, then a member of the council of safety, who informed me that while in captivity, he had procured me a lieutenancy. My heart was otherwise engaged. Morgan the hero! had promised and obtained for me, a captaincy in the Virginia line. Following the fortunes of that bold and judicious commander, my name might have been emblazoned in the rolls of patriotic fame. But alas! in the course of eight weeks after my return from captivity, a slight cold, caught when skating on the ice of the Susquehanna, or in pursuing the wild-turkey among the Kittatinny hills, put an end to all my visionary schemes of ambition. This cause renewed that abominable disorder, the scurvy (which I had supposed was expelled from my system), accompanied by every morbid symptom, which had been so often observed at Quebec, attendant upon others. The medical men of all classes, being engaged in the army, that species of assistance was unattainable, in the degree requisite; lameness, as you now observe it, was the consequence. Would to God! my extreme sufferings had then ended a life, which since has been a tissue of labor, pain, and misery.

THE END.

APPENDIX.

————•————

The following letters written from Canada respecting the Invasion of that Province by Arnold and Montgomery, are taken from the *Pennsylvania Journal and Weekly Advertiser*, Jan. 3, 1776.

Extract of a Letter from an officer under Col. Arnold, dated at Point aux Tremble (in Canada), Nov. 21, 1775.

" The last letter I wrote you was from the Dead river, Oct. 24, which 'tis probable you have never received. At that time our difficulties seemed to increase. We had a very rapid river to encounter with our boats, and a thick wilderness for those that marched by land ; many places, some miles in length, of cedar swamp, hills, etc., but all these were tolerable while our provisions were plenty. At the head of Chaudière lake, which is an hundred and some miles from the Canadian settlements, every man received his allowance of flour, and there was exactly four pints to each. Meat there was none. Upon this small supply we were obliged to push as we valued our lives, and did not know but we should have a powerful army to encounter. Then I first experienced the real advantage of health, being able to keep pace with the foremost, and reached the inhabitants, though in a very weak, half starved condition. Some dogs that had followed us were killed and eat, even the intestines, skin, etc. Many eat their shoes, shot pouches, etc., and some never reached the settlements ; I believe no men ever went through more or greater hardships. Col. Enos, who commanded the fourth or last division of our little army, called a council o war at his entrance into the Dead river, and he with his whole party, consisting of three companies, returned back ; this first caused our distress, a chief of our provision was in the rear under his care. From the last English inhabitants in the province of Maine, to the Canadian settlements, we were thirty-two days marching, and never saw any human being but those of our party, neither do I think it was ever passed, except by Indians and wild beasts. We were at least one month too late for this northern climate, as we suffered much from rains, cold, snow, etc., but our joy upon our arrival among the Canadians is inexpressible, and their kindness and hospitality soon made amends for all our fatigue, though I am sensible it will never be forgotten. From the first inhabitants up Chaudière river, to Quebec, is called ninety miles. We were not permitted to tarry at any place, but marched on as fast as our strength would permit to Point Levi, which is on the river St. Lawrence directly opposite to Quebec, where we found a number of armed vessels, from whom we were frequently complimented with salutes of their cannon.

"The country we last passed through was very thick settled, though every where you see marks of oppression. The people are poor and illiterate and appear to have no other end in view than keeping their souls and bodies together, and preparing for the next world, being exceedingly devout. We tarried at Point Levi near a week, during which time we were busy in preparing to cross the river, being obliged to purchase birch canoes twenty miles distant and carry them by land, the regulars at Quebec having burnt all near them as soon as they heard of our coming. The men of war lay in such a manner as they supposed would prevent our attempt, but on Monday the 13th inst., every thing was ready for our embarkation, and at nine o'clock in the evening, being very dark, the first division set off, and we passed between the Hunter of fourteen guns and Quebec, and landed safely at Point de Pezo. The boats were immediately sent back and continued passing till near daybreak, while the men on this side marched up the hill, at the same place the immortal Wolfe formerly did, and immediately formed. The place we marched up is called Wolfe's Cove, and were you to see the hill, you would think it morally impossible for any thing mortal to get heavy artillery up it. I forgot to inform you that Wolfe had intrenched himself very strongly at Point Levi, the remains of which are very evident, though defaced and much filled up. Near daybreak the guard boat belonging to the man of war was passing from the Hunter to the Lizard, a frigate of twenty-eight guns, at the time some of our boats were crossing, which made us uneasy, and as the guard boat came near the shore we hailed her, and then fired upon her, and could distinctly hear them cry out they were wounded; they pushed off, and the whole garrison was immediately alarmed. After waiting some little time till all our men were over (except a guard stationed at Point Levi), we marched across the plains of Abraham, and at daybreak took possession of some houses, one mile and an half from Quebec; after fixing a strong guard we retired, but were alarmed by their seizing one of our sentinels, whom they carried off. Our army was immediately marched off towards the walls. They fired some heavy shot at us, but without any execution; and our men as usual at Cambridge, picked up a number of them, gave them three hearty cheers and retired to their quarters. On Tuesday they made an attempt for a second sentinel, but were unsuccessful. Our little army immediately turned out, and we took possession of a nunnery in the suburbs within point blank shot, and fixed a strong guard there; they kept up a pretty heavy fire, but fortunately no person received the least injury. We had now in a great measure cut off all communications between the city and country, and I believe they began to feel we were not the most agreeable neighbors. On Wednesday we had two alarms and expected they would have turned out and ventured a battle, but it vanished with the roaring of their cannon. On Thursday evening, as a party were crossing St. Charles river (for Quebec stands on a point between St. Lawrence and St. Charles), one of our men, a Pennsylvanian, and a noble soldier was wounded by a cannon ball in the leg, which was cut off as soon as possible, but he had lost so much blood before the doctor could see him that he expired next morning. We buried him on the plains of Abraham. A noble grave for a soldier, and which his past conduct, since he has been in this department, really merited. Little or nothing material passed on Saturday. On Sunday evening, about seven o'clock, every man received orders to parade at Head Quarters at three o'clock in the morning, with his pack on his back. The boats were dispatched across the river and our guard brought from Point Levi. At the appointed hour we assembled and received orders to retreat. We set off, and in our march passed three different armed vessels, and as the road is on the shore we expected at least a broadside, ut they passed us in peace, and upon their arrival at Quebec, we heard the discharge of a number of cannon, from which we concluded Carleton was on board one of them, or that 'twas for joy of our raising the seige. We marched eight leagues that day, and the colonel found it absolutely necessary to halt here, till he could provide the men with shoes or moccasins, many of them being almost barefoot ; it was the first time I ever wore moccasins on a march, and I assure you from the roughness of the road (it being very hard) I could not, in my opinion, if my life had depended upon it, have marched ten miles next day. It has ever been our fortune from first marching from Cambridge, whenever we were much depressed, fatigued, etc., to hear some agreeable news that would immediately invigorate us, and enable us to proceed with tolerable cheerfulness. At this place we heard the agreeable news of Montreal being in our possession, that Governor Carleton made his escape in a birch canoe, and that he was actually in the ship that passed by here yesterday. In short everything once more seems to conspire in our favor. Gen. Montgomery is on his march for Quebec, and we halt here till he comes up, when we shall return to Quebec again, though whether it will be in our possession this winter or not is uncertain. We hear they are driving in all the cattle, etc., which will enable them to stand a long seige. In this part of the world 'tis time for men to think of winter quarters rather than attacking fortified towns ; however we are *Americans* and *American soldiers.* I have not an objection to visiting the plains of Abraham once more, and 'tis probable shall have good quarters even in Quebec ; at any rate I go with pleasure and sincerely believe every man in our army would rather return and is only sorry that our situation rendered it impossible for us to stay longer before Quebec. Our commander is a gentleman worthy the trust reposed in him ; a man, I believe, of invincible courage ; a man of great prudence ; ever serene ; he defies the greatest danger to affect him, or difficulties to alter his temper ; in fine you will ever see him the intrepid hero, and the unruffled Christian.

"Thus have I endeavored to give you a short sketch of our past and present situation ; I could wish my abilities could have placed it in a more correct light before you ; in my present abode it was entirely out of my power, and it was not a little time before I could procure even thus much paper, which is the leaf of a book, a gentleman had for his journal. In better times expect better fare. Quebec, as I mentioned, stands upon a point, between St. Lawrence and St. Charles rivers, the latter not navigable, except for ferry boats, it consists of the upper and lower town, the latter is immediately on the point or water's edge, and consists of a large number of houses built thick ; the upper town is upon the hill, which is prodigiously high; the town is surrounded on the country part by a wall, from twenty-five to thirty feet high; there are, I think, three gates (though I am not certain), St. John's, Port Lewis, and St. Roque's. On each side the river St. Lawrence, from Quebec to Point aux Tremble (our present camp), the hills, or rather banks, are very high, not much less in general than fifty felt; many places close upon the river ; in some places there is a rich piece. of level meadow, perhaps the distance of half a mile from the bank to the river. The whole from here to Quebec, is thickly inhabited, which I am informed is the case to Montreal. The houses are many of them genteel, rather than otherwise, though in general the inhabitants live very low, and in their dress, manners, stoves, etc., exactly resemble our Germans. Since I left Newbury Port till our march last Sunday, I do not recollect that I have seen an oak tree; I venture to say I have not. In the province of Maine, such part as we came through and Canada, has abounded chiefly with evergreens, such as fir, hemlock, spruce, cedar, pine, birch, maple, etc.; last Sunday I was happy in seeing a few oaks and an apple orchard. The inhabitants few or none speak English. How long we may stay here is uncertain — till our reinforcement arrives, 'tis probable, unless they should venture to attack us from Quebec. Be it as it will I am content, and can remove from place to place with as much resignation as almost any one, having been taught by this campaign to consider no place as my home for more than an hour or a day."

Extract of a letter from a volunteer with Col. Arnold to his friend in this city, dated Point aux Tremble, 21 miles from Quebec, November 21, 1775.

" We arrived before Quebec the 15th inst., after a severe march of about 600 miles ; when we left Cambridge we were eleven hundred strong ; about half way Colonel Enos got frightened, and with three companies, and the sick, which together was about one-half of our number, and the greatest part of the provision, *turned back!* May shame and guilt go with him, and wherever he seeks a shelter may the hand of *justice* shut the door against him ; perhaps I have said too much, but a man that has suffered by him, can hardly refrain speaking. We were about two months on our march, thirty-two days of which we did not see a house, and at short allowance, six days of which we were at half a pound of pork and half a pound of flour per man a day, after which for four days we had only half a pound of flour per day, our pork being gone; two days of which we lost ourselves, marched forty miles, and were but ten miles on our way; our whole stores was then divided, and it was about four pints of flour per man ; a small allowance for men near one hundred miles from any habitation, or prospect of a supply. After having traveled fifty or sixty miles on this scanty allow-ance we came to a river, which we were told was only eight miles from the inhabited parts, here I sat down, baked and eat my last morsel of bread; but, think what was my distress, when I found, after crossing the river, that I had thirty miles to travel before I could expect the least mouthful ; however my dread was soon removed by the return of Col. Arnold, who, with a small party had made a forced march, and returned to us with some cattle he had purchased of the inhabitants ; on these we made a voracious meal, and renewed our march with new courage to Point Levi — from thence we were transported in birch canoes to the plains of Abraham, and from thence retreated to this place to wait for Gen. Montgomery, who, we are told, by express this day, will be with us soon."

" An incessant hurry of business since my arrival in Canada, has deprived me of the pleasure of writing before. This serves to give you a short sketch of our tour, the fatigue and hazard of which is beyond description ; a future day may possibly present you with the particulars. The 15th Sept. left Cambridge, same night arrived at Newburyport 18th embarked and sailed; 19th thick weather and a gale of wind, which divided the fleet ; 20th arrived in Kennebec river, 21st reached Fort Western ; 25th to 29th one division marched off each day, with forty-five days provisions; from 29th to the 8th Oct. the whole detachment were daily up to their waists in water, hauling up the batteaux against the rapid stream, to Norridgewock, fifty miles from Fort Western ; from the 9th to the 16th not a minute was lost in gaining the Dead river about fifty miles ; from 16th to 27th we ascended to Lake Megantic or Chaudière pond, distance eighty-three miles ; 28th Col. Arnold embarked with seventeen men in five bateaux, being resolved to proceed on to the French inhabitants, and send back provisions to the detachment, who are near out, and must inevitably suffer without a supply ; at ten we passed over the lake thirteen miles long and entered the Chaudière river, which we descended about ten miles in two hours, amazingly rocky, rapid and dangerous, when we had the misfortune of oversetting and staving three bateaux and lost all their baggage, provisions, etc., and with difficulty saved the men This disaster, though unfortunate at first view we must think a very happy circumstance to the whole, and kind interposition of providence, for had we proceeded half a mile further, we must have gone over a prodigious fall which we were not apprised of, and all inevitably perished ; here we divided the little provisions left, and Col. Arnold proceeded on with two bateaux and five men with all possible expedition, and on the 30th at night, he arrived at the first inhabitants, upwards of eighty miles from the lake, where he was kindly received, and the next morning early sent off a supply of fresh provisions to the rear detachment by the Canadians and savages, about forty of the latter having joined us ; by the 8th the whole arrived except two or three left behind sick ; the 10th we reached Point Levi, seventy-five miles from Sartigan (the first inhabitants), waited until the 13th for the rear to come up and employed the carpenters in making ladders and collecting canoes, those on Point Levi being all destroyed to prevent our crossing ; having collected about thirty we embarked at nine P. M. and at four A. M. carried over at several times five hundred men without being discovered. Thus in about eight weeks we completed a march of near six hundred miles not to be paralleled in history ; the men having with the greatest fortitude and perseverance hauled their bateaux up rapid streams, being obliged to wade almost the whole way, near one hundred and eighty miles, carried them on their shoulders near forty miles over hills, swamps and bogs almost impenetrable, and to their knees in mire, being often obliged to cross three or four times with their baggage. Short of provisions, part of the detachment disheartened and gone back ; famine staring us in the face and an enemy's country, and uncertainty ahead ; notwithstanding all these obstacles the officers and men inspired and fired with the love of liberty and their country, pushed on with a fortitude superior to every obstacle. Most of them had not one day's provision for a week. Thus I have given you a short, but imperfect sketch of our march. The night we crossed the St. Lawrence, found it impossible to get our ladders over, and the enemy being apprised of our coming we found it impracticable to attack them without too great a risk ; we therefore invested the town and cut off their communication with the country. We continued in this situation until the 20th, having often attempted to draw out the garrison in vain ; on a strict scrutiny into our ammunition found many of our cartridges (which to appearance were good) unserviceable, and not ten rounds apiece for the men who were almost naked, barefooted and much fatigued, and as the garrison was daily increasing and near double our number, we thought it prudent to retire to this place and wait the arrival of General Montgomery with artillery, clothing, etc., who to our great joy this morning joined us. We propose immediately investing the town, and make no doubt in a few days to bring Carleton to terms."

Camp before Quebec, near the General Hospital, Dec. 6.

" I wrote you the 21st ult. which I make no doubt you have received. I then gave you some particulars of our march, proceedings, etc., since which Gen. Montgomery has joined us with artillery, and about 3000 men ; and yesterday we arrived here from Point aux Tremble, and are making preparation to attack the enemy, who are in close garrison, but cannot hold out long, as from the best account they are very much divided amongst themselves, and a prodigious panic has seized them all. Carleton, we are told, is determined to hold out to the very last, as his only hope, for he can expect nothing but punishment from the ministry, whom he has most egregiously deceived, in regard to the inhabitants of this country. All his friends, or rather his courtiers, say, he could not have taken more effectual measures than he has, to ruin the country.

" The 22d ult. he issued a most extraordinary proclamation, strictly ordering all who refuse to take up arms and defend the garrison, to depart the town and district within four days, with their wives and children, under pain of being treated as rebels or spies. In consequence of which a great number of the principal inhabitants came out with their families, but were obliged to leave all their property behind, except some wearing apparel, and a little household furniture, etc. I inclose you a copy of the proclamation. Among the corps who came with Gen. Montgomery, is your worthy friend Captain Lamb, whom I had the pleasure of seeing a few days ago at Point aux Tremble. Our men are in high spirits, being now well clothed with the regimentals destined for the 7th and 26th regiments, who were taken prisoners at St. John's. This is a circumstance which, I believe, the like never before happened to British troops, as two regiments of them to be made prisoners at one time. Providence smiles on us in a most remarkable manner. The Canadians say, ' Surely God is with his people, or they could never have done what they have done.' They are all astonished at our march through the wilderness which they say was impossible, and would not believe our coming, until they had ocular demonstration of it. We are at a great loss for intelligence from the army at Cambridge and other quarters, having had no certain accounts of their movements, nor the least syllable of news since we left Newbury. I am astonished a regular communication has not been opened between Montreal and the colonies, hope you will pay a little attention publicly to it, more especially as there are some scoundrels who, with impunity, open the letters directed to the officers in our army, and I suppose they continue the like infamous practice with the letters which are sent to our friends and acquaintance. The general is now absent sending off an express, by whom I send this. I hope the next time I write you, it will be from Quebec, for if the insulting foe does not surrender shortly, I believe it is the general's intention to carry the town by storm."

ROLL OF CAPT. MATTHEW SMITH'S COMPANY.

On leaving Paxtang this company mustered eighty-seven (87) men. Of this number notwithstanding our researches the names of only fifty-one (51) can be ascertained with certainty. No papers of Smith, Steel, Simpson or Cross, are known to exist. Of Capt. Hendricks's company raised near the same locality, on the west side of the Susquehanna, scarcely a dozen names have been rescued from oblivion. Both companies were of the flower of the country, brave, ardent and patriotic — and no wise daunted by the sufferings of the Arnold campaign — of those who returned nearly all returned to the service:

CAPTAIN.

Matthew Smith, Paxtang.

1ST LIEUTENANT.

Archibald Steel, Donegal.

2D LIEUTENANT.

Michael Simpson, Paxtang, commanded in the assault.

3D LIEUTENANT.

William Cross, Hanover

SERGEANTS.

Boyd, Thomas, Derry, subsequently Capt.-Lieut, 1st Pa.

Cunningham, Robert, Londonderry, d. at Lancaster, of disease contracted in prison, soon after.

Dixon, Robert, killed in front of Quebec, Nov. 17, 1775. Belonged to West Hanover.

PRIVATES.

Ayres, John, Upper Paxtang.
Binnagle, Curtis, Londonderry.
Bollinger, Emanuel, Paxtang.
Black, James, Hanover.
Black, John, Upper Paxtang.

Cavenaugh, Edward, resided in York county, subsequently, " Honest Ned " of Judge Henry.

Carbach, Peter, Paxtang. After return enlisted in Capt. John Paul Schott's Co., March 12, 1777. Discharged at Lancaster, in 1783. Resided in Dearborn Co., Ind., in 1830.

Connor, Timothy, Bethel.

Crouch, James, Paxtang ; afterwards a colonel.

Cochran, Samuel, Paxtang ; afterwards captain of the militia, 1781.

Crow, Henry, died in Derry.

Dougherty, James, Londonderry, captured at Quebec and put in irons eight weeks. Subsequently enlisted 12th Pa.

Dixon, Richard, Dixon's Ford.

Dean, Samuel, served one year, then appointed Lieut. in Col. Harts' regiment, Flying camp. Subsequently 1st Lieut. 11th Pa.

Egle, Adam, Lebanon; wagon-master at Cambridge, Col. Thompson's regiment.

Elder, John, Paxtang.

Feely, Timothy, Dixon's Ford.

Griffith, John, Harris's Ferry.

Harris, David, Harris's Ferry ; subsequently Capt. Pa. Line.

Harris, John, Harris's Ferry ; killed at Quebec.

Henry, John Joseph, Lancaster.

Kennedy, John, Hanover.

Marshall, Laurence, Hanover.

M'Granagan, Charles, Londonderry.

Merchant, George, Donegal.

M'Enally, Henry, Londonderry.

M'Konkey, John, Hanover.

Mellen, Atchison, Paxtang ; resided in Lycoming county in 1813.

Nelson [Nilson], Alexander, Derry ; killed in front of Quebec, Jan. 1, 1776.

Old, James, Derry.

Porterfield, Charles, Hanover.

Ryan, John, Derry.

Simpson, William, Paxtang; wounded August 27, 1775; brother of Michael Simpson.

Sparrow, William, Derry.

Shaeffer, John (drummer) ; resided in Lancaster in 1809.

Smith, Samuel, Paxtang.

Taylor, Henry, Paxtang; captured Dec. 31, 1773, returned Nov. 10, 1776.

Todd [Tidd] John, Hanover.

Teeder, Michael, Hanover ; subsequently enlisted 5th Pa.

Warner, James ; died in the wilderness near Chaudière lake.— Henry, p. 198.

Waun, Michael, Derry ; died at the crossing of the Chaudière.

Weaver, Martin, Upper Paxtang.

Weirick, Valentine, Hanover; resided in Dauphin Co., 1813.

Wheeler, ——— [uncertain] from Paxtang.— *Letter from Dr. W. H. Egle.*

INDEX.

———•◦•———